Rediscovering Renaiss: Witchcraft

Rediscovering Renaissance Witchcraft is an exploration of witchcraft in the literature of Britain and America from the sixteenth and seventeenth centuries through to the present day. As well as the themes of history and literature (politics and war, genre and intertextuality), the book considers issues of national identity, gender and sexuality, race and empire and more. The complex fascination with witchcraft through the ages is investigated, and the importance of witches in the real world and in fiction is analysed.

The book begins with a chapter dedicated to the stories and records of witchcraft in the Renaissance and up until the English Civil War, such as the North Berwick witches and the work of the "Witch Finder Generall" Matthew Hopkins. The significance of these accounts in shaping future literature is then presented through the examination of extracts from key texts, such as Shakespeare's *Macbeth* and Middleton's *The Witch*, among others. In the second half of the book, the focus shifts to a consideration of the Romantic rediscovery of Renaissance witchcraft in the eighteenth century, and its further reinvention and continued presence throughout the nineteenth, twentieth and twenty-first centuries, including the establishment of witchcraft studies as a subject in its own right, the impact of the First World War and end of the British Empire on witchcraft fiction, the legacy of the North Berwick, Hopkins and Salem witch trials and the position of witchcraft in culture, including filmic and televisual culture, today.

Equipped with an extensive list of primary and secondary sources, *Rediscovering Renaissance Witchcraft* is essential reading for all students of witchcraft in modern British and American culture and early modern history and literature.

Marion Gibson is Professor of Renaissance and Magical Literatures at Exeter University and works on witches, magic, paganism and the supernatural in literature. Her previous publications include: *Imagining the Pagan Past* (2013), *Mysticism, Myth and Celtic Identity* co-edited with Shelley Trower and Garry Tregidga (2012), *Witchcraft Myths in American Culture* (2007), *Possession, Puritanism and Print: Darrell, Harsnett, Shakespeare and the Elizabethan Exorcism Controversy* (2006) and *Reading Witchcraft: Stories of Early English Witches* (1999).

Rediscovering Renaissance Witchcraft

Witches in Early Modernity and Modernity

Marion Gibson

 Routledge
Taylor & Francis Group

LONDON AND NEW YORK

First published 2018
by Routledge
2 Park Square, Milton Park, Abingdon, Oxon OX14 4RN

and by Routledge
711 Third Avenue, New York, NY 10017

Routledge is an imprint of the Taylor & Francis Group, an informa business

British Library Cataloguing-in-Publication Data
A catalogue record for this book is available from the British Library

Library of Congress Cataloging-in-Publication Data
Names: Gibson, Marion, 1970–author.
Title: Rediscovering Renaissance witchcraft/Marion Gibson.
Description: 1 [edition]. | New York: Routledge, 2017. |
Includes bibliographical references and index.
Identifiers: LCCN 2017028311| ISBN 9781138025431 (hardback: alk. paper) |
ISBN 9781138025455 (pbk. : alk. paper) | ISBN 9781315147802
(ebook : alk. paper)
Subjects: LCSH: Witchcraft–Great Britain–History. | Witchcraft–United
States–History. | Witchcraft in literature.
Classification: LCC BF1581.G5355 2017 | DDC 133.4/309–dc23
LC record available at https://lccn.loc.gov/2017028311

ISBN: 978-1-138-02543-1 (hbk)
ISBN: 978-1-138-02545-5 (pbk)
ISBN: 978-1-315-14780-2 (ebk)

Typeset in Bembo
by Sunrise Setting Ltd., Brixham, UK

This book is for Margaret Murray, Dr Dorothy Scarborough and Professor Avril Henry.

Rediscovering Renaissance Witchcraft gratefully, if quizzically, marks 100 years since Margaret Murray's Folklore Society lecture on "Organisations of Witches in Great Britain", which changed the way that witchcraft, early modernity and modernity were conceptualised (see Chapters 3 and 4) and it also honours the centenary of the less obtrusive publication of Dr Dorothy Scarborough's pioneering literary history, *The Supernatural in English Fiction*. If we wished to pick a year in which the modern rediscovery of Renaissance witchcraft began, 1917 would be a defensible choice. Professor Avril Henry (1934–2016), together with Dr Gareth Roberts, inspired much of my undergraduate writing.

Contents

Acknowledgements

Thanks to the following people for their help in thinking through the ideas of this book, researching and writing it: G.H. Bennett, Kate Macdonald, Ashley Chantler, Simon White, Tim Cooper, Jo Esra, Ronald Hutton, the students on my Witchcraft and Magic in Literature module, the librarians and archivists at Cambridge University Library, especially the Manuscripts Reading Room, Nottingham University Library Manuscripts and Special Collections, the National Archives, Kew, National Archives of Scotland, Edinburgh, Edinburgh University Centre for Research Collections, Manchester Central Library Archives and Local History collection, University of Leeds Special Collections, Lancashire Archives, Dorset County Museum, Charles Beck, the Shakespeare Birthplace Trust and Exeter University Library Special Collections, Jeanette Winterson, Tanya Stobbs and Vivien Green. Hello to Jason Isaacs. Particular thanks to those who answered my questions about their work: Kate Pullinger, Ruth Warburton, Deborah Harkness, Dulcinea Norton-Smith, Stewart Conn and Caryl Churchill. Thank you to all the writers discussed in this book for your inspiring stories.

A note on interdisciplinarity, terminology and naming

To avoid ambiguity, I use the word "Renaissance" as well as the phrase "early modern" to label the period c.1550 to 1700. Terms such as "Enlightenment" and "Romantic" – both problematic to define but widely recognised – describe aspects of the period c.1700 to 1850. Developments from around 1850 onwards are referred to as "modern", in the popular sense that they point towards contemporary ideas. "Modernism" designates the specific cultural movement of the early twentieth century, also controversial but widely accepted. I also use other literary terms, such as "postmodernism", "magical realism" and "romance". Such terms should not be understood to have a narrow, inaccessible meaning but as being suggestive of attitudes explored in the book, and I'm grateful to the readers for drawing my attention to terms that might need specific discussion. Names are also problematic. A woman can be referred to by her forename as Euphan, Effie or Euphame and by her surname as McCalyane, Macalȝean or Macalzean. I have preserved the spelling chosen by each author because it gives clues about the source of their material and contains noteworthy information about the person named and the person naming them.

Introduction

This book is about witches in early modern and modern literature in Britain and America. It is not a general history of witchcraft in literature; instead, it examines the afterlives of Renaissance texts about witchcraft in fiction written over the last century. Why? Because witches are important in contemporary global culture, from the witch-cities of Ghana, where thousands of women have been living for decades after accusations, to the multi-million-pound *Harry Potter* phenomenon.[1] Witches have a real-life presence in our world, but also an imaginatively rich, money-spinning and politically and socially aware presence in our fiction. Creative industries drive the British economy, which are worth around £84 billion per annum according to a 2016 report by the Department for Culture, Media and Sport, and British fiction represents the United Kingdom to the world, as well as intervening in the lives of viewers and readers globally. So it is significant when, for example, J.K. Rowling's wizard Voldemort haunts the 2012 Olympic Games opening ceremony, pitted against his fellow British witch Mary Poppins by director Danny Boyle. Bad and good witches fought a politically charged battle over Britain's free National Health Service, a significant statement in British politics but also staged as the American President's "Obamacare" provision was being rolled out.[2] As here, fictional witches powerfully incarnate and dramatise our deepest convictions and passions, and this book contends that they have done so since their rediscovery by Romantic radicals in the late eighteenth century.

The book is, to some extent, an attempt to recentre narratives of British and American history and literature around an unexpected figure, that of the witch, to see what happens when we look at western culture from that viewpoint. It gestures towards a version of history that Dipesh Chakrabarty has called "History 2", as set against "History 1". History 1 is a history of capitalism, nation, the banking system, secular governance structure, reasoned decision and all the traditional concerns of European historians of rationality and "enlightenment". History 2 is all the other histories and, as Manduhai Buyandelger sums up, one of these History 2s is a history of "gods, spirits, and other supernatural beings", which would include witches.[3] Bringing together old and new witchcraft fictions on a scale not attempted before, the book's History 2 approach analyses a series of peaks and troughs in depictions of the witch-figure to suggest that witchcraft recurs most frequently in twentieth- and twenty-first-century fiction during periods where radical and conservative forces are in negotiation, the radical in the ascendant. However, witchcraft is also of interest to conservative mythmakers, who build around the figure of the witch new demonologies. Witchcraft depictions in fiction thus function as a cultural barometer, responding to changing pressures around authority, religion, national identity, economics, gender and sex, attitudes to past, present and future, youth and age, science and technology, race and class and our basic understandings of human nature and being.

Even in periods between the Romantic rediscoveries, the writing of witchcraft fictions never altogether ceases, and there are significant overlaps between such periods, where the witch-figure embodies debate. The book thus makes a case for the centrality of the witch in British and American fiction – and culture more generally – in the twentieth and twenty-first centuries, tracing that omnipresence and significance back to their Renaissance roots. Three centuries after the last witch prosecutions, I thus demonstrate the importance of the Renaissance and its literatures today. I also suggest that the continuing relevance of the witch is explained by the way that stories of witchcraft open up special possibilities and tap particular pleasures in the human mind. Their problematic relationship with reality allows this to happen, a philosophical notion that requires a detour into cultural theory before the book commences its cultural history. Whatever their historical status, in different ways, witches are, and are not, real, and stories about them are, and are not, fiction.

For Gareth Roberts, the pioneering scholar of Elizabethan witchcraft fiction in the 1990s, witchcraft could be seen in linguistic terms as a sign without a referent: put simply, "witchcraft" is a *word* that most modern western people think has no real-world *thing* connected to it. Stuart Clark's "Inversion, Misrule and the Meaning of Witchcraft" (1980) and *Thinking with Demons* (1997) explored similar insights, to argue that the notion of the witch is a linguistic construct, a word made out of nothing but a word that when it is spoken makes real the thing it fears.[4] But even in times and places where witchcraft is believed to have a real-world presence, it is always hard to define, prove and document. It remains unreal in many ways because its existence is different from the unarguable, material reality of other crimes (murder, theft and so on). Renaissance demonologists often resorted to classifying it among the illusions of devils or the delusions of women: in important ways both real and unreal. This level of unreality has helped to make witchcraft a compulsive subject of cultural production since. Witchcraft can be recreated each time it is rewritten, it is never closed down or explained away. For the ethnographer Jeanne Favret-Saada, witchcraft was always in story, being retold, a "discourse" where "the act, in witchcraft, is the word" and "the way things are said" is everything: witchcraft's power lies in narrative.[5] Other theorists have also found the concept of the witch empowering, to the extent that Jean-Luc Nancy suggests the notion of the supernatural is inherently subversive of authority.[6] To go back to being a "peasant" or a country(wo)man, in his terms, with fairy tales, deity-filled landscapes and witch-beliefs, is to evade or reconceptualise a whole range of problems connected with capitalist, authoritarian modernity.

This is a potent cluster of ideas. If witches exist in language and story rather than being constrained by reality, then the witch can subvert classification and make language and authority bend to accommodate her or him. They can write their own subversive History 2: a global history of fiction and fantasy. In Gilles Deleuze and Félix Guattari's terms, a witch could be the ultimate "minority". Deleuze and Guattari argued that the notion of a numerical "minority" could be extended to describing any group or individual who refused to conform or was labelled as Other by a dominant culture. In this sense, witches are an ideal minority, so that adopting the identity of a witch, however ironically or metaphorically, is a process of "becoming minoritarian", standing out and resisting oppression. Because s/he exists in language, such a witch can be always unfixed and surprising. To use another Deleuzian phrase, also adopted by Miriam Wallraven, s/he can always be "becoming witch" because s/he cannot be pinned down. In the 1990s, Diane Purkiss wrote about "choosing to be a witch", suggesting that despite its dangers, witch-hood offered power to those early modern people who confessed.[7] With this in mind, this book examines elements of "choosing to be a witch" in modernity. I suggest that writers began to choose witchcraft themes as a subversive step during the First World War and that this conception of the witch has continued and developed into the present day. But without Renaissance witches as a pattern, this reinvention could never have occurred.

The relationship between history and modernity in witchcraft fiction is interestingly paralleled in contemporary realities globally, as recent anthropological work has suggested that contemporary witchcraft accusations occur where modernity meets history in some obvious way. In 2013 and 2016, the anthropologist Peter Geschiere argued that in some African contexts "the notion of *sorcellerie*" is "constantly 'provoked' by its coexistence with a scientific discourse propagated by the mission, the schools, modern health care, and other institutions". He suggested that despite (or even *because of*) the apparent certainties offered by these institutions, witchcraft accusations respond to the sense that "nowadays something basic is going wrong and that things are getting out of hand". Geschiere concluded that "witchcraft or shamanism is about a lack of certainty, something that defies explanation, a gap that is difficult or even impossible to fill".[8]

Another anthropologist, James Siegel, suggested that witchcraft beliefs "insist on the continued presence of an unknown" in work on witchcraft accusations in Java in the late 1990s, despite the apparent scientific certainties of the modern world. Believing witchcraft to be a real force, Siegel argued, depends on suspicion that is only strengthened by "introducing a term – 'witch' – that is incapable of doing more than designating that something is at work which is not understood".[9] We are back once again with the notion that the word "witchcraft" has no referent, exists only in language and story, but demands constant reiteration to fill a descriptive gap. In modern societies across the world, there is the expectation of explanation in scientific terms. Where this fails, the word "witchcraft" pops up, "signifying nothing" as Macbeth might put it, but offering the prospect of making sense of things by naming and dealing with a witch.[10]

The connection made here made between Javanese anthropology and trans-atlantic fiction is a two-way street, because Siegel locates the unknowable aspect of witchcraft belief in the western literary notion of the sublime. Romantic writers of the late eighteenth century, such as Edmund Burke, defined the sublime as an experience of astonishment, terror and "obscurity" or that which is "dark, uncertain, confused". For Siegel, witchcraft is sublime in that both provoke emotions and sensations where "we feel overcome" by something broadly indefinable. Favret-Saada agreed: her experience of witchcraft was one where "*something in this cannot be coped with*".[11] This notion of sublimity has long been important to literary fiction. The Romantic poet William Wordsworth, for example, processed overwhelming experiences by describing sublime "spots of time" during which he felt elevated and transformed – negatively or positively – and he (and his fellow-poet Samuel Taylor Coleridge) spoke about the "emotion recollected in tranquillity" that enabled him to later discuss these experiences and form them into poems.[12] I argue in this book that it is no coincidence that he and his fellow-Romantics were fascinated by witchcraft in history: as Siegel suggests, witchcraft was part of the literary sublime then, and still is today.

After all, even in societies that do not, or do not any longer, believe in witchcraft, stories of it continue. Even if a particular world view is rejected, the stories of that world view still have a life of their own. For believers in the phenomenon of witchcraft, as Octave Mannoni put it, "the belief must survive its refutation, even if it thereby becomes impossible to grasp and one can see nothing but its utterly paradoxical effects".[13] And so the telling of witchcraft stories has outlived the phenomenon of witchcraft accusation. Where there are no witches, we are left with stories that conjure up the witchcraft sublime, motivating rediscoveries, retellings, reimaginings, parodies and writings back to old stories. This continued "New" Romantic response is what drives today's fictions of witchcraft, just as it drove those of earlier Romantics. Rewritings of witchcraft stories today are thus poetic examples of emotion recollected in tranquillity.

Witchcraft in European history, once so firmly consigned to a medieval or Renaissance past, is made modern by these rewritings. As I have suggested, they began with the Romantics, Wordsworth's contemporaries – and have recurred during periods of resurgent Romanticism thereafter. In each rediscovery of witchcraft, the sublime relationship between witchcraft, excitement and trauma is foregrounded, as well as the ways witchcraft stories can transform reality, affecting the world around them. Drawing on these ideas, this book argues that the trauma of the First World War and the exhilarating changes brought on by the War released a new wave of interest in witchcraft – a new Romantic rediscovery. Many witchcraft fictions of this period are an attempt to process the overwhelming emotions of the War and the breakdown of supposed Victorian certainties of reason and religion. The book goes on to argue that more recent writings relating to witchcraft are still responding to that re-enchantment, either in reaction or reinforcement – further rediscoveries.[14] What emerges is a magical realism that transcends the narrow literary-theoretical use of that term to embrace a wider range of texts about magic and witches set in a world where belief in these as realities has ceased.

Because of the constantly changing understanding of witchcraft over time, and the fluid relationship between past and present, rediscovering witchcraft is thus not about tradition or backward-looking alone. It is about tradition-with-modernity, continuity-with-change, looking back and looking forward (perhaps looking back in order to look forward). In Deleuze and Guattari's terms, it is about "becoming" rather than being a stable fixity, a nicely demarcated temporal state. In the case where a real-life accusation is made, a recourse to witchcraft is a very destructive means of achieving this precarious balance between modernity and history. In modern British literature, the focus of most of this book with an excursion into American literature in Chapter 6, the conflicts played out are less acute, but still deeply felt, so that a magical transformation is needed to overcome them. Disbelief must be suspended, or a risk taken, in order to write about witches, but there are also important rewards. As creative writers, folk-lorists, anthropologists and historians, we still need witches in modernity and postmodernity and will do into whatever comes next. The rediscovery of witchcraft is in this way a kind of radical nostalgia, the sense that despite the horrors of the past something valuable may have been lost with its passing and a better future might be modelled on elements salvaged from this better past.[15]

With these ideas in mind, this book examines the dialogue of modern texts with those of the Renaissance to suggest that a preoccupation with the modern retains and indeed "provokes" a rediscovery of witchcraft.

Notes

1 Whitaker; Laary. On *Harry Potter* see Chapter 7.
2 Vaizey and Department for Culture, Media and Sport (the report mentions, among other witch-fictions, Gabaldon's *Outlander* series as a highlight); Stebner.
3 Chakrabarty, 1601, 5151–74, 5208–28, etc. (Kindle) – the notion of two histories draws on Marx; Buyandelger, 13.
4 Roberts, "Descendants" 185; Clark's "Inversion" focuses on fictive literature including texts discussed in this book, *Thinking* on demonology: modern witchcraft studies would be unthinkable without either.
5 Favret-Saada, 3, 9, 23, 175.
6 Nancy, 55–7.
7 Wallraven, 75; Purkiss, chapter six.
8 Geschiere, 2013 *passim*; quotations summarising his argument in 2016, 243, 244, 247.
9 Siegel, 25.
10 Shakespeare, 5.5.27.
11 Burke, 55; Siegel, 23; Favret-Saada, 22.
12 Wordsworth, *Pedlar* 51; Wordsworth and Coleridge, 111; see also "Goody Blake and Harry Gill", *Works* 134, 135.
13 Mannoni in Rothenberg, Foster and Žižek, eds, 82.
14 On re-enchantment, see Landy and Saler, eds, and Jenkins.
15 For a discussion of radical nostalgia see Bonnett.

1   Renaissance witchcraft

This chapter discusses the records of early modern British witchcraft trials, examining the stories from the archives that shaped so much future literature. It sets the scene for the discussion of two reinventions of this material, one by Renaissance creative writers and one by writers working in the last hundred years. The first reinvention is the subject of Chapter 2, the second occupies the rest of the book. This chapter looks at both manuscript trial records – where these exist – and published documentary accounts of such trials, which often used legal documents in their account. This is not to ignore the differences between manuscript sources and published accounts: indeed, these could be quite different. What Chapter 1 will do, however, is treat both manuscript and published accounts from the period of the witch trials as primary sources. Both contain original, documentary material that is as close as subsequent creative writers – both immediately after the events and in later generations – could get to the events they wanted to transform into literary texts.

In most cases, manuscript records would not have been available to contemporary creative writers: the records went straight to judicial archives or were discarded. They did not circulate widely during the Renaissance because of the logistical challenges of copying. But, as I explored in *Reading Witchcraft* (1999) and *Early Modern Witches* (2000), they were sometimes made available to hack journalists or publicised by wealthy victims of witchcraft attacks. Therefore, some appeared in news pamphlets, either in full or excerpted. These pamphlets, and some of the original records, were then discussed and published by scholars from the Romantic period onward, giving nineteenth- and twentieth-century creative writers increasingly easy access to them. I have discussed the pamphlets and their manuscript sources extensively in previous books and articles, challenging their claim to offer verbatim access to witchcraft interrogations and exploring their status as collaborative, creative, generic and unreliable narratives. That scepticism still stands. But in this book, I reframe them as the texts that, whatever their flaws as factual evidence, embodied the Renaissance image of the British witch as it was handed down to later generations of writers.

Scottish witches: the North Berwick case

By far the most influential account of a British witchcraft trial is the body of records produced when a group of supposed witches were accused in 1591 of trying to murder the Scottish king, James VI. The records are notable because of the sensational nature of the accusations – attempted regicide and treason sponsored by the devil in person – and because James published his own reflections on witchcraft in *Daemonologie* in 1597. James VI, who became James I of England in 1603, passed a new Witchcraft Act in 1604, and Shakespeare adapted elements of the case in *Macbeth* in around 1606. With this confluence of cultural currents, the Scottish witches of 1591 became subsequently (in)famous. But there is also another reason for their notoriety in their transmission from the Renaissance to modernity. The witches' stories emerged early into the scholarly limelight, when the records of their trials were rediscovered by Scottish Romantics and included in Robert Pitcairn's nation-defining legal history *Ancient Criminal Trials in Scotland* in 1833. From Pitcairn's edition, their story travelled through the minds of other scholars, popular historians and creative writers with diverse results.

The indictments (dittays) of the North Berwick witches, and supporting pre-trial documents, survive in the National Archives of Scotland.[1] Also informative is the pamphlet *Newes from Scotland*, published for an English readership a few months after the trials in 1591. *Newes* tells us that a maidservant, Geillis Duncane, was the first suspect. In November 1590, she had been absent at night from the home of her employer, David Seaton, and had started offering healing services which he thought unnaturally acquired. Illegally, Seaton tortured Duncane with the pilliewinks (thumbscrews) and by binding her head tightly with rope. He also had her searched for a witch's mark, and when a blemish was found, she confessed and named others.[2] The pre-trial records appear to confirm the story told in *Newes*, suggesting that Duncane was the first suspect questioned. However, the records start with a list of questions mentioning material from other depositions and a note stating that she was confronted with another witness accusing her, so the exact sequence of events is not clear. It is also mentioned that other people had recently been burnt as witches: evidently, there is a backstory to the 1591 trials that we can no longer access.[3]

However, her ordeal began; her depositions show that Duncane spoke of meeting the devil and attending witch-sabbaths. But her evidence was soon surpassed by a torrent of information from another suspect, Agnes or Annie Sampson or Tompson. Sampson was a widow who, her statements suggest, lived by selling healing prayers and magical advice. A contemporary history calls her a "wyse wyff", a name for a magical practitioner or "cunning" person. Sampson's dittay from January 1591 gives details: she diagnosed by examining the sarks (shirts) of sick people, combated spells of witches and the odd "warlach" (warlock) and "elf-schot" (affliction by evil fairies or spirits). She said she was helped by a dog-shaped spirit, called "Elva" or "Eloa".[4] As well as describing her healing spells, Sampson added to Duncane's story, naming other witches who met with the devil and raised a storm to stop the Queen coming "home". In these first depositions, we encounter the royal aspect of the case. The witches were accused of trying to stop King James bringing home his new bride, Anne of Denmark, to Scotland.

James' wedding was at the centre of the 1589 to 1591 witchcraft fears. He was beset by rival claimants to his throne and sectarian violence. As a young ruler, he had been subjected to kidnap and murder attempts, and accused by Calvinist churchmen of favouritism bordering on homosexual infatuation with the Earl of Lennox. So his marriage to Anne was vital: he could produce heirs and refute scandal, but only if he and his wife were fertile and healthy, their children lived and at least one was male. The precious royal couple were married by proxy in Denmark in August 1589 and Anne sailed for Scotland. But storms drove her fleet to Norway and tension mounted: what if the new queen never arrived? Demonstrating his authority and virility, James went to fetch her and married her in person in Norway, with another ceremony in Denmark in January 1590. The thrice-married King and Queen arrived in Scotland on 1 May, triumphant. But this final journey too was disrupted by storms, and another vessel carrying wedding gifts for the Queen was sunk off Leith. As the saga continued, both Danes and Scots began to suspect James' enemies were causing the storms by witchcraft.[5]

Sampson's statements explained how she supposedly became involved in this plot. Years before, in newly widowed poverty, she had given herself to a spirit who told her that if she served him, she would never want. Presumably this was "Eloa": he marked her, and visited her in human form. Sampson had asked Eloa to tell her about the heirs the King would have, and recently they had discussed the Queen's journey to Scotland, which Sampson had then tried to impede. This story can be imagined as being prompted by the anxieties of Sampson's questioners, who included the King and his ministers, but it might also reflect public anxiety and rumour. Sampson seems to have known ladies in the royal penumbra, as clients of her magical practice, and exchanged information with them. In *Newes*, it was even reported that she had been able to tell the King accurately the private words he had spoken to his wife on their wedding night.[6] This knowledge suggests a community of eavesdropping and gossip operating between courtiers and the wider world. Nobles and gentry sought power from magical practitioners through having their fortunes told, investigating the fates and inheritances of others and buying magical remedies, spells and perhaps even poisons. This is a pattern that we will see recur in fictional representations of witchcraft.

In the North Berwick case, two upper-class women in particular – Ewfame Macalʒean and Barbara Naipar (or Macalzean and Naper, as *Newes* calls them) – were accused of seeking love-charms and cures from Sampson and others, and more deadly magic. They were tried in May and June 1591, both refusing to confess anything. Macalʒean's dittay accuses her of using charms "that will owthir [either] caus your husband love yow, or ellis gett your will of him" and of poisoning him. It itemised her "undewtifull behaviour", and "traffiking" with witches, and claimed that her husband was "wereit [wearied] of his lyffe, be [by] the daylie truble he had in youre cumpany". She was also accused of seeking a replacement husband "under culloure and cloik [cloak] of mariage with youre dochter", and of other murders and harm. *Newes* reveals that one victim was her "Godfather" and another "one of the Lords and Justices of the Session" (a judge of the body later known as the High Court of Justiciary, which tried the witches). Sampson had helped her and had also been consulted by Naipar, initially on behalf of Lady Angus, who was suffering morning sickness. Naipar wanted to secure Lady Angus' favour, so Sampson "inchantit be hir sorcerie, ane lytill ring" for her. She was also accused of plotting to kill the Earl of Angus by melting "ane bony small pictour of ȝallow walx [yellow wax]". Once James attracted the witches' attention, a wax image was also made representing the King.[7]

Duncane, Sampson, Macalȝean and Naipar, along with a group of other witches, were thus accused of a range of activities focused upon subverting authority, masculinity and good order within state, society and family. These have been central themes of the scholarly exploration of their activities – by Christina Larner, Stuart Clark, P.G. Maxwell-Stuart, Gareth Roberts and Lawrence Normand, Julian Goodare, Thomas Brochard and others – and for many of the creative writers who have read their trial records and *Newes*.[8] At the summit of the national patriarchy, the King was to be attacked in multiple ways: by sinking his ships, by melting a wax image, by casting a poisonous toad into his path and using its venom to smear his discarded clothes. Another accused, Jonet Stratoun, said Sampson had hung up the toad to extract poison from it which she stirred into a mixture heated over a fire. In *Newes* is an illustration of a group of women heating and stirring liquid in a vessel over a fire and a passage in which Sampson confesses this, with variation: she says she gathered the toad venom in an oyster shell. But Sampson was also said to have despaired of bewitching the King, concluding that the devil could not hurt him. *Newes* contextualises this claim in a way that was useful for James politically: it states that Sampson's devil told her "the king is the greatest enemy he hath in the worlde".[9]

This juxtaposition of king and witch, one chosen by God, the other by Satan, structured many later adaptations of these stories. In particular, *Newes* stressed the connection between James and Agnes Sampson: she had secret information about him and was "the onelye woman, who by the Divels perswasion should have entended and put in execution the Kings Majesties death". But the story has always been told selectively in creating this binary relationship. In practice, the other conspirators were equally linked with James (or, if one disbelieves the evidence, *not* linked with him). For example, Macalȝean is described as ordering the wax image of the King to be made, not Sampson, and there is confusion about responsibility and chronology. The usual account of the case also leaves out other central figures – Robert Greirsoun the "Comptroller" of the witches, and so on – because only the four dittays of Sampson, Macalȝean, Naipar and another suspect, Dr John Fiene, have survived, together with *Newes*, and only these dittays were printed by Pitcairn. Even with the pre-trial documents added, Sampson, Macalȝean and the others are surprisingly elusive figures in the records and their roles are enhanced and tidied in retelling: alternative names "Annie" and "Agnis Tompson" disappear, along with key details, like Sampson's initial denial of all the accusations made against her – documented in *Newes* – and her pre-trial denial that she knew her accuser Duncane at all.[10]

Duncane and Sampson's story is actually full of holes, suggesting it was not an account of a real coven as some have supposed, but produced in response to pressure, collaboratively with their accusers. These co-authors each had their own agenda, but together they produced a story resonant with the fears and desires of their situation, especially royal fears about marriage and patrilineal succession. *Newes* reveals the nature of the pressure to contribute something useful to this narrative. As we saw, Duncane was tortured to obtain her initial confession. Sampson was shaved, her head was bound with tightening rope and once her "privities" were searched and a supposed devil mark found, "she immediatlye confessed whatsoever was demaunded of her". Fiene (also known as Cunningham) had his leg-bones smashed with hammers and his fingernails pulled out. Unsurprisingly, confession followed, and the story solidified: the witches had menaced James, and done so at the instigation of Francis Stewart Hepburn, Earl of Bothwell, James' cousin and a rival for the throne. All the key players were executed, except perhaps Naipar, who pleaded pregnancy, and Bothwell, who escaped prison, was tried in 1593 on his own terms and acquitted. Macalȝean, whom (as Normand and Roberts note) is portrayed in her dittay as particularly "unnatural . . . malicious and vengeful", was with especial cruelty burned alive.[11]

Along with the horror of this injustice and the relationship between witches and kings, the details of the supposed witches' sabbaths have been of interest to creative writers retelling their story. One in particular was a gala occasion: Sampson said that over 100 people, six men and the rest women, had attended an All Hallows Even "conventioun" at North Berwick kirk. They had done homage to the devil there. Fiene, the witches' "Clarke" or "Regester", had appeared "missellit" (disguised), led dancing and ritual turning "widderschinnes" (anti-clockwise) and brought lights "lyke mekle [big] blak candillis" to the kirk. He had taken notes of the meetings' attendees and is shown in *Newes'* woodcut writing at a table. Duncane had played music on a "trump" with the witches "singing all with one voice". Then the devil had entered the pulpit looking "lyke ane mekle blak man", and held roll-call: each witch "kist his erse" in homage. Satan asked for reports of action since the last meeting. There was an argument about the image of the King during which, prompted by "Effie MacCalȝan", Robert Greirsoun "ffand grit fault with the Dewill" for not providing the figure and "Barbara [Naipar] and Effie MacCalȝane gatt þan [then] ane promeis of þe [the] Dewill, that his hienes [Highness'] pictour sould be gottin to þame twa [them two], and that rycht sone [right soon]". This testy exchange over, the witches opened graves and stole bones for making magic powders, after which, adjourning the meeting, they parted.[12]

Their plot to attack the King with the long-promised wax effigy menaced his body, but also his ships, and the association of witches with storms had long-term literary consequences. Sampson's dittay explained how the "sisteris" raised an "ewill wind" on a regular basis, once sailing in a boat "lyke ane chimnay" to attack a ship named the *Grace of God*. *Newes* adds that in order to attack the ship carrying jewels for the Queen, they sailed in "riddles or Cives", taking with them a christened cat tied to parts of a dead body, which they threw into the sea. In the pamphlet's illustration, a ship is shown sinking as a result.[13] Fiene, a young schoolmaster, expanded on Sampson's account of magic using body parts. His dittay enumerates the religious aspects of the crime of witchcraft, as conceived in Renaissance Scotland: denying God, adoring the devil, attempting to convert others to demonic worship and dismembering dead bodies and "bairnis [children] unbaptesit". Such unnatural acts of butchery accompanying the witches' apostasy were supposed to destabilise and fracture the natural world, causing tempest and shipwreck.

As well as this chaos-causing witchcraft that fed the fears of his questioners, in *Newes*, Fian (the pamphlet's spelling) is also unexpectedly portrayed performing love-magic in a way that sounds like a folk tale interpolated into the political material of his wider confession. In his love-spell, he used what he mistakenly thought to be the pubic hair of a "Gentlewoman" whom he desired. But, in fact, the young woman's mother had discovered the plot, and substituted the hair of a cow. Once Fian had "wrought his arte upon them", the bewitched cow followed him around the town "leaping and dauncing . . . to the great admiration of all the townes men".[14] This tale of trickery – a moment of light relief among the tortures and perversions described in the pamphlet – suggests the entertaining potential of magic, an element frequently exploited by creative writers both in Renaissance and modern times. Thus, the story of the North Berwick witches brought together and publicised a number of key elements in the portrayal of witches that, selectively retold, went on to have long afterlives.

Other Scottish cases

The trials of the North Berwick witches were in some respects unique, which is why their imprint is so easily detected in later fiction. There were plenty of cases that were unlike them in many ways. For example, the trials of Bessie Dunlop in 1576 and Isobel Gowdie in 1662 focused on evidence of ghosts and fairies. In evidence published by Pitcairn, Gowdie told of flying about on a straw, of transformation into animals and birds, of orgies with a "meikle, blak, roch [rough] man" and a visit to the fairy court. Her vivid confessions have been celebrated, partly because they extend the image of the witches' convention described by the North Berwick witches. Like them, Gowdie's "coven" (a word not in fact used in the earlier account) met in the kirk, and membership began with a covenant, after which there was sex, arse-kissing, spell-casting with unbaptised babies and clay pictures, and grave-robbing. But, even more so than the North Berwick witches, Gowdie spoke about the coven's constitution, in a way that was influential in later anthropological understandings of witchcraft as paganism. Each coven had rules and calendar festivals, she said. Members were punished for failure to conform. There were always thirteen members, including two named roles, "maiden" and "officer". Gowdie's confession was, as Emma Wilby calls it, "exceptional" and "idiosyncratic", particularly in its suggestion that witchcraft was a cultic religion, but it was very influential with later writers.[15]

Gowdie may echo the North Berwick story, integrating aspects of it into her own vision, but one case prefigures it strongly, establishing several key tropes for later trials. In 1590, Katharene Ross or Roise, Lady Fowlis, was accused of bewitching and poisoning her own relations. First, she attacked Robert Monro, Laird of Fowlis and Marjorie Roise, Lady Balnagoune, by making "twa pictouris of clay", and shooting them with "elf arrow heides" (Neolithic stone weapons, thought to be elvish). Lady Fowlis "schott twa schottis with the said arrow heid" at one and her fellow-witch Loskie Loncart shot three at the other: both shattered. Additionally, Lady Fowlis attacked her stepson Hector Monro with poison, attempting to wipe out a bloodline so "that [her] awin bairnis sould succeed to the hous of Fowlis". There was also a counter-accusation: Hector Monro was accused of killing Lady Fowlis' son George Monro. He, allegedly, performed a rite during which he was buried in a grave whilst cunning folk transferred his sickness to George.[16] Both accused were acquitted, but their dittays remained to tell a story that, when published in later times, influenced some later fiction. It shares the North Berwick themes of an attack on patriarchal authority and rightful succession, with Katherene Roise prefiguring Ewfame Macalʒean and her associates, but is far less well-known.[17]

The fame of the North Berwick witches and their many afterlives suggest that if a story was reimagined by a creative writer in Renaissance Britain, particularly if that writer was Shakespeare (see Chapter 2), it was likely to appear repeatedly in fiction thereafter. Meanwhile, other stories were lost for centuries before their rediscovery, like that of Lady Fowlis and Isobel Gowdie, but each had its day, thanks largely to Pitcairn's edition (see Chapter 3). With its influences on *Macbeth* and related plays, *Newes from Scotland* is the best example of a long, vivid afterlife for what was effectively an early modern newspaper story. But it was one of dozens of witchcraft pamphlets published from the mid-sixteenth century onwards.

English witches: Elizabethan origins

Most of these pamphlets were English. Their stories are almost all of neighbourly dispute in small villages, unlike the Satanist regicide and revolt imagined in the Scottish capital and that nation's great houses in the 1590s. In England, publishers printed what came to them in dribs and drabs from the courts and other informants. These sources included statements given to magistrates, descriptions of courtroom testimony and evidence collected by clerics and gentlemen – people such as the poet-translator Edward Fairfax, who accused several women of bewitching his daughter in 1621. In the 1620s to 1630s there was a lull, followed by a spate of publishing in the 1640s to 1650s in response to a series of large-scale trials across eastern England inspired by godly gentlemen like the "Witch Finder Generall" Matthew Hopkins.[18] Through the later seventeenth century, witchcraft stories were also incorporated into pamphlets and treatises that were part of sectarian dispute over the nature of God's providence, the role of fundamentalism or "enthusiasm" in political life and the nature of matter and spirit. Combatants in that dispute, such as the Somerset rector Joseph Glanvill and Francis Hutchinson, Suffolk vicar and later Bishop of Down and Connor, cited pamphlet stories regularly, and prompted the publication of new accounts of witchcraft trials.

As with the Scottish sources, a few English accounts were especially influential. In 1579, *A Detection of Damnable Driftes, Practized by Three Witches* publicised the stories of Essex women tried at the county's summer Assizes. One, Mother Nokes of Lambourne, whose indictment under the name Alice Nokes survives in the National Archives, Kew, fell out with neighbours over what they thought to be trivial matters:

> a Certaine Servant to Thomas Spycer of Lamberd Ende in Essex yoman, sporting, and pasing away the time in play with a great number of youth, chaunced to snatch a paire of Gloves out of the pockette of this Mother Nokes Daughter being a yong woman of the age of xxviii yeres, which he protesteth to have done in jest. Her Mother perceivyng it . . . [said] to her Daughter, lette him alone, I will bounce him well enough, at what time he being soudainely taken, and reft of his limmes fell doune.

Mother Nokes' accusers added that she had killed a child, and bewitched a plough horse because the ploughman would not speak to her: she was executed.[19] A neighbour told how Mother Nokes spoke of one "Tom" as someone who was always on her side, and he believed she meant a "fiend".[20] Familiar spirits in the shape of animals were a favourite theme of English and some Scottish accounts: quarrels that preceded an accident or illness were taken to have caused it, and a familiar was suspected as the agent of the harm.

In 1582, another pamphlet, *A True and Just Recorde*, publicised the trials of a group from the Essex village of St Osyth and their familiars, who had supposedly caused agricultural and medical problems in their community for years. This pamphlet was intended to have influence beyond the immediate consumption of its story: it was prefaced with a plea for a change in English witchcraft law to make the crime punishable by burning. Witches, the prefacer wrote, should be "rygorously punished", "most cruelly executed" as heretics. Foreign magistrates punished witches proportionately "burning them with fire, whome the common lawe of Englande (with more measure of mercie then is to be wished) strangleth with a rope". The pamphlet went on to detail how witches such as the suspects Ursley Kempe and Elizabeth Bennet kept familiar spirits shaped like black and grey cats, a lamb, a toad, a black dog, two little colts and a red lion. They were named "Tyffin", "Tittey", "Pygine", two "Jacke"s, "Robbin", "Suckin" and "Lyerd". Some of the women confessed. The magistrate Brian Darcy was told stories of how the familiars afflicted fellow-villagers and their animals (miscarriage, paralysis, aching bones, tumours and so on). They had killed children, caused brewing and churning processes to fail, carts to get bogged down and other costly misfortunes.[21]

One woman, Bennet Lane, detailed transactions with her neighbour Annis Herd, which seemed to have led to domestic difficulty:

> Annis Herd beeing at her house she gave her a pint of milke and also lent her a dish to beare it home, the which dishe she kept a fortnight or 3 weekes, and then ye girle of the said Annis Herds came to her house on a message: and she asked the girle for the dish, and said though I gave thy mother milk to make her a posset I gave her not my dish.

When, following this incident, Lane was unable to skim her milk and make butter:

> shee tooke a horse shue and made it redde hote, and put it into the milke in the vessals, and so into her creame: and then she saith, shee coulde seath [boil] her milke, fleete [skim] her creame, and make her butter in good sort.

Lane's ritual was intended to ward off Herd's supposed attack: fire and iron were countermagical tools.[22] Her story suggests both generosity and guilt at its limitations: both were "poore" women, and while Lane helped Herd by giving her milk, she was unwilling also to donate her precious dish. The English pamphlets repeatedly document complex interactions of this kind, and the feelings that accompanied them: guilt, anxiety, resentment, trust, hope, fear. These churning emotions – part of the witchcraft sublime that I discussed in the introduction – would flavour witchcraft fictions of the twentieth century, appearing alongside specific details such as the names of familiars and particular transactions of food, drink and housewares.

As stories of witchcraft evolved over time, some later cases pitted whole families against each other. In 1589, five children of Robert and Elizabeth Throckmorton of Warboys in Cambridgeshire accused all three members of a neighbouring family, Alice and John Samuel and their unmarried daughter Agnes, of sending spirits to torment them. A pamphlet, *The Most Strange and Admirable Discoverie of the Three Witches of Warboys*, was produced in 1593, relating the agonies of the bewitched. After years of accusatory confrontations, Alice Samuel confessed that she was a witch and although her husband and daughter Agnes stoutly resisted, all three Samuels were hanged. Agnes was urged by onlookers to plead pregnancy and prolong her young life, but she retorted that she would not: "it shall never be sayd, that I was both a Witch and a whore". Readers of this and other such accounts have often suspected the Throckmorton children of shamming and sadism: Joan Throckmorton carried on dialogues with spirits only she could see and Jane scratched Alice Samuel so savagely that her nails broke. Some of the children would only be well when they were allowed to play games, but began convulsing as soon as Bible readings began.[23] Concerns over proper godly behaviour, and sectarian tensions, frequently animated such pamphlet accounts, and children ventriloquised adult concerns about salvation, prayer, the Word and other Christian touchstones.

English witches: the Pendle case

One influential Jacobean trial driven partly by sectarianism was documented by Thomas Potts, clerk at the Lancaster Assizes of summer 1612. Two groups, the "Pendle" and "Samlesbury" witches, were tried. The latter were acquitted when the evidence of their 14-year-old accuser, Grace Sowerbutts, collapsed. It emerged that Sowerbutts had been tutored by Christopher Southworth, a Jesuit who had also ministered to the accused (Sowerbutts' grandmother and aunt Jennet and Ellen Bierley and one of the priest's own relatives Jane Southworth). All had been Catholic recusants and they suspected they were accused because they had begun attending Protestant services: a bitter, pragmatic conclusion. Another reading might be that Sowerbutts, like the Throckmorton children, was living in an intensely pious atmosphere and begun to manifest symptoms of supernatural sickness as part of the group's belief that their sect was under Satanic assault. The same would be true of other "possessed" persons such as the "Boy of Burton", Thomas Darling, from 1597. Usually this kind of case occurred in an extreme Protestant (rather than Catholic) context, although there are exceptions like the Samlesbury accusations.[24]

Whatever the motivation, Sowerbutts' stories were coloured by Catholic demonologies, and thus unusually florid for an English witchcraft trial – more like the horrors and ecstasies of the North Berwick case than the St Osyth or Warboys ones. In an episode apparently drawn from Giovanni Pico della Mirandola's demonological writings, Sowerbutts said Jennet Bierley "thrust a naile into the navel" of a baby, "and afterwards did take a pen and put it in the said place, and did suck there a good space".[25] When the child died and was buried the witches exhumed its body, and:

> did boile some therof in a Pot, and some did broile on the coals, of both of which the said Jennet and Ellen did eate . . . [and] did seethe the bones of the said child in a pot, & with the Fat that came out of the said bones, they said they would annoint themselves, that thereby they might sometimes change themselves into other shapes.

Indeed, Jennet Bierley often transformed herself into a dog, Sowerbutts said. The witches also allowed "black things" to "pull downe the said three Women, and . . . abuse their bodies". The cannibalism and racy sexual content were untypical, so much so that Sowerbutts was not believed. She was dismissed as an "impudent wench" by Potts, who ridiculed both Christopher Southworth and his "scholler", accusing them of "villainie", "Trecherie" and "Conspiracies".[26]

However, another young witness, 9-year-old Jennet Device, accuser of the "Pendle" witches, was believed, and many of those she named were hanged. Like Sowerbutts, these included her grandmother (Elizabeth Southerns or Demdike), but also her mother, brother and sister (Elizabeth, James and Alizon Device) and some of their neighbours. Speculation about Jennet Device's motives preoccupies many later accounts of the case, influencing the portrayal of all the accused.

As the matriarch of the family, Demdike attracts much odium. In this, later writers follow Potts, who describes Demdike as about 80, blind and "a Witch for fiftie yeares". He imagines her taking "great care and paines" to get her descendants "to be Witches" and labels her a "general agent for the Devill" – a designation suggesting a commercial intelligence context that was amplified by later editors of his work. Yet Demdike's confession to the examining magistrate Roger Nowell extends back only two decades: she says that "about twentie yeares past" she gave her soul to a devil called Tibb in return for "any thing that she would request". Tibb appeared "in the shape of a Boy . . . about Day-light Gate" (twilight) and later as a dog, sucking blood from Demdike against her will.[27]

Demdike further told Nowell that she did not request anything of Tibb until "Christmas last", when she asked for "revenge" against the miller Richard Baldwyn. Demdike had been led to the mill by her grand-daughter Alizon to beg, but Baldwyn had retorted "get out of my ground Whores and Witches, I will burne the one of you, and hang the other". After this quarrel, Tibb disappeared permanently. Exploring this revenge story, Nowell must have asked Demdike about the techniques of witchcraft, and she said that:

> the speediest way to take a mans life away by Witchcraft, is to make a Picture of Clay, like unto the shape of the person whom they mean to kill, & dry it thorowly: and when they would have them to be ill in any one place more then an other: then take a Thorne or Pinne, and pricke it in that part of the Picture you would so have to be ill: and when they would have any part of the Body to consume away, then take that part of the Picture, and burne it. And when they would have the whole body to consume away, then take the remnant of the sayd Picture, and burne it.[28]

The fact that Demdike knew this much about witchcraft led later writers to conclude that she was a witch, and that the next suspect whose examination Potts prints was her longtime rival in magical business.

This woman, Anne Whittle or Chattox, was also elderly and her family disliked the Demdike-Devices. Yet she claimed that Demdike had persuaded her to become a witch fourteen years ago. Chattox gave her soul to the devil in the shape of a man named Fancie, and entertained a dog familiar – they promised her gold, silver and a "Banquet", she said. Chattox and Demdike then together killed Robert Nutter and Richard Ashton, both wealthy young men. Nutter was killed because he was a threat to Chattox's family: he "did desire [Chattox's] Daughter" Anne Redferne, "to have his pleasure of her", her mother explained. This threatening proposition was rejected, and Nutter had planned to evict the Redfernes from his land. Explaining the background of the family's rivalries to Nowell, James Device gave further details of the Chattox clan's magic: they had exhumed "three Scalpes" (skulls) and used the teeth, buried alongside a "Picture of Clay" representing Robert's kinswoman Anne Nutter.[29] Meanwhile, another member of the family, Alice Nutter, was – confusingly – accused by Jennet Device of siding with the witches. Potts speculated about her motives: perhaps "a desperate desire for Revenge" caused this "rich woman" to descend to a "wicked course of life". Yet before she was accused of killing Henry Mitton, she was "in the common opinion of the world, of good temper, free from envy or malice". He admitted his puzzlement whilst affirming that "she was guilty", like her indigent accomplices.[30]

The Demdike-Devices were indeed very poor: Alizon Device told several stories of begging for small items. In March 1612, for example, she met a pedlar, John Law, who refused to give or sell her pins (accounts differed). She asked her black dog familiar to "lame him", he fell down speechless and was paralysed on the left side. When Law accused her of witchcraft, Alizon pleaded guilty. Interestingly, her familiar was nameless, and James Device explained why. The witches had held a feast on Good Friday, he said, "for the naming of the Spirit, which Alizon Device . . . had", but they "did not name him, because shee was not there". By then Alizon was in prison in Lancaster Castle. The witches therefore plotted to rescue her and her co-accused, and "blow up the Castle" in a gunpowder plot. Their Good Friday sabbath was portrayed as a northern and likely Catholic conspiracy, involving witches from as far away as Yorkshire, in the person of Jennet Preston of Gisborne. Preston came to Pendle for help in killing an enemy who, she said, had "maliciously prosecuted" her – another attack on order, justice and piety, as Potts saw it. This reading of witches as inverting all good order, and rebelling because they are poor and marginalised, appears consistently in fictions based on Potts' pamphlet *The Wonderfull Discoverie*. The result was a mass execution: Elizabeth, James and Alizon Device, Anne Chattox, Anne Redferne, Alice Nutter, Jennet Preston and a number of others were hanged. Elizabeth Demdike had already died in prison.[31]

English witches: other Jacobean cases

Later Jacobean pamphleteers also often framed their accounts with Potts-like moralising on the subversiveness of witches. In 1613, *Witches Apprehended* told the story of Mother Sutton and her "wicked and lewde" daughter Mary, who was swum in a millpond after being suspected of bewitching a "Gentleman of worship".[32] In 1619, an account of seven witches in Rutland, Lincolnshire and Leicestershire spoke of their "malicious disposition against their betters or others thriving by them". These women had conspired against the Earl of Rutland, Francis Manners, killing his two male heirs, Lord Roos and his younger brother. Contrasting the witches' rancour with the beneficence of their victims, the pamphleteer extolled the Earl's and Countess' virtues: never "denying the accesse of the poore", making their home "a continuall Pallace of entertainment". Two of the witches, Margaret and Phillip (Philippa) Flower were employed there until neighbours said their mother Joan was "a plaine Atheist", "her demeanour strange and exoticke", that Margaret was stealing from the Earl and that Phillip had bewitched another man into obsession with her. At last, Margaret was dismissed when "the Countesse . . . discover[ed] some undecencies both in her life and neglect of her businesses . . . yet gave her 40 s[hillings] a bolster, & a mattresse of wooll". Thus, the witches are portrayed as ungrateful and impossible to please. They are also represented as physically remarkable: a woodcut shows hard-featured, bearded women, leaning on crutches and sticks, surrounded by familiars.

These creatures had helped them bewitch the Earl's children. Phillip said that Margaret "by the commaundement of her mother, brought from the Castle the right-hand glove of the Lord Henry [Roos]" and Joan "rubd it on the backe of her Spirit Rutterkin", a cat. They then boiled the glove in water, "pricked it often, and buried it". Joan also boiled "feathers and blood together" cursing the Earl's family. They repeated the procedure with a glove belonging to the younger boy, and with gloves that were a present from one of Joan Flower's enemies, Mr Vavasor. As well as Rutterkin, the sisters confessed they had familiar spirits that sucked their breasts and "within the inward parts of [their] secrets": both were executed. Joan Flower died before her trial, choking on bread after she had "wished it might never goe through her if she were guilty": the pamphleteer does all he can to convince readers that she was. He may be Samuel Fleming, the Rector of Bottesford, and chaplain to the Earl: certainly, Fleming helped to examine the witches, as the pamphlet relates.[33]

Another chaplain, Henry Goodcole, was responsible for the influential account of Elizabeth Sawyer, the "Witch of Edmonton". Goodcole served at Newgate Prison in London, exploiting his position to sell true crime stories such as his *The Wonderfull Discovery of Elizabeth Sawyer* (1621). Eight days after Sawyer's execution, Goodcole published an account of her confession. He described her as "a very ignorant woman", one-eyed, "crooked and deformed" by demonic poetic justice and addicted to "cursing, swearing, blaspheming . . . imprecating" and "lying".[34] He explained that Sawyer bewitched her neighbours simply because they "would not buy Broomes of her" and because one had struck her sow. These neighbours gave evidence in court, but Sawyer's guilt was finally determined when she was searched for a demonic sign; a "private and strange marke" was found near her "fundament", taking the form of "a thing like a Teate" which "seemed as though one had suckt it". Sawyer explained that the devil "in the shape of a dogge" called "Tom" had sucked her body and Goodcole pursued this point. Did she, he asked, "pull up her coates" to facilitate this intimacy? No, she said, "the Divell would put his head under my coates".[35] The suspicion of demonic sexual contact hovered around Goodcole's account, as with the contemporary story of the Flower family.

English witches: Matthew Hopkins, "Witch Finder Generall"

The most sensational of seventeenth-century witchcraft events are the trials connected with Matthew Hopkins, the "Witch Finder Generall". Hopkins, the son of a Suffolk minister, undertook witch-hunting activities in the south-eastern counties of England in the mid-1640s, starting at his own home, Manningtree in Essex, in March 1645.[36] The Civil War had brought chaos and violence across Britain, and the period saw widespread witchcraft-panic. Around 200 people were executed between 1645 and 1648 according to John Stearne, one of the witch-finders working with Hopkins. The term "panic" is – in this instance – justified. For example, in April 1645 Anaball Durrant alleged that Mary Johnson had killed her child. But when her husband called her "to make her ready to go before the...Justices", he suddenly announced that "Johnson would be his death", began sweating profusely and writhing in pain. When a noise "like a Hornet" was heard, he began screaming: "It comes, it comes, Now goodwife Johnsons Impe is come, Now she hath my life". At that moment, part of a wall in the Durrants' house collapsed. Here is the witchcraft sublime in all its terror. At least eighteen people were hanged in the ensuing trial.[37]

By then, Hopkins had set up as an expert. He assembled like-minded interrogators and "searchers" who stripped suspects and examined them. A wart, wen or pile could be identified as a teat sucked by a familiar – as in Sawyer's case twenty years before. Manningtree women were employed to search female suspects, whilst Stearne, a godly man from Long Melford in Suffolk, searched men. Hopkins and Stearne travelled together and separately through eastern England, testing anyone brought to them.[38] As well as the spurious science of searching, they introduced methods of interrogation not known to have been used in other English pre-trial hearings. These were authorised by the Manningtree magistrates, Sir Harbottle Grimston and Sir Thomas Bowes, and thereafter used until the witch-finders were stopped from applying them. John Gaule, a Huntingdonshire vicar, describes how groups of witch-finders "watched" suspects, holding them in an "uneasie posture . . . without meat or sleep for the space of 24 hours" or more, searching and questioning them. Suspects were also swum – like Mary Johnson in 1613 – to see if they floated, in which case they were guilty. This, along with stress and deprivation methods akin to torture, likely prompted compliant confessions, Gaule argued, and he opposed Hopkins' visit to his village.[39]

Hopkins' is the best-known name from the trials of the 1640s. He was in his mid-twenties, godly and ill: Stearne tells us he died of "a Consumption" in 1647. But under normal circumstances, his activities might not have led to mass executions: pre-War attempts to begin witch-hunts had failed.[40] Because of the War, however, some judicial safeguards were suspended. Vigilantism and unusually constituted courts produced unusual outcomes. A high-church Suffolk vicar, John Lowes or Lowis, was accused, swum and confessed to Hopkins that he had suckled Satanic imps, sunk a ship and killed cattle.[41] He was executed – an unimaginable outcome only a few years before. A puritanical Ipswich woman, Mary Lakeland, was burned for "petty treason", the murder of her husband by witchcraft. Later writers often assume that burning was the accepted punishment for witchcraft and associate it with Hopkins: but it was not, and he was not there. Many of the atrocities associated with the "Hopkins" cases were thus atypical and committed by others than Hopkins.[42] As at Salem fifty years later, a court of Oyer and Terminer was commissioned to manage the multiplying accusations, and failed: even structures that mimicked pre-War norms could not recreate order in the changed circumstances of the time. Among others, Diane Purkiss, James Sharpe, Malcolm Gaskill and Peter Elmer have examined the ways that the Civil

War can be seen as unleashing and stimulating varied kinds of hatred – particularly sectarian and gendered kinds associated with witchcraft.[43]

Some facets of the trials were, however, Hopkins' responsibility. One of the episodes reworked by later writers is the interrogation of the first suspect, Elizabeth Clarke, as described by Hopkins himself and Stearne. Imprisoned at Manningtree, watched for three days, searched and questioned, Clarke eventually offered to summon her spirits. Hopkins' 1647 treatise *The Discovery of Witchcraft* discussed them and included a woodcut depicting, among others: Holt, a cat-like creature; Jarmara, a dog; Sack and Sugar, a rabbit (although elsewhere described as a toad); and Vinegar Tom, a greyhound with extra-long legs.[44] The latter would become especially famous. Accounts differed about whether he had the head of an ox and turned into a child (Hopkins' final word on him) or was an ordinary dog (Hopkins' first version of him, in another account). In the woodcut, Vinegar Tom accompanies Clarke and another woman, probably her fellow-accused Anne West, who are introducing their animals with the speech-bubble "My Imps names are", while "Matthew Hopkins. Witch Finder Generall" stands over them, iconic. At least eight witnesses claimed they had seen some of Clarke's imps: the woodcut makes them and Hopkins himself as vivid as possible for the reader.[45]

Equally sensational was an account of a sabbath – mild by Scottish standards, but clearly depicted as Satanic worship. Rebecca West told Hopkins that she, her mother Anne, Clarke and their co-accused "spent some time in praying unto their Familiars" while others "read in a book". Rebecca received a spirit as lover, husband and "her God". Many confessions similarly focused on perversions of the puritanical culture of eastern England. Stearne noted "many of these Witches made outward shews, as if they had been Saints on earth", "seemed to be very religious people" and attended "all Sermons neer them". Mary Lakeland was described as "a professour of Religion, a constant hearer of the Word".[46] These godly behaviours were inverted by Satan: Stearne described how in Huntingdonshire, John Winnick called his spirits "Lords and Gods", while John Clarke had told another man, "I doe not believe you are a Witch, for I never saw you at our meetings", as if upbraiding a sporadic church-goer. Elizabeth Weed's devil "came to her . . . with a Paper, and asked her whether she were willing to seale the Covenant", just as Puritans often covenanted with God.[47] Later, some scholars such as Margaret Murray saw these stories as descriptions of real-life meetings of a devil cult (see Chapter 3), whilst others such as James Sharpe, Malcolm Gaskill and Sheilagh Ilona O'Brien reflected on the ways the Hopkins trials demonstrated that despite some differences of tone, scale and focus, English witchcraft was not greatly dissimilar to Scottish or wider European models and Hopkins was no aberration.[48]

Hopkins and Stearne appear as bogeymen in modern fiction, and although often inaccurate in its detail, this image is not unfair. Even by 1647, the pair were being attacked as inhumane charlatans. In his *Discovery*, Hopkins rebutted accusations made against him at the Norfolk Assizes: "that he must needs be the greatest Witch, Sorcerer, and Wizzard himselfe, else he could not [find out witches]", that his witch-marks were "natural excrescencies", he had "used unlawfull courses of torture" and that "all that the witch-finder doth, is to fleece the country of their money".[49] Stearne's *A Confirmation and Discovery of Witch-Craft* also carefully presents himself as "a plaine country man" dedicated to "truth", but suggests he is being sued for the return of witch-finding fees. The pair's fanaticism and cruelty are not mythic. Hopkins described those who defended accused witches as "Sticklers", adding that he preferred to "persist without controle". Stearne defended the accusation of an 8-year-old boy, boasted of the 200 people executed and explained that he only swam witches in *warm* weather. Both men complain about the financial costs of their inquisitions.[50] It is unsurprising that horrified response to their activities colours the portrayal of other witchcraft trials that were quite different, as this brief account of some other English trials suggests.

American witches: Salem

The English trials of 1645 to 1648 are closely related to American trials, which had begun as early as 1626 with the accusation of Joan Wright in Virginia. They intensified after 1647, when Alse Young was executed in Connecticut. Whilst American witchcraft events and their afterlives are not the focus of this book (they are the theme of my 2007 book, *Witchcraft Myths in American Culture*) they do need to be mentioned because their story is intertwined with that of the British cases discussed here.

The "Salem" trials of 1692 to 1693 are best known, primarily because of their influence on American literary giants such as Nathaniel Hawthorne and Arthur Miller, who, in turn, influenced later British writers. Spreading through communities around Salem Town in Massachusetts, these accusations began in the house of Salem Village's minister Samuel Parris. His young daughter and another girl, Abigail Williams, began to accuse an "Indyen" woman servant, Tituba, and several fellow-colonists of attacking them by witchcraft. Accusations proliferated until nineteen people had been hanged and one man pressed to death for refusing to cooperate with the court, with hundreds of suspects jailed. The case prompted soul-searching in the godly communities who came to believe that they had murdered innocent people.[51] As well as the Hopkins trial pamphlets, the Salem prosecutors had available to them more recent English publications: *A Tryal of Witches* (1682), the record of a case of witchcraft in Bury St Edmunds, Suffolk, in 1664; several pamphlets recounting the story of the Bideford witches, Devonshire, such as *A True and Impartial Relation of the Informations against Three Witches* (1682) and *The Full Trials, Examination and Confession of Four Notorious Witches*, dealing with the Essex witches, Rose Hallybread and Susan Cock (1690).[52] The close relationship between American and British ideas of witchcraft continues today.

Renaissance witchcraft: summary

This chapter has summarised a range of primary sources that were influential in creating the image of the Renaissance witch in Britain. As can be seen, the best-known Scottish stories were different from most English ones and English ones differed among themselves, with a few cases becoming especially famous. But, despite this diversity, a number of themes tie together early modern British understandings of witchcraft: witches were thought to attack their neighbours out of revengefulness, envy or misconceived malice; they were usually women, sometimes defying powerful men outright; they embodied fears for the safety of kings and nobles, succession and wealth; they prompted sublime emotions of overwhelming terror and hatred; they challenged notions of submissiveness and proper sexuality; they focused sectarian fears of religious error; and their stories made it clear that Satan could appear to such sinners in animal or human form, tempting them to revolt and pledge themselves to evil and even to formal devil-worship. Witches inverted socially prescribed norms, unsettled and challenged established authorities and promised boundless empowerment and freedom to those willing to join them. Readers may already have recognised images, names or tropes from witchcraft stories retold in modernity or from early modern plays and poems. It is certainly true that material from the courts and the Renaissance popular press suffuses creative writing about witchcraft in modernity and that is often because Renaissance creative writers borrowed extensively from real-life events around them in creating their own witchcraft texts. These early redis-coveries are the theme of the next chapter.

Notes

1 NAS JC2/2, JC2/3 (High Court of Justiciary, Books of Adjournal), JC26/2 (High Court of Justiciary processes, depositions). JC26/2 is currently unfit for production, so that unfortunately I have not been able to check transcripts against the original records.

2 *Newes* A4–B; modernised transcripts in Normand and Roberts, eds, 135–289, includ-ing the dittays (transcribed in their original spelling by Pitcairn – see below) and pre-trial papers not transcribed by him. On modernisation see also Normand. A few pieces of information mentioned during my account did not reach the public domain until 2000 (there have been four main releases of information: the dittays used in court [1591], *Newes* [1591], Pitcairn [1833] and Normand and Roberts [2000]), but they are included here as context, with Pitcairn's text as the main, quoted source because his is the most influential account for later creative writers (see below). The account here is not the full story of the case, but focuses on the elements re-used by later writers. Normand and Roberts, eds, 22.

3 Normand and Roberts, eds, 135, 136, 151.

4 Normand and Roberts, eds, 137, 138, 145, 155, 156, 231–46; Pitcairn, ed., Volume 1, Part 3, 230 quoting the *Historie of King James the Sext*, and Volume 1, Part 3, 231–7; Pitcairn read "Elva" (e.g. 235), Roberts and Normand read "Eloa" (e.g. 137).

5 Normand and Roberts, eds, 29–38, *Newes* C.

6 Pitcairn, ed., Volume 1, Part 3, 232; Normand and Roberts, eds, 139, 233; *Newes* A4.

7 Pitcairn, ed., Volume 1, Part 3, 250, 252, 240; Normand and Roberts, eds, 245, 262, 263; *Newes* B2. The letter ȝ is called yogh and is an Old Scots/Middle English letter.

8 Larner's pioneering *Enemies of God* discusses political power structures and the relationship of royal authority with witchcraft in the act of nation-building, themes continued in her *Witchcraft and Religion*; Clark's "Inversion" analysed texts including

Daemonologie, Newes from Scotland and *Macbeth* using structuralist, Foucauldian notions of binary opposition and power; Roberts and Normand continued this broadly new historicist work highlighting themes of subversion and containment in the North Berwick trials (see above). Among others, Goodare, Levack, Maxwell-Stuart, Wasser and Hughes continue to debate issues of monarchical and court power whilst Wilby, Martin and Cordey examine the relative powerlessness of the accused, and their agency; for recent work see Goodare, ed., *Scottish Witches* and Goodare, ed., *Scottish Witch-Hunt*.

9 Normand and Roberts, eds, 171, 172, 185, 274 (Stratoun's evidence was not included in Pitcairn's edition of the dittays: these documents only appear in Normand and Roberts); *Newes* A2v, A4-v, B4.

10 *Newes* B4-v; Normand and Roberts, eds, 137, 171, 229, 162 (including pre-trial material not in Pitcairn), *Newes* Bv ("Anne", "Anny", "Agnis Tompson", etc), 142–4.

11 *Newes* B3, C-C2, D2-v; Normand and Roberts, eds, 39–49, 218; Naipar's fate is uncertain: for her pregnancy see Pitcairn, ed., Volume 1, Part 3, 243 and Normand and Roberts, eds, 252. Normand and Roberts suggest she was executed in 1591 (216) although she was apparently still alive on 4 December of that year (she is not described as "umwhile" or "deceased", whereas Macalȝean is, 198). Yeoman's "North Berwick witches" surveys biographical information on five of the accused, concluding that Naipar had died by 10 December 1600, on the evidence of NAS GD16/41/117 (misnumbered 112), an escheat document relating to the transfer of her estate to the crown.

12 Pitcairn, ed., Volume 1, Part 3, 238, 239, 246; *Newes* title page, Cv-2, B3; Normand and Roberts, eds, 147, 257, 258. The letter þ is called thorn and is an Old English/Old Norse letter.

13 Pitcairn, ed., Volume 1, Part 3, 235, 236, *Newes* B4v-C; Normand and Roberts, eds, 237, 238. There is some confusion over the ships: Sampson's dittay mentions two christened cats and the Queen's ship (Normand and Roberts, eds, 240), but nowhere the later-famous sailing sieves.

14 Pitcairn, ed., Volume 1, Part 3, 213; *Newes* C3-4.

15 Pitcairn, ed., Volume 1, Part 2, 49–58 and Volume 3, Part 2, 603–13, 616; see also NAS JC2/10; Wilby, *Visions* 55. Gowdie's best-known afterlife is orchestral, James MacMillan's *The Confession of Isobel Gowdie* (1990) but see also Brodie Innes, *Devil's* (and Chapter 4).

16 Pitcairn, ed., Volume 1, Part 3, 192–6, 202–23.

17 Yeoman, "Hunting"; Brochard, 51, 52, 58.

18 See Fairfax, *Daemonologia*; see Gibson, ed., *Early Modern* for editions of the English pamphlets up to 1621; for facsimiles, Gibson, ed., *Early English*, Gaskill, ed., *Matthew Hopkins* and Elmer, ed. For discussion of all the sixteenth- and seventeenth-century pamphlets, Millar. For recent corpus linguistic approaches see Suhr, and Chaemsai-thong.

19 *Detection* A5v, Bv; National Archives PRO ASSI 35/21/4 indictment for murder, showing her supposed victim as Elizabeth Barfott, perhaps the child. Unless otherwise stated, original Assize and Quarter Sessions records for English witches have been lost. See Gibson, ed., *Early Modern*.

20 *Detection* B2-v.

21 *Recorde* A3v, 2A4, C3v, B3, B8v, C7v, D5, 2A2, B4, D8, E3v, D7, 2A. See Gibson, ed., *Early Modern*.

22 Gibson, ed., *Early Modern* 113, 114; Rosen, 147, 148; National Archives PRO ASSI 35/24/1, Herd was indicted for bewitching John Wadde's sheep and acquitted. Ursley Kempe and Elizabeth Bennet were both executed (Gibson, ed., *Early Modern* 83–7).

23 *Warboys* O3. See Gibson, ed., *Early English* and Almond 2008 for an account of the case.

24 Potts, M2v, M4v. See Almond 2016 and Poole, ed., for an account of the Lancashire case and further discussion, and Gibson, ed., *Early Modern* for this and Darling (on which also *The Most Wonderfull and True Storie* and Gibson, *Possession*). Walsham, 160.

25 Stephens, *Demon* 278; Almond, "The Lancashire Witches" and 2016. Stephens "Skepticism" explores the contest of believers and sceptics in *Strix*, which prefigures that surrounding Grace Sowerbutts.

26 Potts, L2, K4v, L2v, M3-v, N2v.

27 Willis, 15 discusses Demdike as a malign educator; see also Crossley, ed., who adopted the language of Victorian commerce to describe her and her rivals (xlvi–xlviii); Potts, Bv, B2-v.

28 Potts, B3-v.

29 Potts, E4, E3, D2, D3-v, B4-v, D3v, E3v-4.

30 Potts, O3-P2v.

31 Potts, R3v-Sv, G4v, C3, X4v-Yv, I2v.

32 *Witches Apprehended* A4, C.

33 *Wonderfull Discoverie* B2-v, C2v-4v, F, F3, F4, G, D2v. See Borman for an account of the case.

34 Goodcole, C, A4v-B.

35 Goodcole, Bv, B2, B3-v, C3v, C2v, C4.

36 Hopkins, 2; Stearne, 61; see Gaskill, *Witchfinders* for an account of the case.

37 H.F., 20, 21.

38 Hopkins, 10; Stearne, 11.

39 Gaule, 78.

40 Gibson, *Possession*; see also Richard Galis, *A Brief Treatise* (London, 1579).

41 Notes of pre-trial examinations, B.L. Add. MS 27402, printed in L'Estrange Ewen, *Witch-Hunting* 300, 301; Stearne, 23, 24; *A True Relation of the Araignment of Eighteene Witches* (London, 1645) 3.

42 *The Lawes against Witches and Conjuration . . . Also The Confession of Mother Lakeland* (London, 1645) 7, 8. Contextually, see P.G. Maxwell Stuart, *Witch-Hunters* (Stroud: Tempus, 2003).

43 Purkiss, "Desire"; Sharpe, "Devil"; Gaskill, *Witchfinders*; Elmer, *Witchcraft*, chapter 4.

44 Stearne, 14, 16; H.F., 4; Hopkins, 2.

45 Hopkins, 2, 10; F.H., 2; Stearne, 15 (Stearne says eight people were present).

46 H.F., 12, 15; Stearne, 39; *Lawes* 7.

47 Stearne, 16, 38; F.H., 11–15; Davenport, 1–4, 9, 15; on godliness, see Gaskill, *Witchfinders* 58–61.

48 Sharpe, "Devil" and *Instruments* argue for a greater emphasis on diabolism in England; Gaskill, *Witchfinders* moves beyond Hopkins to his community, and see also his "Witchcraft and Evidence" especially 36. See also on specific episodes, Gaskill "Witchcraft and Power", Jackson, "Witches" and Timbers, which analyses the Wests' "sabbath" in detail.

49 They were notorious enough to inspire forgery: in Deacon's *Matthew Hopkins*, an inauthentic document called "The Tendring Witchcraft Revelations" appears, Cabell's *Witchfinder General* reiterates this material; Hopkins, 1–9.

50 Stearne, A3v, 18, 20, 58, 60; Gaule, A3-v; Hopkins, 10.

51 Trial and related records can be found here: http://salem.lib.virginia.edu/home. html: see particularly the oft-cited Examinations of Sarah Good, Sarah Osburn or Osborne and Tituba, Tittuba or Titibe (Salem Witchcraft Papers numbers 63.6, 125.4 and 125.5).

52 On Bury St Edmunds see Geis and Bunn; on Bideford, Gent.

2 Witchcraft in Renaissance literature

Renaissance creative writers left a rich but skewed body of fictional work about witches. Their rewritings of the already problematic texts discussed in Chapter 1 introduced new biases, often skirting issues of guilt and justice and favouring the spectacular over the documentary. They drew material from the works in Chapter 1, but also from other places, including histories such as Raphael Holinshed's *Chronicles* (editions in 1577 and 1587) and demonologies such as Reginald Scot's *The Discoverie of Witchcraft* (1584) and George Gifford's *A Dialogue concerning Witches and Witchcraftes* (1593). The latter were works embodying the English understanding of witchcraft in the 1570s to early 1590s, whilst Holinshed echoed the English and Scottish medieval texts that were his sources. Holinshed's focus on the relationship between court life and witchcraft prefigured the North Berwick story (which is in many respects a medieval survival), whilst Scot and Gifford concentrated on contemporary village witchcraft stories, giving writers of Renaissance witchcraft fiction at least two traditions to choose from. Further, Scot and Gifford treated witchcraft as essentially unreal, a product of demonic delusion, trickery and human superstition. This was a stance that decisively shaped English Renaissance fictions. Most of these imply that witches are at least as entertaining as they are threatening and they are often metaphorical rather than realistic, inhabiting a blurry space beyond lawcourts and gallows.

For instance, John Lyly's *Mother Bombie*, Robert Greene's *Friar Bacon and Friar Bungay* and George Peele's *The Old Wives Tale* (late 1580s to early 1590s) are all plays relating to witchcraft but also "festive comedy", in C.L. Barber's definition, relating to seasonal revelry such as tale-telling, fairs and mumming.[1] Lyly's Mother Bombie is a cunning woman "who yet never did hurt", more sibyl than witch, so much so that some readers hesitate to describe her as one.[2] *Friar Bacon* features a magician with a comic servant and tricksy devils: it draws on the news pamphlet *A Most Wicked Work of a Wretched Witch* (1592) for an amusing story of a bewitched man flying. The audience marvel at feats of supernatural science, including a talking brazen head, suggesting magic's potential to prompt the creation of theatrical spectacle. The head is meant to assist Bacon, but as it speaks ("Time is", "Time was" and "Time is past") it malfunctions and is destroyed. Nothing in the play is really threatening, much less Satanic.[3]

Such plays are also in dialogue with each other: they were written in what appears to be a clubbable culture of fashion-conscious collaboration and competition, so that certain tropes recurred frequently. For example, there is another talking head that rises out of a well in *The Old Wives Tale*, suggesting a relationship between it and *Friar Bacon*. *The Old Wives Tale* self-consciously retells other stories throughout, as its title suggests, and it was influential itself so that there are elements of *The Tempest* (c.1611) in it as well. The ill-defined "Conjurer", "wise man" or "cursed sorcerer" Sacrapant anticipates Prospero as well as recalling Friar Bacon: he causes a storm, enslaves his victims and once stripped of his accessories loses his power. There is a dance of harvestmen, and a *Tempest*-like gesture towards "forgiving" and "sheer fun", as Mary Ellen Lamb calls it. Criticism of the play often refers to the joyful poetic justice of mummers' plays and folk tales.[4] As this comparison suggests, the witches and magicians of the Elizabethan stage were often the benign guides or comic villains of popular romance, revolving around what Jackson Cope called "mowing and sowing . . . a little death and a little beginning".[5] In this, they influenced many later works.

There are, of course, exceptions to the comedic frame of reference of Elizabethan magical plays. Shakespeare's two early *Henry VI* plays (c.1591) contain two witches, Joane la Pucelle and Margery Jordane or Jourdemayne, who are truly dangerous and are executed.[6] Whilst Christopher Marlowe's *Doctor Faustus* (early 1590s?) also echoes popular festivity, overall it resists this gentle trend.[7] The play shows the German scholar Faustus invoking devils, making a devil-pact, summoning spirits – with one of whom, in the shape of Helen of Troy, he copulates – and succumbing to damnation by being torn apart, engaging horrifyingly with learned European demonological preoccupations.[8] Paul Kocher was right to suggest that Faustus is a witch. That is not all he is, but he strongly recalls *Newes from Scotland*'s Dr Fian (or Fian recalls Faustus, depending on which came first). Both the schoolmaster and professor demonstrate the consequences of over-reaching in learning; both speak familiarly with the devil, organising his worship; both see magic as a means to sexual fulfilment; both are associated with broken bodies. *Newes'* subtitle, describing Fian's *Damnable Life and Death*, also echoes *The Historie of the Damnable Life, and Deserved Death of Doctor John Faustus*, the title of the English Faust book.[9] Yet *Doctor Faustus* is a deeply ambiguous text, and Marlowe also invites the audience to enjoy magic, not simply condemn it. In this, the play prefigures Jacobean witchcraft drama.

Macbeth (c.1606) shares with *Doctor Faustus* a connection with Scottish source material and an uneasy horror-comedy, so much so that its grotesquely ambivalent witches led Diane Purkiss to accuse Shakespeare of creating an "exploitative collage of randomly chosen bits of witch-lore".[10] But Holinshed's *Chronicles,* a key source, is itself a patchwork: its most notable witchcraft-related borrowing is Andrew of Wyntoun's mid-fifteenth-century phrase "Werd Systrys".[11] Holinshed was so extensively adapted by Shakespeare that in 1952, Robert Adger Law created a three-page table of references to the *Chronicles'* "Makbeth" story alone. Centrally, Shakespeare reworks Holinshed's account of the lords Macbeth and Banquo meeting "three women in strange and wild apparell, resembling creatures of elder world". Later we read in Holinshed that Macbeth fears his fellow-thane Macduff because:

> he had learned of certeine wizzards, in whose words he put great confidence (for that the prophesie had happened so right, which the three faries or weird sisters had declared unto him) how that he ought to take heed of Makduffe.

Shakespeare thus draws from Holinshed such phrases as "so wither'd, and so wilde in their attyre", "weyard sisters", the number three and questions of ontological and spiritual status ("not like th'Inhabitants o' th'Earth . . . Live you . . . ? what are you?"). On stage, his sisters may even have resembled Holinshed's fairies more than immediately recognisable witches, for the astrologer Simon Forman, attending a performance in 1610/11, recorded them as "feiries or Numphes [nymphs]".[12] Even this description is ambiguous.

Other material in *Macbeth* is more straightforwardly witchlike. In that, it is indebted to the North Berwick story, most persuasively in this passage:

> First Witch[13]: A Saylors Wife had Chestnuts in her Lappe,
> And mouncht, & mouncht, and mouncht:
> Give me, quoth I.
> Aroynt thee, Witch, the rumpe-fed Ronyon cryes.
> Her Husband's to Aleppo gone, Master o'th' *Tiger*:
> But in a Syve Ile thither sayle,
> And like a Rat without a tayle,
> Ile doe, Ile doe, and Ile doe.
> Second Witch: Ile give thee a Winde.
> First Witch: Th'art kinde.
> Third Witch: And I another.
> First Witch: I my selfe have all the other,
> And the very Ports they blow,
> All the Quarters that they know,
> I'th'Ship-mans Card . . .
> Though his Barke cannot be lost,
> Yet it shall be Tempest-tost.
> Looke what I have.
> Second Witch: Shew me, shew me.
> First Witch: Here I have a Pilots Thumbe,
> Wrackt, as homeward he did come.[14]

The "Syve"-sailing appears to be modelled on *Newes'* "cives", and the "tempest" and "contrary winde" deployed there by the devil belongs here to the sisters. The *Tiger* recalls James' ship – "Tempest-tost" but indeed not lost, because the pamphlet tells us that the King's "faith . . . prevailed above their ententions". The Pilot's homeward-coming ship also suggests James and Anne's voyage, as well as the ship the North Berwick witches actually did sink off Leith. Finally, Shakespeare's image of the Pilot's dead and disintegrated body sums up Scotland's fate if it were left without a king, the equivalent of the Pilot and Master in different ways. What if, as *Newes* puts it at the end of the page bearing the signature "C", from which these notions all stem, "his Majestie had never come safelye from the Sea"? Shakespeare's borrowings are precisely focused on this key page from *Newes*, which is themed on witchcraft, tempest, shipwreck and mastery.[15]

But the North Berwick trials shape the play's mood and content elsewhere too. *Macbeth* begins with reference to a storm: "in Thunder, Lightning, or in Raine". Holinshed omitted mention of the weather in his description of the meeting with the "three women", so these repeated images of tempest seem likely to come from *Newes*; and its witch-created storm seems to have haunted Shakespeare's imagination, as we shall see later in the chapter.[16] The fact that the weird sisters are clearly described as "Witches" in stage directions ("Enter three Witches" in 1.1, for example) is further evidence of *Newes'* influence: Holinshed's descriptions do not suggest this label fits them at all well. Shakespeare took the phrase "weird sisters" ("weyward, weyard" in the Folio text) from him, but not the label "Witch". Yet, despite this label, the play creates space for doubt about the guilt of the sisters. Whilst they are described as Witches in the stage directions, they do not accept the name themselves. One of the characters refers to herself as a "Witch" at 1.3.7, but she is quoting the sailor's wife's invective. The word appears in the sisters' speech only as a slur, although that abuse does prompt a magical attack that may justify its use. On the other hand, a fairy might respond in a similar way.

Macbeth is very clearly about witchcraft; yet it makes witches difficult to define. It also problematises the other half of North Berwick's demonological binary, kings. In 1.2 we hear that Ross "seemes to speake things strange" and then his first utterance is "God save the King". Like North Berwick's devil, Ross makes the conventional connection between royalty and godliness, the King as Satan's adversary, but *Macbeth* makes "strange" this notion. God fails to save King Duncan and allows Macbeth and his "Fiend-like Queene" to supplant him. Macbeth is a king who consults witches, sending us back to *Newes* with awkward observations, not least that James himself could be said to have consulted the North Berwick witches in questioning them. Their responses suggest he interrogated them in person seeking information about himself. Accordingly, they told him the devil feared him, and related a fact about himself that he believed they could only have known by witchcraft (his wedding night words to Queen Anne). Banquo's question "What, can the Devill speake true?" is apposite if Shakespeare was considering the truth of these demonic claims about James. Macbeth is a version of *Newes'* Bothwell, tempted by "supernaturall solliciting" to treason but, as Banquo's descendant, the Scottish king James is the ultimate beneficiary of the witches' prophecy. The breakdown of the magical binary bequeathed to *Macbeth* by *Newes* is evident here, as kings and witches are linked in uncomfortable union.[17]

Macbeth is another play that was in dialogue with its contemporaries. John Marston's *Sophonisba* (1604–6?) also explores the too-close relationship between royalty and witchcraft when its Libyan King Syphax is bedded by the illusionist witch Erictho. Marston added this "practical joke" episode to his classical sources, suggesting it had topical relevance for him.[18] The play contains numerous echoes or prefigurings of *Macbeth* (again it is unclear which came first) and its king–witch mirroring may be one of these. Certainly after revealing her bed-trick, Erictho "slips into the ground" like the earth-bubble witches of *Macbeth*: but here, the witch has essentially raped the royal enquirer.[19] Other early modern plays also reflected upon connections between supposedly evil, inverted witches and supposedly normal people, the "Hurley-burley" of confused ontology and power structures that *Macbeth* staged so fully.[20] In Ben Jonson's *The Masque of Queenes* and Thomas Middleton's *The Witch* (1609 and c.1613–16) witches frolicked for audiences including James, Anne and their courtiers.

Jonson's masque, a Candlemas entertainment that he describes as being written at the request of the Queen, opposes witches with queens, extending the king–witch binary in a different direction. The witches personify enemies of good reputation (they are named Suspicion, Malice, Slander and so forth), and are misruled by a Dame, inverting all good governance and repute. The masque's action sees them banished by Heroic Virtue, giving way to a show of virtuous and famous queens who were played by Anne and her ladies. But the masque has attracted critical suspicion that the queens are insufficiently unlike the witches.[21] This is clearer when it is viewed alongside the slightly later play *The Witch*, whose witches – Hecate, Puckle, Hoppo, Hellwain and Stadlin – are regularly consulted by supposedly heroic characters, and appear at times more trustworthy and sane than their allegedly virtuous clients. They sing entertaining songs and enact slapstick comedy, offering other characters a space outside the court where fun and feasting occur and dark deeds are done. This heterotopia – an "other place" of dangerous freedoms – recalls the place where Macbeth and Banquo meet the weird sisters in its ability to grant wishes. Middleton's witches' wishes are sometimes murderous but more usually sexual: they indulge, as Julia Garrett points out, in an amusing proto-feminist exploration of "female erotic pleasure", not unlike Erictho, seducing whom they like. But much of their magic is done to help courtiers indulge *their* desires. Therefore, in *The Witch*, as in *Macbeth* and *Sophonisba*, witches are represented as very like the well-reputed courtiers of *The Masque of Queenes*.[22]

So clear are these similarities that many readers believe *The Witch* responds satirically to the *Masque* and to the real-life events of the Essex annulment scandal, which titillated Jacobean London. In a series of hearings, it was alleged that the Countess of Essex – Frances Howard, one of the player-queens in Jonson's masque – had resorted to witches herself.[23] She had rendered her husband impotent, forced an annulment and remarriage, and inspired the poisoning of an opponent of the new match: a murder supposedly effected by the cunning woman Anne Turner, who was hanged for the crime in 1615.[24] These events are all echoed in *The Witch*, and in other contemporary satires that, as Alastair Bellany documents, touched every aspect of court life from the King's sexuality to the colour of ruffs.[25] Back-reading the Essex case and Middleton's satire onto

Jonson's masque is risky but, taken together, the two works and the earlier *Sophonisba* offer a powerful demonstration of the persistence with which Renaissance drama returned to the relationship between court and coven, theatrical performance and sabbath. From *Newes from Scotland* through a series of interrelated texts art imitated life and vice versa. The ways in which fictions of witches dramatised concerns about corrupt authority and provided a fantasy of empowerment for nonwitches are important for later works, with *Macbeth* being the best known and most obvious conduit for these ideas into the future.

The uncannily echoing dialogue between witch and nonwitch exists not just at the plot level in Renaissance drama, but also in the transformative language of witchcraft.[26] The ways in which the weird sisters' speech infects or colours that of *Macbeth*'s other characters has often been remarked. When Duncan comments that what the Thane of Cawdor has "lost, Noble Macbeth hath wonne" he is echoing the Second Witch's "When the Battaile's lost, and wonne". The sisters' "faire is foule and foule is faire" is echoed in Macbeth's "so foule and faire a day I have not seene".[27] Like a witch, Lady Macbeth calls on "Spirits, That tend on mortall thoughts". Although they are murderers by daggers rather than witchcraft, Macbeth and Lady Macbeth are also sometimes thought to be demonically possessed, or bewitched – perhaps metaphorically, because the sisters' words have "the power to bend reality, to shape the imagination". Macbeth is tempted by a vision towards his first crime ("is this a Dagger, which I see before me ... ?") and both experience visionary torments afterwards: Banquo's ghost and "Out damned spot". Lady Macbeth's guilt is partly expressed in witchy sing-song: "the Thane of Fife, had a wife: where is she now?" The weird sisters are *Macbeth*'s most obvious witches, but Macbeth and Lady Macbeth might be considered part of their coven. Macbeth attends a sabbath; Lady Macbeth invokes spirits; both speak like witches.[28]

The case for Lady Macbeth as a witch is stronger. Like Agnes Sampson in *Newes*, Lady Macbeth is "the onelye woman, who by the Divels perswasion should have entended and put in execution the Kings Majesties death". She invites spirits to interfere with her sex, "fill" her body and "take" her milk, evoking images of demonic copulation and transformation, possession and suckling. But her husband's sabbath attendance in the "cauldron" scene echoes the woodcut image in *Newes from Scotland*, and even his communication with her by letter recalls Dr Fian acting as "Regester" to the devil. *Newes* makes play of Fian's literacy as a "Clarke": he also reads and signs his own confession, an act referred to on three occasions in the pamphlet.[29] There is no letter sent by Macbeth to his wife in Holinshed, making the literary act of writing and reading about witchcraft a significant Shakespearean innovation – is it there because of Fian, because Shakespeare was thinking about the relationship between witchcraft, words and writing? Lisa Hopkins discusses Macbeth's letter's status as deceptive and, further, in recording the sisters' activities, he acts like one of their number, spreading their ambiguous oracle.[30] So we might see Macbeth and Lady Macbeth as the Fourth and Fifth Witches, if we choose. Some criticism even sees Macbeth's call to his man Seyton in 5.3 as a summoning of Satan, although there has been well-argued resistance to this.[31] More generally, readers have long identified one or both Macbeths with or as witches: in my reading, they are made more witch-like by their echoes of *Newes*.[32]

However, if they are witches they might have to take numbers Eight and Nine. A further complicating factor is the appearance of another four witches, or three witches and a witch-goddess, Hecate. In 4.1 they enter as "Hecat, and the other three Witches", making a total of seven with the three weird sisters. Hecate appears as "Mistris" of the other witches' "Charmes" and "close contriver of all harmes". But whilst Hecate is mentioned elsewhere by Macbeth ("Witchcraft celebrates Pale Heccats Offrings" and "black Heccats summons") her appearance as a *dea ex machina* and association with the sisters seems forced, metrically by its tetrameter couplets and in plot by its unnecessary nature.[33] Because in 3.5 and 4.1 material appears in *Macbeth* that also appears in or strongly recalls Middleton's *The Witch*, including a witch-leader character named Hecate, it has long been thought that *Macbeth*'s text survives in a version either written by Shakespeare in collaboration with Middleton, or modified by Middleton at a date between 1606 and its appearance in the 1623 Folio. The fact that around 3.5 and 4.1 the play's chronology is disrupted might indicate interpolations, especially taken alongside the way the witches speak.

The witches' speech is influenced by Scot, once again suggesting his ubiquity as inspiration, and by the pamphlets that helped to spark his *Discoverie of Witches*. One of Middleton's sources was thus *A True and Just Recorde*, probably as quoted in Scot's *A Discourse of Divels and Spirits*, appended to his *Discoverie*. The song "Blacke Spirits, &c." – which also appears in *Macbeth*'s 4.1 – includes names from *A True and Just Recorde*, which Scot discusses:

> he spirits and shee spirits, Tittie and Tiffin, Suckin and Pidgin, Liard and Robin . . . white spirits and blacke spirits, graie spirits and red spirits, divell tode and divell lambe, divels cat and divels dam.

Compare *The Witch*:

> Black spirits, and white; Red spirits, and gray;
> Mingle, mingle, mingle, you that mingle may.
> Titty, Tiffin, keepe it stiff in;
> Fire-drake, Puckey, make it luckey;
> Liard, Robin, you must bob in.[34]

Compare also *Macbeth*, 1.1 or 1.3, as quoted above. The plays rework the names, rhyme, repetition and rhythm of Scot's list, originally conveying his contempt for the evidence as childish nonsense, into a special witch-speak. This is characterised by heavy patterning: alliterative iambic chanting in unpredictable but thumping metres, triplicate forms and couplets, moving sinisterly towards a crisp closure. The stage witch-speak recalls Geillis Duncane's song in *Newes*, as Purkiss notes, and like her colleagues, *Macbeth*'s weird sisters speak and sing "all with one voice".[35]

This eerie patterning would prove one of the play's main legacies in witchcraft fiction: "haunting and unforgettable". Purkiss argues that such witch-verse signifies evil "like the villain's black hat in a western", but also wonders if it is meant to be funny, reductive, and if the witches of *Macbeth* are a "comic sub-plot", which returns us to the start of this chapter and the comedy of *Mother Bombie* or *The Old Wives Tale*. Indeed, whilst L.C. Knights described the speech of *Macbeth*'s witches as a "sickening see-saw", in this Scot–Middletonian section of the play, it is also child's-play in the belittling sense.[36] Whatever its effect, comedy and sublime horror are not mutually exclusive, and witches often evoke both in their speech and acts. Another key legacy of early modern witch-plays is thus their sense of disgust edged with amusement: cauldron-scenes typify this. Both *Macbeth* and *The Witch* feature these, and how far the same mind shaped both is, again, unclear. In particular, *Macbeth* draws on the all-out horror of the "bairnis unbaptesit", jointed corpses and venomous toads deployed at North Berwick, and the uncanny imagery of English pamphlets with their demonic cat familiars.

In 4.1, *Macbeth*'s sisters fill their cauldron with loathsome and cruelly obtained ingredients:

> First Witch: Thrice the brinded Cat hath mew'd.
> Second Witch: Thrice, and once the Hedge-Pigge whin'd.
> Third Witch: Harpier cries, 'tis time, 'tis time.
> First Witch: Round about the Caldron go:
> In the poysond Entrailes throw
> Toad, that under cold stone,
> Dayes and Nights, ha's thirty one:
> Sweltred Venom sleeping got,
> Boyle thou first i'th'charmed pot.
> All: Double, double, toile and trouble;
> Fire burne, and Cauldron bubble.
> Second Witch: Fillet of a Fenny Snake,
> In the Cauldron boyle and bake:
> Eye of Newt, and Toe of Frogge,
> Wooll of Bat, and Tongue of Dogge:
> Adders Forke, and Blinde-wormes Sting,
> Lizards legge, and Howlets wing:
> For a Charme of powrefull trouble,
> Like a Hell-broth, boyle and bubble . . .
> Finger of Birth-strangled Babe,
> Ditch-deliver'd by a Drab,
> Make the Grewell thicke, and slab.[37]

Remembrance of the cauldron scene tends to colour memory of the whole play (which is why it is so interesting that Forman did not remember it – was it, therefore, not in the early version that he saw?). Its emphasis on the physical artefacts, processes and substances of witchcraft is especially potent. As Chris

Laoutaris points out, the play is "staging the circulation of familiar objects in ways which result in their defamiliarisation and mystification".[38] Mixing familiar and unfamiliar, especially in imagining foraging, cooking and consuming, the sisters define the uncanny. From their homely-but-horrific brew they conjure unexpected apparitions: like *The Old Wives Tale* and *Friar Bacon*, an armed head, along with a bloody child and a child crowned, with a tree in his hand, followed by the show of eight kings. These visions embody fragmentary images of dynastic succession and war. The latter theme in particular would recur in the twentieth century in connection with a reinvented witchcraft.

As this chapter's focus has suggested, *Macbeth* is the Renaissance text that features most frequently in modern rediscoveries of witchcraft in Britain and America. The complex of works related to it, from *Newes* to *The Witch*, is also therefore important. But with the flowering of magical realism in the later twentieth century, works that imagined magic in contexts of oppression and poetic resistance emerged "writing back", and *The Tempest*, rather than *Macbeth*, lent itself to these rediscoveries. *The Tempest*'s witch Sycorax is ideally fitted for reimagining because she never actually appears and we hear of her only through the magician Prospero's abuse. He calls her a "fowle Witch", "damn'd Witch" and "hag", whom he alleges had sex with the devil and carried out "mischiefes manifold, and sorceries terrible", working by "potent Ministers". Her son Caliban adds that Sycorax worshipped a god named Setebos; he confirms that Sycorax used "Charmes" and himself curses like a witch, although ineffectively.[39] Sycorax-as-witch has been reclaimed by such readers as Abena Busia, Leah Marcus and Purkiss, and regarded as the victim of Prospero's demonisation.[40] But Prospero himself is called a "Sorcerer" by Caliban, and throughout the play he summons and commands spirits using the Faustian magical paraphernalia of book, robe and staff. He raises the dead too, he tells us, Medea-like. In his final speech to the audience, he admits freely that he has used "Charmes" like Sycorax, taking over her "Spirits to enforce" and using his "Art to inchant": now he pleads for forgiveness.

Prospero's most obviously witch-like act is to cause a sea-storm, like the North Berwick witches, an aspect of his magic not usually discussed in this context. In this, as well as his literacy and orderliness, he might remind us of Dr Fian as well as Doctor Faustus, sitting in his study with his books. Yet Prospero's practices were traditionally considered benign in comparison with Sycorax's. In addition to Frank Kermode's famously polemical introduction to the 1954 Arden edition, which pits Prospero as "theurgist" against Sycorax as "goetist", C.J. Sisson, Hardin Craig and Robert West – to choose just three examples from the 1950s to 1960s – all regarded his magic as broadly neo-Platonic or "white". Ellen Belton explored the possibility that Prospero is a hypnotist; for Jasmine Lellock, he is an alchemist transforming human potential; Robert Reid sees *The Tempest* as most decisively shaped by Christian passion plays and so on. The fact that Prospero is the play's internal dramatist, and an avatar of the playwright himself, produced further readings focused on the joyously transformative potential of magic.[41]

Despite these persuasive readings of Prospero's art as largely benign, it is also clear that in choosing a sea-tempest as the titular image of his play, Shakespeare returned to the North Berwick trope of the witch-raised storm. That choice places Prospero in the same situation as Agnes Sampson and her fellow-witches and *Macbeth*'s weird sisters, which makes Prospero more like Sycorax than most critics are willing to concede. There is even an alluring further parallel: in 1823, Charles Lamb found an account of an Algerian witch said to have caused a sea-storm in 1541 that saved Algiers from invasion – was that story, he speculated, a source for Sycorax? No direct link to Shakespeare has been proven, but even without this storm-raising similarity, many readers link the magics of Sycorax and Prospero.[42] Is Prospero a witch? Genevieve Guenther compares Prospero with the definitions of witchcraft in King James' *Daemonologie*, finding numerous simi-larities, although she does not quite say that Prospero resembles Sampson.[43] In 1985, prompted by Anthony Harris' "rash" conclusion that Prospero was a Faustian figure, Cosmo Corfield summed up the debate about Prospero's possible witchcraft by suggesting that the word "rough", as in the "rough magic" that he abjures in 5.1, was the crux of the matter.[44] Depending on how we read its roughness, Prospero's magic might mean that *The Tempest* shows us two kinds of witch.

Before moving on to look at the afterlives of the witches of Shakespearean drama, it is important to consider briefly a sample of the related witches of Elizabethan poetry. In contrast to the subtleties of Shakespeare, Edmund Spen-ser's *The Faerie Queene* (Books 1–3, 1590) seems simpler, containing neatly labelled witches who reappear in fragmentary form in later texts. Like Erictho and Prospero, these are witches with classical roots. Duessa is "cruell" and "wicked", a witch who can change appearances, enfeeble and entrance her victims like Medea or Circe. Although she appears beautiful, she is in reality "a filthy foule old woman" with "neather parts . . . misshapen, monstruous" and part-animal, shown when she is stripped. Here, witchcraft is figured as deceit, doubleness, duality – the qualities associated a year later with Ewfame Macalȝean. Another version of Duessa, Acrasia, appears in Book 2, luring knights into joyous, lustful idleness that transforms some into animals. Unlike Duessa, Acrasia is not false: she really is desirable. Instead, the threat seems to be that what she offers is truly good in many ways – pleasurable, beautiful, precious – yet it must be resisted if one is to remain virtuous, so much so that her bower must be destroyed (as explored by Stephen Greenblatt and Gareth Roberts).

In Book 3, Spenser offers us a third encounter with the meaning of witchcraft. This witch is so stereotypical that Katherine Briggs called her "the most complete witch in the regular English tradition". We see:

> A little cottage, built of stickes and reedes
> In homely wize, and wald with sods around,
> In which a witch did dwell, in loathly weedes,
> And wilfull want, all carelesse of her needes;
> So choosing solitarie to abide,
> Far from all neighbours, that her devilish deedes
> And hellish arts from people she might hide,
> And hurt far off unknowne, whom ever she envied.[45]

This witch is ugly and old, poor and anti-social, like the witches described in English pamphlets, and she is obviously so. There are no deceitful surprises behind words such as "loathly . . . wilfull . . . devilish" and "hellish", and there is nothing alluring either. But Spenser's third witch is like Duessa and Acrasia in other ways: she is associated with lust. When her son unsuccessfully pursues the beautiful fugitive Florimell, the witch sets a hyena-like creature on her, representing the consuming of female flesh.

However, the witch also has unusual traits. Unexpectedly, when Florimell escapes her, the witch behaves like a male magician, a Friar Bacon or Doctor Faustus. She fabricates a false Florimell to comfort her son. This creature is a Petrarchan simulacrum, made of snow, wax and metal, but also a succubus powered by a masculine "wicked Spright". As Patrick Cheney suggests, the witch's sudden deployment of traditionally masculine manufacturing skill and learning is unsettling. He sees the witch as an allegory of aspects of the neo-Platonic imagination, but she is also something worse, a female projector, alchemist or natural philosopher. This unnamed but powerful witch and her son may be prototypes for Sycorax and Caliban, a luridly potent hag and her unloved, sexually predatory offspring: their activities certainly inform later texts.[46]

The "wilfull want" of Spenser's third witch caricatures the unwilling poverty of many suspected witches, but the final text that is self-evidently influential in later rediscoveries of witchcraft presents a much more realistic portrait of such a poor, old woman. Elizabeth Sawyer, in John Ford, Thomas Dekker and William Rowley's *The Witch of Edmonton* (1621), is guilty of the crime, for which she is executed at the play's end. However, the audience is also encouraged to sympathise with her as the victim of her neighbours' aggression, which drives her to witchcraft. On one level, her story is a classic revenge tragedy, inflected by *Doctor Faustus* and an anonymous play, *The Merry Devil of Edmonton* (1608), with its depictions of a male conjuror, Peter Fabel, and his devil Coreb.[47] But it also has a vivid social realism and remains partly true to the life of its historical model, Elizabeth Sawyer of Edmonton. As we saw in Chapter 1, her confession was documented in Henry Goodcole's pamphlet *The Wonderfull Discovery of Elizabeth Sawyer*.

The playwrights used Goodcole's carefully recreated dialogue with the witch as inspiration for their character's meeting with a demonic dog familiar, and her close relationship with him. But they changed her familial circumstances to make her more indigent and isolated (the real Sawyer had a husband and children), as well as changing the nature of her crimes (the real Sawyer practised regular *maleficium*, whilst in the play her witchcraft prompts uxoricide and suicide in others). This "representational ambivalence" – between fact and fiction, condemnation and sympathy – means that, as David Stymeist argues, the play both critiques and reinforces established Renaissance notions of witchcraft.[48] Like all the plays and masques discussed so far, it reimagines the stories told in its sources but also moves them from supposed fact to definite fiction, provoking consideration of the reality (or not) of witchcraft acts.

One of *The Witch of Edmonton*'s innovations, perhaps drawing on *Doctor Faustus* with its tempting devil Mephistopheles and its Evil Angel, is to incarnate Sawyer's devil-dog Tom and put him onstage. Goodcole's Tom is an absent presence, long gone by the time the witch is in her Newgate cell. In the play, Tom is embodied by an actor who must have been costumed as a dog and who speaks many of Goodcole's best lines. The audience sees and hears the temptation of a demonic familiar, who disconcertingly offers not just revenge on enemies, but play and cuddles like a real dog. The play's Tom also changes perceptions of Goodcole's devil in other ways. He moves between the narrative strands of the play, enabling more dramatic sinfulness to afflict the community of Edmonton than the real-life accusers could envisage. Tom rubs against the bigamist Frank Thorney, who decides to kill his first wife. He admits he cannot kill good people such as Old Farmer Banks, one of Sawyer's "chief Adversaries", "whose blows", she says, "have lam'd me". Even if he has behaved badly to Sawyer, Banks is "loving to the world, And charitable to the poor" and thus protected. Instead, Tom calls a succubus to tease Banks' son. Masquerading as "a sweet, lovely Maid", the succubic spirit – akin to Faustus' Helen or the false Florimell – leads young Cuddy Banks into a pond. It is hard not to enjoy the devil-dog's pranks, in part simply because the audience enjoys watching an actor imitate a dog.

The play also adds to Goodcole's account by changing the relationship between Sawyer and her neighbour Anne or Agnes Ratcliffe. In the stage version of the story, the witch is made responsible for not just the sickness but the suicide of her neighbour, a new level of witch-attack that focuses on the soul of the victim. As Katherine O'Mahoney points out, the play's Sawyer is not just imperilling her own soul, but those of others because suicide was damnable. Ratcliffe's suicide acts as an intensifier of community feeling, so that the play's villagers turn on Sawyer viciously: "Burn the Witch", they chorus, "beat her, kick her, set fire on her". Sawyer's response is one upon which the audience is invited to reflect:

> If every poor old Woman,
> Be trod on thus by slaves, revil'd, kick'd, beaten,
> As I am daily, she to be reveng'd
> Had need turn Witch.

This amplifies the complaints with which she enters the play in 2.1:

> And why on me? why should the envious world
> Throw all their scandalous malice upon me?
> 'Cause I am poor, deform'd and ignorant . . .
> Some call me Witch,
> And being ignorant of my self, they go
> About to teach me how to be one.[49]

As Julia Garrett argues, *The Witch of Edmonton* does not exonerate the witch – it retains enough of Goodcole's censure to prohibit that – but its "compassionate depiction" does go some way towards explaining her conduct. Anyone faced with her circumstances, the play suggests, might become a witch. The name "witch" itself is thus also exposed as a metaphor for all kinds of sinful empowerment – as in Middleton's *The Witch* – so that Sawyer lists courtesans, lawyers, scolds and seducers as "witches" alongside herself. "A Witch?" she scoffs – "who is not?" Other readers observing these broadly satirical passages have regarded the play as outright "sceptical" (Michael Hattaway) and "subversive" of traditional witchcraft discourse (Viviana Comensoli).[50] Barbara Traister suggests more hesitantly that the play responds to the later Jacobean atmosphere of scepticism towards straightforward accounts of witchcraft as a threat. Most interestingly for our consideration of the rediscovery of witchcraft in the twentieth century, David Stymeist suggests the playwrights of *The Witch of Edmonton* – all of whom had suffered at the hands of the law – found common ground with the witch in writing her story, even though they also conclusively affirmed that she had been justly hanged.[51] Thus, even in Jacobean stagings, the witch was already being interpreted as a metaphorical figure, who could be appropriated to dramatise, and encourage reflection upon, the trials of her re-creators. Such a figure, with no stable referent or meaning, encourages us all to consider who is and is not also a witch.

Renaissance witchcraft in fiction: summary

This chapter has discussed the diverse representations of witches in Renaissance fictions, with a focus on well-known, canonical texts such as *Macbeth* and the cluster of plays and one masque that responded to, and perhaps in some instances informed, them. The influence of *Newes from Scotland* on many of these texts is evident: images of grave-robbing and sieve-sailing, sea-storms, cauldrons and cats, clerkly and hedonistic sabbath-attendees, singing, dancing, making images of intended victims, attending to demonic admonitions, subverting and seducing authority figures and other magical activities all relate back to the North Berwick witches. The ways that several plays and the masque use elements of the North Berwick story to problematise the relationship between witches and kings is important: in later fiction, witches and witch-hunters continue this vexed association, where the roles of hero(ine) and villain may easily be reversed or conflated. The chapter has suggested that despite some egregious exceptions, witches emerge from Renaissance fictions as very much like other people in their sins and follies: as Elizabeth Sawyer says, "a Witch? who is not?" The influence of early English demonologies by Scot and Gifford is likely to be one reason for this: both constructed the witch primarily as a pitiable sinner or victim of injustice rather than as an enemy of the state, God or even her community in any straightforward way. We have therefore seen in this chapter early indications that it is possible to empathise with a witch and/or be amused by her or his antics, a trend that has continued and strengthened into modernity.

The rest of this book now explores the rediscovery of the Renaissance witch, with the discussion now shifting to twentieth- and twenty-first-century fiction.[52]

Notes

1 Dean, 263; Barber, xiii, 3 – although I am extending Barber's definition beyond Shakespeare, which he specifically rejects.

2 Early English Books Online, 1594 edition, http://quod.lib.umich.edu/cgi/t/text/text-idx?c=eebo;idno=A06622.0001.001, with line references from Scragg, ed., 3.1.29; Scragg, 30.

3 Towne emphasises the play's demonic element; Early English Books Online, 1594 edition, http://quod.lib.umich.edu/e/eebo/A02127.0001.001/1:2?rgn=div1;view=fulltext, with reference from Seltzer, ed., XI: 53, 64, 73; on sources that inflect the play see Walsh (Spenserian resonances, see also below); Senn; Hieatt; Gibson, "Greene's *Friar Bacon*"; Ardolino, "History of Oxford"; and LeGrandeur. On the head, see Dahlquist.

4 Early English Books Online, 1595 text, http://quod.lib.umich.edu/e/eebo/A09232.0001.001/1:2?rgn=div1;view=fulltext with line references from Whitworth, ed., 1.1.291, 318; Lamb, 37; Renwick; for wider religious resonance see Ardolino, "Protestant Context".

5 Cope, 337.

6 Shakespeare texts are quoted from the First Folio (1623) online facsimile at: http://firstfolio.bodleian.ox.ac.uk/book.html; on Joane, see Tricomi; on the *2 Henry VI* conspirators, Levine.

7 Pettitt, "Folk-Play"; although, contradictorily, Stevenson emphasises the "comic core".

8 Macdonald, "Calvinist"; on passion, see Streete; on animal-human and other boundaries transgressed by magic, Pettitt, especially 300–3, and on natural philosophy, Sugar.

9 Kocher argues that the play has a sound "witchcraft basis", 9 and *passim*. As Marlowe's play's date is unclear, the relationship between the texts is speculative. But it does appear strong, and the story of Fian and the heifer – which appears in *Newes* but not in the pre-trial paperwork, some of which is lost – recalls Faustian pranks.

10 Purkiss, *Witch* 207; on *Macbeth*'s Scottishness, see Clark and Mason, eds, 26–35.

11 Wyntoun, 225, line 20.

12 Line numbers are from Brooke, ed., 1.3.40–53; Benecke, 248.

13 The Folio text simply numbers the characters 1, 2 and 3.

14 Brooke, ed., 1.3.4–29.

15 *Newes* C.

16 Brooke, ed., 1.1.2; Calhoun discusses some of the witchcraft sources of the play, but attributed *Newes* to James' personal authorship, and is imprecise about *Macbeth*'s borrowings from witch-lore across Europe.

17 Brooke, ed., 1.2.47–8, 1.3.108, 132.

18 Roberts, "The Crone" 128.

19 Early English Books Online, 1606 edition, http://quod.lib.umich.edu/cgi/t/text/text-idx?c=eebo;idno=A07083.0001.001, line numbers from Corbin and Sedge, ed., 5.1 stage direction after line 21; Richardson, 106. Corbin and Sedge, eds, discuss Erictho's origin in Lucan (6).

20 Brooke, ed., 1.1.3; see also Heywood and Brome, whose *Late Lancashire Witches* stages similar inversions (on which see Willis, "Witch-Family" and Coffin).

21 www.bl.uk/collection-items/autograph-manuscript-of-ben-jonsons-the-masque-of-queens-1609.

22 The term, explored by Foucault, has been translated as both "other" and "different" spaces. *The Witch* was not published until 1778 – see below.

23 Purkiss, *Witch* 199–225; Sermin Meskill; George; Roberts, "Re-Examination"; Bromham; Garrett, "Witchcraft and Sexual Knowledge" 32. More generally, Lancashire discusses *The Witch*'s role as political satire and the Overbury scandal.

24 For general histories see Lindley and Somerset.

25 Similarities are summarised in Schafer, ed., xvi, xvii; see also Corbin and Sedge, eds, 13–20; Bellany, 152–8; and www.earlystuartlibels.net/htdocs/overbury_murder_section/H0.html.

26 On witch-language see Byville, and Richardson, chapter 2.

27 Brooke, ed., 1.2.67, 1.1.4, 1.1.9, 1.3.38; see Doran, Walton Williams, Juhasz, Kranz, especially 346, and Hope and Witmore.

28 Brooke, ed., 1.5.40–6, 2.1.33, 3.4, 5.1.35, 42; Fishlin, 6.

29 Brooke, ed., 5.1; the witches' letter does not appear in *Newes* but Fian's writing does: title page, C2, D, D2, B4-v.

30 Hopkins, "Reading" 5–7.

31 For instance, Nosworthy, 217, Davidson and Greenblatt, 32 (categorically "Macbeth is not a witch").

32 On Lady Macbeth's common imagery with witches see Adelman, "Born of Woman" and *Suffocating Mothers*; Marcus, *Puzzling Shakespeare* 104; Callaghan, 358; Dolan, 227; more generally on witch imagery and infanticide meeting in Lady Macbeth, Willis, *Malevolent Nurture* and Chamberlain; see also Laoutaris, below.

33 Brooke, ed., 3.5.6–7, 2.1.51–2, 3.2.43.

34 Scot, 455; from the first edition, 1778, www.bl.uk/collection-items/first-edition-of-middletons-the-witch.

35 *Newes* B3; Purkiss, *Witch* 199, 200

36 Frye, 250; see also Kranz, 352–4; Purkiss, 210; Knights, 20.

37 Brooke, ed., 4.1.1–36.

38 Laoutaris, 176.

39 Kermode, ed., 2.1.258, 263, 264, 269, 275, 340, 374.

40 For pioneering rereadings of Sycorax, see Busia, Marcus, Purkiss 1996; more recently, Go explores Sycorax' highly mobile origin, this time as a Scythian/cannibal witch; see also Gibson and Esra, eds, entry on Sycorax.

41 Sisson, especially 76; Craig; West; Kermode, ed., xl; all these refer to Curry. Belton, 127; Lellock; Reid; Egan; Ettin, especially 284–9; Giorno. See also Mowat.

42 Kermode, ed., 3.2.41, 1.2.187–8, 193, 245, 246; Epilogue 1, 14; Lamb.

43 Guenther, and compare Mzeil, 116, which does; Davis, which links Scottish and Irish witches with Sycorax; and contextually Mac Cárthaigh.

44 Harris, 135; Corfield, 32.

45 Briggs, 75; Roche, ed., 1.2.33, 1.5.27, 1.2.40–1, 1.8.45–6, 3.7.6.

46 Roche, ed., 3.8.5–8; Cheney; on Spenserian magic generally, Gross.

47 See Walker, ed.

48 Stymeist. On contradiction see also Dawson.

49 Early English Books Online, 1658 edition: http://quod.lib.umich.edu/e/eebo/A57764.0001.001/1:5.2.1?rgn=div3;view=fulltext with line references from Corbin and Sedge, eds, 4.1.15, 27, 78–81, 3.1.70–91, 2.1.1–10, 16, 31, 150–64. O'Mahoney argues that by showing Sawyer prompting suicide, the play demonises her more than Goodcole does.

50 Garrett, 327; Hattaway, 50; Comensoli, 59; Ford *et al.*, 4.1.78–154.

51 Traister; Stymeist, 44–6.

52 Later plays, such as Heywood and Brome's *Late Lancashire Witches* (1634) are also important in the story of rediscovering witchcraft, but are seldom directly referenced in later texts. See Pudney for a much wider range of plays with a witchcraft element.

3 "Where the place?"

Renaissance witchcraft rediscovered in Scotland

As the two previous chapters' focus has likely suggested, the rediscovery of Renaissance witchcraft begins with Scotland, with the dittays of the North Berwick witches, *Newes from Scotland* and *Macbeth*. It moves through an English reworking of these materials towards a complex reimagining of an interwoven British history and culture, one that privileges sublime stories of subversion and resistance, associating them with witches. Later, wholly English, European and American materials are drawn into the mix, as will be discussed in later chapters, together with the occasional Welsh, Irish or Manx influence. But to understand the rediscovery we need to begin with Scotland, and specifically with Romanticism and the Scottish Enlightenment.

As I said in the Introduction, Romantic priorities are central to an understanding of the rediscovery of witchcraft in the late eighteenth century. Siegel's suggestion that a witchcraft event is a manifestation of the sublime usefully indicates that Romantic historians were attracted to witchcraft histories because of their sublimity: their passion and drama. The dramatic, theatrical potential of witchcraft events is also important to their Romantic rediscovery because of the shadow cast over them by *Macbeth*. With its intense uncanny atmosphere, *Macbeth* was a frequent reference point for writers evoking the "weird"-ness of witches. The play's setting, contrasting with its origin, was important too: *Macbeth* is often called "the Scottish play" but was written, as far as we know, in England. In this it has a dual, uncanny identity like the weird sisters: a doubleness shared by other works discussed in this chapter. This uncanniness mirrors the role of witchcraft in Scotland's political history and its uneasy relationship with England. The Anglo-Scottish relationship is thus an important factor in the Romantic rediscovery of witchcraft.

The first writers on Scottish witchcraft looked back to the seventeenth century as a period of legal self-definition and the loss of independence (with regal union in 1603 and the Act of Union in 1707) to explore issues of freedom, legal process and jurisdiction. They were often lawyers themselves. But, partly because of its nationalist implications, the history that was written was far from dry. Instead, it is a passionate recital of tyranny, injustice and rebellion, often exploring witches' role in the nation's past. Witches appeared as early victims of state tyranny, prototypical Romantics persecuted by an aggressive monarchy, nobility and church. The history of Scottish witchcraft thus became a personally empowering model for some of its Scottish rediscoverers, just as it had been for some of the English Jacobean writers discussed in Chapter 2. Later, as this chapter and the next show, this capacity for empowerment extended to the indulgence of passions and freedoms not encouraged by English convention, either social or literary. Rediscovering witchcraft through Scottish texts, rather than English ones, meant that the history of witchcraft became a literature of passion, national soul-searching and sublime subversion.

Writing Scottish witchcraft history

Scottish witchcraft history is inescapably shaped by the fact that Scotland's king, James VI (later James I of England), questioned the North Berwick witches and wrote *Daemonologie*. In England and Wales, no monarch played anything like a similar role in witchcraft prosecution. James also presided over the culture that produced the 1604 Witchcraft Act and *Macbeth*, so that the history of his reign, and of the united Scottish–English monarchy by extension, is also more generally a history of witchcraft. As we saw in the first two chapters, this king/witch binary has influenced the writing of literature and history ever since, a historiographical trend two centuries old that continues today.[1] And, as James Sharpe notes, "it was the Scottish hunts which first attracted sustained scholarly attention". Sharpe cites Walter Scott's *Letters on Demonology and Witchcraft* (Edinburgh, 1830), John Graham Dalyell's *The Darker Superstitions of Scotland* (Edinburgh, 1834) and Francis Legge's "Witchcraft in Scotland" in the *Scottish Review* 18 (October 1891: 257–88) as pioneers, as well as a republication of a work by Charles Kirkpatrick Sharpe (the "Introduction" to his edition of Robert Law's *Memorialls* [Edinburgh, 1818] which became *A Historical Account of the Belief in Witchcraft in Scotland* [Glasgow, 1884]).[2]

To this can be added *A Collection of Rare and Curious Tracts on Witchcraft* (Edinburgh, 1820), John Mitchell and John Dickie's *The Philosophy of Witchcraft* (Paisley, 1839) and George Moir's *Magic and Witchcraft* (London, 1852), as well as Hugo Arnot's *Collection and Abridgement of Celebrated Criminal Trials in Scotland from A.D. 1536 to 1784* (Edinburgh, 1785), the earliest really influential work.[3] The most oft-cited, however, is Pitcairn's *Ancient Criminal Trials in Scotland* (10 volumes, Edinburgh, 1829–33, see Chapter 1). There are more broadly focused Scottish works too, such as Charles Mackay's *Extraordinary Popular Delusions and the Madness of Crowds* (London, 1841), which has a chapter on witchcraft. A number of these publications, and scholarly editions of the earlier works, were produced by the Bannatyne Club, founded by Scott, Pitcairn and others in 1823 with the aim of enriching Scottish historical knowledge. Witchcraft was a central occurrence in that history, as we have seen, but Club members were particularly interested in its interconnections with the ethics of governance and justice, as their wider catalogue of publications demonstrates.[4] It was this context that set the direction for later witchcraft historiography in Scotland.

For these Scottish Enlightenment figures, witchcraft had a contemporary relevance that was not matched anywhere else in Britain. Until recently, witchcraft had been seen by some Scots as a prized national difference from the English. Ian Bostridge explains that to Scottish witch-prosecutors and some politicians:

> the campaign against witchcraft...played a symbolic role in Scottish opposition to English intellectual and religious colonisation of their kingdom ... For many Scots, the English were both leaguers with the devil and an impediment to godly resistance to witchcraft.

Bostridge and Owen Davies both highlight James Erskine, Lord Grange, who in February to March 1736 spoke in the Lords against the repeal of the Witchcraft Act out of a combination of religious zeal and Scottish patriotism. Erskine thought the English establishment figures promoting the repeal were deists and anti-Scottish: why should they determine Scottish demonological policy?[5] He was not alone in his views. In 1743, secessionist Presbyterians in Edinburgh published their opinion that the repeal of the Witchcraft Act had been a "national ... sin ... contrary to the express law of God". Answering, the radical lawyer Arnot noted that "the Seceders comprehend a very large body of the populace in Scotland". He deplored their document, its reading from pulpits and its reprint in Glasgow "so late as the year 1766", and his disgust at relatively recent events such as this (just nineteen years before) fuelled his scholarship on the history of witchcraft.[6]

Arnot's concern is obvious in his work: portrayals of the English as witch-loving enemies of God imply that to be Scottish is to hunt witches. This was the antithesis of the progressive Scotland that he promoted. For instance, in his history of Edinburgh he praised recent improvements – libraries, hospitals, welfare societies, free schools – contrasting these with a Scottish history that seemed "barbarous" and "bigoted', its monarchy a "tyranny".[7] In his *Celebrated Criminal Trials* "Euphan McCalzeane" thus appears as "barbarously" punished, in a sequence of trials both "absurd and iniquitous", demonstrating "fanaticism ... barbarity ... bloody zeal". Agnes Sampson, was "a grave, matron-like woman, of a rank and comprehension above the vulgar", accused of ludicrous crimes. Such witches were "human sacrifices" on "the altar of the Fatal Sisters, – Ignorance, – Superstition, – and Cruelty", victims of "legal murder". For Arnot, this history of witchcraft led to one "important conclusion": only "Science" and "Civil Liberty" could protect the subject's "sacred rights". He also described McCalzeane as one of the "Weyward Sisters", a nod to the pervasive influence of *Macbeth* and its witch/king binary. In real life, Arnot argued, McCalzeane had fallen victim to a corrupt king: "to move the wheels of his Majesty's conscience" after her execution, her children had "to grease them" with payment.[8] That was Scotland's past, a tragic drama of royal vainglory: her future must be different.

Arnot's work thus reforged the link between Scotland and witchcraft, relocating witches from the discourse of demonology into that of legal history, a history of horrors that evoked the sublime passions of pity and revolutionary rage. He also pushed their crime from reality into fiction, using the reference to *Macbeth* as a marker of that shift. Altogether, he positioned witchcraft in a less harmful space, and his successors followed his lead. A review of Arnot's book condemned the "atrocity" displayed in "every part of the state" in the past, including Tarquin-like "tyranny, rapacity, and absurdity in the government" and "religious madness". Pitcairn believed some of the witches deserved their fate, but described their torture (specifically Fiene's) as a "disgrace to this country".[9] Mitchell and Dickie regretted that "in no country did the flame of witchcraft burn brighter, or were victims more easily procured for the sacrifice, than in our own" and Moir echoed them: "in no country . . . did this gloomy superstition assume a darker and bloodier character than in Scotland".[10] Even Kirkpatrick Sharpe, a royalist who was accused of levity for his attempts to make history amusing, spoke of Scotland's past as "disgraced" by witchcraft prosecution.[11]

Some writers reflected anxiously on comparisons between Scotland's and England's witchcraft history. Dalyell spent five pages wondering how "this cruel innovation on reason [witchcraft prosecution] was introduced into Scotland", desperate for an external source. He was pleased that although the swimming test had "disgraced the English rabble . . . south of the Tweed" he found no evidence of it in Scotland, despite its appearance in the King's *Daemonologie*. The English also "probably" invented the pilliewinks, he hoped.[12] But Scott's was the strongest statement of Anglo-Scottish comparison, notable for its self-accusing difference from Dalyell's. In his *Letters on Demonology and Witchcraft*, there are neighbouring chapters on English and Scottish witchcraft. Whilst Scott recounted English cases – Warboys, Bury St Edmunds, the Hopkins trials – he praised "sensible and courageous" Englishmen who minimised persecution.

Discussing Hopkins, Scott opined:

> the boast of the English nation is a manly independence and common sense, which will not long permit the license of tyranny or oppression on the meanest and most obscure sufferers. Many clergymen and gentlemen made head against the practices of this cruel oppressor of the defenceless.

Further, "it must be admitted, that the most severe of the laws against witchcraft originated with a Scottish King of England" and that "for many years the Scottish nation had been remarkable for a credulous belief in witchcraft". Scott regretted that in Scotland, the "system" of witchcraft was different from the English conception, "subsisted to a later period, and was prosecuted with much more severity". Apologetic throughout, he made the conventional gesture towards the literary, the saving grace of Scottish witchcraft that transformed the national horror into dramatic art. He hoped readers would be interested in Scottish witches because they "were the countrywomen of the weird sisters in *Macbeth*". In his novels, he also likened Scottish witches to their English literary forebears: in *Waverley*, for instance, where Janet Gellatley is compared with Spenser's witch in her "gloomy hollow glen".[13]

Eighteenth- and nineteenth-century Scottish historians thus attempted to cleanse Scotland of the stain of superstition by emphasising the improvements of modernity and repositioning the narrative of the trials in history alongside Renaissance fiction. Each felt the sublime emotions of witchcraft events, but strove to turn them from a persecutory energy into an impulse towards compassion. Ironically, each also deepened the association between Scotland and witchcraft by his antiquarian researches and their distribution in print. Scottish Romantics thus both founded modern witchcraft studies and provided the raw material for many of the later fictions that are the subject of this book. In 2002, Julian Goodare suggested that "there is surely more to be said on the relationship between witchcraft and intellectual ideas in this formative period between the Reformation and the Enlightenment".[14] This is still true. But Arnot's role is a key one. He made the crucial connections between Scottish witch-trials and governance in a forthright radical voice, rehabilitating witches as victims of state oppression. He also framed them in a patriotic discourse of national progress, of emotion recollected in liberal and humane tranquillity.[15]

Even more conservative Scottish writers such as Pitcairn drew on this legacy. It was these legal historical works that provided the crucial access to original records – especially the dittays of the North Berwick witches – which creative writers found so fascinating in later times. Often Scott provided an introduction, either by his historical or fictional works. For instance, one of the first writers to dramatise Scottish witchcraft in a recognisably modern way was the Scottish poet Joanna Baillie. Baillie moved to Hampstead, London, around the turn of the eighteenth century, and there wrote a play, *Witchcraft* (1836). *Witchcraft*'s events are fictional, dealing with the wrongful accusation of an innocent heroine and three deluded old women, and Baillie cited Scott's novels as her inspiration. But she also used material from a Renfrewshire trial of 1697, likely sourced from Arnot and Scott's *Letters*, as Alyson Bardsley has shown, as well as more detailed accounts of the case by Francis Grant in *A True Narrative* (1698) and in an anonymous *History of the Witches of Renfrewshire* published in Paisley in 1809. *Witchcraft* is also heavily indebted to *Macbeth*: for its three witches, and many words and phrases of dialogue (newts and adders, "mawkin" cats, rhyming spells, thunder and lightning and so on). As Janet Handley suggests, *Witchcraft* thus sits between fact and fiction.[16] And Baillie's movement from Scotland to England – from the territory of Bothwell to that of Shakespeare – also places her work in a liminal space. It mirrored the cross-border journey that Scottish witchcraft stories undertook in modernity.

This chapter now examines how British writers in the twentieth century mined these Scottish sources. They rediscovered stories of sublime passion not available to them in the history of English witchcraft, and they also found ways to discuss new liberties in witchcraft stories, as Arnot had done.

Scottish witchcraft viewed from England

Just as *Macbeth* haunted Scottish accounts of witches, English writers often rediscovered Renaissance witchcraft through Shakespeare. In the early twentieth century, the new professions of folklorist and literary critic both examined how Shakespeare's work reflected the supernatural beliefs of his time. The new bibliography and Poelite stagings, which tried to recreate the original textual and theatrical experience, provided studies of key passages and stage effects.[17] Early Shakespeare films applied a new medium to old plays: in 1908, for example, *The Tempest* showed Ariel vanishing through a cutting trick. In this historicist, nostalgic climate, Shakespeare became part of a debate about modernity and liberal values, the (ir)rational and unconscious, the pagan and the folkloric. Early scholars of the Shakespearean supernatural included Henry Neele, W. Carew Hazlitt, Hall Caine, T.A. Spalding, T.F. Thiselton Dyer, Albert Tolman, Alfred Nutt, Felix Schelling, Margaret Lucy, Arthur Quiller Couch, Henry Wheatley and H.W. Herrington. There was keen interest in publishing their work: Chapman and Hall, Griffith and Farran, *PMLA* and *Folklore* all contributed. The Liverpool publisher William Jaggard, working on the *Shakespeare Bibliography*, which would be published in 1911, compiled a booklist on "Folk-lore, Super-stition and Witchcraft in Shakespeare" in 1906 containing 97 items.[18]

Shakespeare was often presented as a Renaissance folklorist by these scholars. Quiller Couch (Q) summed up this attitude: in "The Workmanship of *Macbeth*" (1914) he argued that Shakespeare was not a witch-hunter or witch-believer.[19] Instead, he was a craftsman, absorbing James VI and I's interests, mingling them with folk tales and transforming them into an ambiguous dramatic vision, sug-gestive, not superstitious and fictive, not factual. Q and his fellow-critics thus participated in the Anglophilic denial noted before in this chapter: surely English dramatists, unlike Scottish kings, never truly invested in witchcraft beliefs? Instead, they transmuted them into works about tolerance, possibility and interpretation. In *Macbeth*, it was suggested, Shakespeare had created an unbreakable link between Scotland and witchcraft in the public mind, but had remained untainted himself. The idea that witchcraft was something sublime, un-English and exciting that belonged elsewhere was common in the period. It is not wholly unfair – as we have seen, most English prosecutions were small-scale, with a primarily domestic focus, and the loss of records relating to the Hopkins trials means that a particularly vicious period of witch-hunting is under-represented in English histories. But small scale and domesticity do not mean insignificance, and later writers would present these microhistories of witchcraft as just as sinister as any Scottish sabbath.

The notion that witchcraft belief was not part of mainstream English culture was, however, endemic in early twentieth-century England. In particular, it did not belong in metropolitan modernity. In 1908, Oliver Madox Hueffer mocked belief in magic as belonging among Romney marshlanders, suburban lodging-house keepers and "silly servant-girls".[20] Magic appeared in the press as an anthropological curiosity, a relic. When Edward Lovett of the Folklore Society lectured on his collection of charms in 1914 and 1917, press coverage expressed surprise at several charms from London's docklands, which were made to counter the U-Boat threat.[21] A *Times* article on "Superstition in Essex" in 1915 quoted a correspondent's letter reporting stories that a woman had been feeding "niggets" (familiars) with chopped grass in an Essex village: "fancy such things going on forty miles from London!" it exclaimed.[22] The working classes – servants, landladies, seamen, agricultural labourers – were the target of comment here, with a prevailing opinion that "we" (*Times* readers, an urban intelligentsia) would naturally not believe in witchcraft. Meanwhile, "we still hear of people in remote villages who complain of being overlooked", as a rare curiosity. The focus of such reports was a narrative of progress unchanged since the eighteenth century, with an added implication that the London elites were especially rational.[23]

Witchcraft was fascinating, therefore, but forcefully marginalised: it belonged in fiction and on the far-away peripheries. This was not a uniquely English phenomenon. Speaking of the Normandy *bocage*, Jeanne Favret-Saada joked about a similar Parisian perception in the mid-twentieth century: "how convenient that there should be a district full of idiots, where the whole realm of the imaginary can be held in".[24] Owen Davies has examined a similar discourse, denying-yet-documenting the continuation of supernatural beliefs, especially in cities, in the American press.[25] Also in America, Philip Gould and Lawrence Buell have connected this stereotype to nineteenth-century patrician fear of the democratic "mob".[26] Such projections of anxiety can be seen to reflect concern about a witch-hunting lower class, external to official circles and worryingly backward. Educated, publishing elites thus continued throughout the early twentieth century to regard themselves as guardians of rationality, despite ample evidence that supernatural beliefs flourished among all classes of society (see Chapter 4).[27] But as well as an element of class snobbery, we can see that there is a geographical dimension to these projections of a superstitious Other: witchcraft always happens somewhere else (rural Essex or Suffolk, the East End).

With this pattern of centre/periphery distinction mapped onto the traditional association between Scotland and witches, it is unsurprising that a frequent location for fictions of witchcraft was north of the border. Britain's "Celtic" nations and regions were often a focus of enquiry into belief in fairies, paganism, Druidry and witchcraft. Scottish, Welsh, Irish and Cornish scholars were disproportionately represented among eighteenth- and nineteenth-century antiquaries (John Toland, Edward Lhuyd, Edward Davies, William Borlase and others) and their work responded to, and influenced perceptions of, Celtic survivals in far-flung places. The furore over the role of Irish fairy and witch beliefs in the murder of Bridget Cleary at Clonmel in 1895 and the work of folklorists such as Walter Evans Wentz and John Rhys on Cornish and Welsh fairy mythology continued the association into modernity. And, put simply, Scotland's witchcraft history was rolled into this stereotype of Celtic mysticism.[28] As Eliza Lynn Linton suggested in 1861, "Scotland was always foremost in superstition . . . saddest and darkest and unholiest of all was the belief in witchcraft . . . which was nowhere more bitter and destructive than among the godly children of our Northern sister".[29] In this English stereotype, Scotland remained trapped in the witchcraft sublime, distant, irrational and persecutory.

Scotland was not just a magical threat, of course. It was also a political one, with the two threats acting as proxies and intensifiers for each other. Early movements towards Scottish devolution began in the late Victorian period, and culminated in the 1913 Scottish Home Rule Bill, intended by the Liberal government to strengthen the Union by allowing Irish-style Home Rule to Scotland. However, the Bill was abandoned during the First World War and by its end, fears about "Red Clydeside" had emerged from industrial unrest among Scottish shipyard workers. Whilst recent historians have suggested these fears were an over-reading of revolutionary potential, it is true that Scottish political debate after 1900 was often centred on the need for "social regeneration" in a way that was different from England.[30] Scotland thus represented a radical alternative in the English political imagination, ever-present at the centre (as many English MPs at Westminster represented Scottish constituencies, including the Prime Ministers H.H. Asquith and Winston Churchill) but politically peripheral. The same was true of Wales to a lesser extent, with David Lloyd-George as its representative. Revealingly, the ethnically Welsh Lloyd-George was nicknamed "the Welsh wizard" – thus a "Celtic" politician advocating devolution and progressive legislation was labelled using old stereotypes.[31]

Celtic polities, especially Scotland, were thus the early twentieth-century Other in a way that Victorian theorists of culture such as Matthew Arnold or Robert Knox would have recognised easily. Celts were consumed, in Knox's opinion, by "furious fanaticism; a love of war and disorder, a hatred for order and patient industry . . . restless, treacherous, uncertain". Arnold's warmer formulation labelled the Celtic imagination as fey and unrealistic, troubled by a "perpetual straining after mere emotion": poetic, but problematic.[32] Celts were thus perceived as uncannily British but not English, and Scotland as a repository for sublime emotions, along with sublime scenery and backward superstition: a heterotopia where the English imagination could play. When this Celtic stereotype was combined with the rich heritage of scholarship on witchcraft trials that we have seen in this chapter, Scotland proved an irresistible location for witchcraft stories. It also provided ideal export material for the exploration of wider issues of difference, change and threat in England.

Inventing a Scottish paganism in England

One of the most prominent theorists of this heterotopia was the Egyptologist Margaret Murray. Murray worked on cultic religion and myth, and during the First World War she transferred her understanding of Egypt to Renaissance British, especially Scottish, materials, apparently regarding them as equivalently exotic. Murray began lecturing on witchcraft beliefs in 1917, speaking to the Folklore Society on 18 April about "Organisations of Witches in Great Britain". In her talk, Murray argued that the people prosecuted for witchcraft in Renaissance Britain had not been innocent victims of demonologists' fantasies. Instead, they had been members of a pagan cult, surviving from prehistory. It was not a wholly new idea (see Chapter 4), but its detail was new and its assertive clarity startling. Even in its early years, some people disbelieved Murray's theory, criticising it as "misleading" and "completely mistaken", "based on preconceived notions in the exploitation of which, fact or fiction is unhesitatingly drawn upon to prop up the vain imaginings".[33] But her imaginings caught the mood of many of her contemporaries and they circulated widely.[34] Mimi Winick calls this "imaginative quality" in her work "fantastic scholarship", arguing that it belongs to a scholarly genre that "valued interpretation over evidence" and stimulated readers to fantasy. And certainly, this fantastical quality brought Murray's work to the attention of writers as diverse as Sylvia Townsend Warner, John Buchan, Robert Graves and H.P. Lovecraft.[35] Each found in her witch-cult a reservoir of creative potential.

Murray argued that "among the witches we have the remains of a fully organised religious cult, which at one time was spread over central and western Europe, and of which traces are found at the present day". Her stress on organisation, geographical spread and long survival – summed up in the idea of "fullness" – suggest the recovery of a lost wholeness and unity. In 1917, this was especially welcome, offering the rebuilding of a divided and broken European world: "pleasurable belief in a meaningful system... a sophisticated form of enchantment" as Winick calls it.[36] Murray's lecture was delivered 2 years and 258 days into the War, a count that *The Times* updated daily. The Second Battle of Arras was under way, the Czar had been overthrown in March and the United States had entered the war in early April. At home, bread rationing had begun and the day before Murray's talk, 17 April, was the first day of compulsory meatless menus in hotels.[37] In the midst of a war in which established certainties were collapsing, the appeal of such a forcefully articulated truth-claim is clear. Murray expanded her ideas in her 1921 book, *The Witch -Cult in Western Europe*. And her primary building blocks for the witch-cult were – of course – Scottish texts, so that a further pleasure of her witch-cult was its Great Britishness: perhaps the English could borrow a little witchcraft sublime in this time of emotional need?

While Murray draws on French and English material throughout her work, Scotland dominates. In the *Witch-Cult* chapter on "The God", England receives approximately three pages of consideration, Scotland eighteen. Much of this recites "the most interesting case" of the North Berwick witches. As her footnotes show, Murray rediscovered Agnes Sampson, John "Fian", "Effie McCalyane" and Barbara "Napier" in Pitcairn. She focuses on what she sees as organised religious features in their activities: "admission ceremonies", formal dances, the exchange of letters, the taking of minutes, the "Conventioun", "the devell ther maister" and his sermon delivered "in liknes of ane blak man". Murray especially enjoys the organisational breakdown over the provision of a wax image, noting how "the said Barbara and Effie McCalyane gatt then ane promeis of the Dewill, that his hienes pictour sould be gottin to thame twa, and that rycht sone". From her reading of Celtic myth and the evidence of Isobel Gowdie, she imagined a calendar of "joyous" witch-festivals: Beltane, Lammas and so on. And she argued that the "devil" was a human being, dressed up for performance like a stage Satan. As the witches named Bothwell as their leader, Murray concluded it was him: "by changing the title 'the Devil' by which he was known to the witches, to the title 'Earl of Bothwell' by which he was known outside the community, the man and the motive are manifest". The witches died as faithful martyrs to their "Master" Bothwell, whom they regarded as "God Incarnate", she concluded.[38]

Murray's ideas were publicised widely by others: in 1925, by both the folklorist J.W. Wickwar, who quotes her almost verbatim without attribution, and the Catholic historian Montague Summers.[39] In his *History of Witchcraft*, Summers praised Murray's "tireless industry", but condemned her cult-witches as Satanists instead of tolerating them as pagans: "the immodesty of the witch-cult" disgusted him. To Summers the witch was:

> an evil liver; a social pest and parasite; the devotee of a loathly and obscene creed . . . a blasphemer . . . a charlatan . . . a bawd; an abortionist; the dark counsellor of lewd court ladies and adulterous gallants; a minister to vice and inconceivable corruption . . . an anarchist.[40]

And so on. Summers had been an Anglican minister until about 1909, when he converted, allegedly after being accused and acquitted of pederasty at the Anglican church where he officiated. The details of these accusations have not survived, but they may be related to his 1907 book *Antinous and Other Poems*. Antinous was a youth deified by Hadrian and associated with homosexuality in *fin de siècle* culture: Summers portrayed him in strikingly homoerotic terms.[41] Given these associations, something of the complex nature of Summers' conservative religio-sexual energy, directed against witches, might be inferred.

Despite differences of emphasis, Summers was responding to the same cultural change as Murray and Wickwar, one that he described as the "rationalistic superstition dying fast", and which Joshua Landy and Michael Saler would call "re-enchantment".[42] Summers' sense that an age of rationalism – the one described by *The Times* and Madox Hueffer – was ending was articulated in his "Introduction": a "heavy and crass materialism . . . so prominent a feature during the greater part of the eighteenth and nineteenth centuries in England" was by the 1920s, he thought, being eroded by new spirituality and, regrettably, "modern Witchcraft, for frankly such is Spiritism" (spiritualism).[43] This insight will be further explored in Chapter 4. And in recognising this new mood, Summers predictably drew on Scottish material, which helped to shape his understanding of witchcraft as subversive and anarchistic. In his autobiography, he explained that his interest began with "a long account of witchcraft in Charles Mackay's *Memoirs of Extraordinary Popular Delusions*", as well as the work of the English demonologist Joseph Glanvill. In particular, he recalled Mackay's comments on James VI and I.[44] Summers thought Mackay wrong to describe witchcraft belief as a delusion, and like his fellow popular historians, he had begun to recognise that in various forms, it could be resurgent in Britain after the First World War.

Whether imagining a cult of joyousness and martyrdom or anarchy and obscenity, Murray, Wickwar, Summers and their fellow-historians reimagined their witches from Renaissance, and especially Scottish, materials. Their version of the Renaissance witch as a passionate religious zealot, sexually and politically liberated, poetic, Celtic, sublime and free caught the imagination of creative writers in the 1920s in a moment of new Romanticism. Murray's influence can be traced almost word for word in some post- First World War fictions. Summers, too, was influential, in ways that he would not have wished to foresee. In the final section of this chapter, I shall look briefly at the influence of Murray and Summers on three novels of the post-First World War period, as an introductory case study in the wider story of transmission from early modernity to modernity of Scottish witchcraft material. The connection between Murray and several of the novelists' work is transparent, and has been highlighted by Kate Macdonald in a pioneering article.[45] Also of interest is the fact that a number of novelists take their con-demnatory approach to witchcraft from Summers. But, finally, there are some examples where both the Murray and Summers schools of thought have been bypassed. Here, creative writers have gone straight to Renaissance records via the first wave of rediscoverers of witchcraft, the Scottish Romantics.

"A Scotch philosophaster with a turn for witchroasting": Scotland and witchcraft in three British novels

The quotation above is from James Joyce's avant-garde experiment *Ulysses* (1922), but in the mid-1920s, a series of middlebrow novels drawing on Scottish witchcraft appeared.[46] For instance, in the Scottish novelist John Buchan's *Witch Wood* (1927), a seventeenth-century kirk minister discovers a "coven" and experiences a witch-hunt. Buchan's debt to Murray is evident. At a "Beltane" festival, Buchan's witches dance and play music, "the women half-naked, but the men with strange headpieces like animals". At Lammas comes a gravely celebratory processional dance and so on. Here is Murray's witches' calendar, whose "feasts and dances" suggest, in her words, "a joyous religion". Buchan's pagans' rites also echo her contention that "the Devil was a man, wearing either an animal's skin or a mask in the form of an animal's head". Later in the novel, a woman accused of witchcraft becomes "a human sacrifice made by the Coven to their master" and we hear of the role of this man: "Francie Stuart was one – him that was Earl of Bothwell in the days of James the Saxt, and he had a braw Coven".[47] This is, of course, a North Berwick reference.

Buchan's reading of Murray can be followed page-by-page. Buchan's "hound-faced leader" sacrifices a red cockerel and begins to preach about "Abiron". He marks his followers' foreheads in blood, inverting Christian baptism and com-munion. In her ten-page section on sacrifice, Murray reproduced the English witch Jone Waterhouse's confession from 1566 that she offered her dog-shaped devil "a red kocke", and added details of demonic baptism from Scotland. The name Abiron, from a French source, occurs one page later. Buchan's witch-leader then reads names from a book in a "roll-call" like that of Dr Fiene's register and the worshippers dance: "figure would clasp figure and then fling apart, but in each circuit [the minister] noted that the dancers kissed some part of the leader's body, nozzling him like dogs". This is a polite account of the North Berwick-style anal kiss, transmitted through Murray's similar verbal formulation: "kissing the Devil on any part of his person that he chose to indicate". What Buchan's kirk-minister has found is a precisely dramatised version of Murray's witch-cult, particularly her chapters on "The God", "The Assemblies" and "The Rites". Yet despite his exemplary close-reading of Murray, Buchan describes the witch-cult's activities as "obscene" and "bestial lust", just as Summers did. Murray provides the content, Summers the tone.[48]

As Macdonald points out, Murray's theory was not used unproblematically as a blueprint by writers: each also brought their own additional reading and creativity to bear on her material. Most famously, Murray's *Witch-Cult* influenced Sylvia Townsend Warner's *Lolly Willowes* (1926), in which an English gentlewoman, Laura, becomes a witch. But what is most interesting to me about *Lolly Willowes* is that Townsend Warner transplants Murray's Scottish materials to England, completely changing their context. Critics have hitherto missed *Lolly's* Scottishness. Thus, readers such as Jane Garrity have felt that "Lolly consolidates her Englishness".[49] Yet Murray's *Witch-Cult* is not the only Scottish source: as Townsend Warner explained, "my interest in witchcraft had been evoked...by the charm of the spells and invocations quoted in Mackay's *Popular Delusions*" before, many years later, she "harked back" to this "interest" upon reading a "remarkable book... *The Witch Cult in Western Europe* by Margaret Murry [sic]". She also mentions Pitcairn as providing "the actual speech of the accused", which suggested to her that "these witches were witches for love, that witchcraft was more than Miss Murray's Dianic cult".[50] We will discuss what that "more" was in the next chapter.

From Murray, Mackay, Pitcairn and other sources, Scottish witchcraft animates *Lolly Willowes* from cover to cover. From *Macbeth* comes Laura's "once the hedgepig whined. Harper [sic] cries, 'Tis time...'" and her reference to Dunsinane; from Arnot, via Pitcairn or Scott to Mackay and Murray comes the reference to "a matronly witch like Agnes Sampson", and from Murray, Pitcairn and probably Scott, Laura gathers her courage to defy the devil, as "Euphan Macalzean had rated [scolded] him".[51] Laura, a quiet English spinster who has defied her male relations to live alone, is suddenly linked with the scandalous Macalȝean, supposedly adulteress, murderess and Satanist. But Townsend Warner transplants these Scottish thrills across the border, in a manner universally unsettling, and blends them with English and European stories.[52] I suggest that this blended witchcraft is part of what Garrity rightly identifies in other contexts as "bi-location" in Townsend Warner's work, a metaphorical ability to be in two places at once.

Garrity uses this concept of bi-location – the phrase is Townsend Warner's – to discuss *Lolly Willowes'* blended literary traditions (realism, fantasy) and the encoding of a lesbian subtext in what appears an innocuously traditional *Bildungsroman*. "When is a witch not a witch?" asks Garrity, suggesting that we read "the witch as a code for lesbianism" when, for instance, at the village sabbath, Laura dances with the "young slattern" Emily, whirling "fused together like two suns". Garrity also identifies Murray as offering Townsend Warner an image of lesbian sexuality in her *Witch-Cult*. Murray thought the human representing the devil could be "occasionally a woman" and that the devil used an "artificial phallus". In *Lolly Willowes*, Garrity suggests, this image informs Laura's mis-recognition of Satan at the sabbath as female, having "the face of a very young girl", a "girlish throat" and "mincing like a girl". When he turns out to be male, she is repulsed by his heterosexual attentions.[53] We might extend Garrity's reading and see bi-location as bisexuality – at the time of writing *Lolly Willowes*, Townsend Warner was in a heterosexual relationship.

But there are also geographical, national ways to read Laura's bi-location, between places and intermediate. Garrity sees Laura as an "intermediate type", using Edward Carpenter's term for homosexuals, whom he linked with magic as witch-doctors, priests, prophets and "female wizards, or witches". But "inter-mediate" is also a deliberately hazy term echoing the themes of geographical travel that I have traced here in witchcraft fiction of the period. As James Harker argues, Laura does not think her way into being a witch, crossing a boundary, but realises she *is* already one: she has already arrived somewhere else, somewhere heterotopic. Not coincidentally, she celebrates her freedom by throwing away her map and guidebook. Jennifer Poulos Nesbitt argues that discarding the map is a mistake but, in fact, it is part of Laura's journey towards a fantastical, inter-mediate self.[54] However we imagine Laura's witchy "bi-location" sexually, it is also a geographical state, maplessly free, hovering between England and Scotland. Laura turns her Scottish witchcraft loose in Buckinghamshire, bringing the witch and all her significances home to the Home Counties.

In particular, the North Berwick witches haunt *Lolly Willowes*, as can be seen from Laura's explicit references to Macalȝean above. There are similarities of form, theme and detail between these witches' stories and Laura's. Like the North Berwick witches, her initiation is expressed as covenant: "she, Laura Willowes, in England, in the year 1922, had entered into a compact with Satan". Like them, the devil appears to her as a human man, metaphorically "a kind of black knight . . . succouring decayed gentlewomen" like Macalȝean and Naipar. Like them too, Laura performs image magic, with scones shaped "into likenesses of the village people". She keeps a cat familiar named Vinegar, a more English than Scottish tradition, based on Hopkins, but one that also echoes the christened cat in *Newes*. Her landlady Mrs Leak is likened to Agnes Sampson, as a "matronly . . . chaperone". At the sabbath, Laura dances a "Highland Schottische" and, as we have seen, like Macalȝean and Naipar, she upbraids Satan. In fact, Laura goes one better: it is she who preaches a sermon to the devil, inverting the relationship between the preacher of North Berwick kirk and his listeners.[55]

Whilst Murray was an important source for Townsend Warner, she read well beyond *The Witch-Cult* in ways that intensified the Scottishness of her witchcraft tropes. The English fascination with Scottish witchcraft in the 1920s was not simply a response to Murray, but existed in other forms. Una Silberrad's *The Book of Sanchia Stapleton* (1927), for example, takes its material directly from Pitcairn without any Murrayite elements. Silberrad's witches are unproblematically guilty sorcerers, not pagans, a view drawn straight from Pitcairn. Although he deplores the "unhappy period" of the witch-hunts as a "strange infatuation", he opines that Lady Fowlis – Silberrad's chosen focus – did "enter . . . into compact with . . . a crew of miscreants" and attempt "horrible practices". Her acquittal "can only be attributed to the very powerful influence of the parties" on trial. Silberrad concurs. Katherene Roise becomes Catherine Renwick in her novel, a gold-digger and adulteress who marries the Master of Ravensrigg in her pursuit of wealth and power. Soon the heroine, Sanchia, finds her in a barn with "a strange small bow in her hand" shooting an "elf-arrow" at "a little figure made of wax". This, helped by poison, kills Catherine's husband, and she then attempts to cure her lover's illness with a magical ritual based on digging two graves. Once her plot is foiled, Catherine is justly executed as a witch.

However, despite Catherine's role as a villainess, the reader is struck by her daring, intelligence and ambition. Further, by the novel's end, the heroine Sanchia has become more and more like Catherine. Beginning as a humble servant-girl, she rises through the use of her skills – literacy, detective work and physical bravery – to inherit Catherine's home and family when she marries Catherine's stepson, the new Master of Ravensrigg.[56] The novel is in a number of ways a rewriting of Charlotte Brontë's *Jane Eyre* and like Jane in Sandra Gilbert and Susan Gubar's famous reading of that novel, Sanchia trumps and succeeds her would-be nemesis (Bertha/Catherine) by becoming more like her and taking her place. Witchcraft empowers women in these two final fictions, Townsend Warner's and Silberrad's, even as in the latter it appears to be represented as a traditional threat. And despite her dependence on Pitcairn, Silberrad, like Townsend Warner, also migrated her Scottish story south to England, in this case, Westmorland. Once again, a novel that seems to be about English witches is based on specifically Scottish material.

So what did Scottish witchcraft mean?

In this chapter, we have seen how records of Renaissance Scottish witchcraft were filtered through *Macbeth* and other Jacobean drama, transcribed by anti-quarian historians such as Arnot, Pitcairn and Scott and then transformed by their modern rediscoverers like Murray and Summers in the years during and after the First World War to produce a hybrid British witchcraft. This often presented itself as English, but was, in fact, very largely Scottish. So what does Scottish witchcraft mean in these fictions?

Most obviously, Scottish witchcraft is associated with aspects of Britishness linked to Celtic stereotypes: sublimity, poetry, freedom, imagination and sub-version. Among the novels discussed in this chapter, Laura Willowes' subversion – her sexuality and her refusal to remain confined by "custom, public opinion, law, church and state" – has received the most critical attention.[57] This has never, however, been linked to the Scottish origin of the novel's witchcraft sources. From Scotland, and from the North Berwick witches in particular, Laura draws her willingness to defy even Satan, and also some of her emphasis on undermining patriarchy. Ewfame Macalʒean is an important inspiration. Macalʒean may also influence Silberrad's portrayal of Catherine Renwick, a murderously rebellious wife and step-mother, taking a lover under cover of maternal match-making and exhibiting all of Macalʒean's "undewtifull behaviour" like the more precise source of Silberrad's character, Lady Fowlis. Catherine is, of course, also a traitor to her King, like Macalʒean. Whilst Silberrad condemns her, the similarities of intelligent agency between Catherine and the novel's heroine Sanchia are also clear.

Buchan too found in the Scottish histories a means of dramatising rebellion against constraint – his Calvinist rebels are Satanists after Murray's model, political rebels like Summers' witches.[58] But the novel is also about more intimate rebellions against unreasonable aspects of church and state. Buchan's young minister, David Sempill, is ultimately a tragic figure who is destroyed by defying a community run by corrupt elders. He regards the witches' freedoms as repugnant, but is forced to accept that relatively speaking, he is less empowered than they are and wishes to be. Murray Ewing thus describes the book as showing "an idealistic young man learning to see the world's hypocrisy . . . in all its disillusioning glory", whilst Macdonald sees it as "attacking contemporary fundamentalism and social corruption".[59] Sempill is no witch, but the witches' presence in the novel helps the reader to address issues of freedom of conscience, justice and the power balance between old and young, wealthy and poor, as in *Lolly Willowes* and *The Book of Sanchia Stapleton*.

In these ways, post-First World War witchcraft fiction dramatises the concerns of young women and men struggling against convention and corruption, which threatened the new freedoms that they wished to claim. Bruce Knoll prefers the term "resistance" for describing Laura Willowes' activities, whilst Macdonald uses "non-conformity" for her and David Sempill, arguing interestingly that their stance against convention has Christian roots (Sempill is, after all, a Non-Conformist minister).[60] But in this chapter, I have suggested that the relationship of these modern witchcraft texts to Renaissance witchcraft sources strengthens their resistance or non-conformity, and indeed, turns it into outright subversion based on the reputation of Scottish witches for regicidal, patricidal treason, the inversion of all good order and piety, sublime passion and power. "Rebellion", the Bible points out, "is as the sin of witchcraft" and set alongside each other and their predecessors, the witches of 1920s novels become more subversive by association. After all, the North Berwick witches planned regicide, mariticide, infanticide and devil-worship, as well as regular old murder, seduction and *maleficium*.

Renaissance witchcraft, Romanticism, Scotland: summary

This chapter has begun to explore the ways in which importing early modern Scottish witchcraft stories into England also imported subversive notions, tracing their roots back to Romantic-era radicals such as Arnot. In the works of Buchan, Townsend Warner and Silberrad, witches bring with them a Celticised disturbance, a sublime passion and unpredictability that was ideally suited to the ruffled sensibility of post-War fiction. In the next chapter, I shall continue this examination, looking at how the War itself, and the transformations that fuelled and resulted from it, further shaped the radical witchcraft texts of the period, moving them away from antiquarian Celtic territory and into new sublime literary worlds of science fiction and fantasy.

Notes

1 See Chapter 1 for a discussion of the recent historiography.
2 Sharpe, "Witch-hunting" 183. See also Brodie Innes in Chapter 4.
3 Maclaurin's (M'Laurin's) *Arguments and Decisions* contains several witchcraft cases but offers no comment. *Rare and Curious Tracts* was anonymous, and is now attributed to David Webster (Henderson, 342).
4 Laing, ed., catalogues the works.
5 Bostridge, "Witchcraft Repealed" 326–8; Davies, *Witchcraft, Magic and Culture* 2. *House of Lords Journal* vol. 24, 585–606; for Erskine's interventions see www.british-history. ac.uk/lords-jrnl/vol24/pp585-595, www.british-history.ac.uk/lords-jrnl/vol24/pp595-598 and www.british-history.ac.uk/lords-jrnl/vol24/pp598-606.
6 Arnot, *Collection* 369, 370.
7 Arnot, *History* iv, 228, 229.
8 Arnot, *Collection* 349–51, 354, 361, 366, 368, 369, 371, 394.
9 Anonymous review, *Edinburgh Magazine* (September 1785) 155–8; Pitcairn, vol. 1, 219. See also reviews of the *Collection* in the *English Review* (October 1785) 286–91 and *Monthly Review* 77 (September 1787) 213–16 for similar comments.
10 Mitchell and Dickie, 16; Moir, 48.
11 Kirkpatrick Sharpe, *Memorialls* xxi; *Edinburgh Monthly Review* 1:6 (June 1819) 681–707.
12 Dalyell, 617–22, 632, 636, 648.
13 Scott, *Letters* 245, 257, 258, 282, 283, 287; *Waverley* (1814) in *Novels and Tales* vol. 2, 148. Among other Romantic works, Spenser's witch is also a source for Percy Shelley's 1820 "The Witch of Atlas" on which see Baker and Clark.
14 Goodare, "Introduction", *Scottish Witch-Hunt*, 12.
15 See also Levack, 79, 80 and elsewhere, Goodare, *Scottish Witches* 212, Bardsley, etc.
16 Baillie, 613, 615, 616, etc. (she mentions *The Bride of Lammermoor*); Scott, 334, 335, which reprises Kirkpatrick Sharpe almost verbatim; Bardsley 247, 248, 250–5, 259. The witch Mary Macmurren's son recalls *The Witch* too. Handley, 71, 74, 75.
17 The new bibliography was a school of criticism dedicated to the material text of (primarily) early modern works, stripping later editorial changes and restoring original readings for debate, see Maguire, chapter 2. William Poel was the founder of the Elizabethan Stage Society (1895) – on stage magics in the period see Nilan.
18 His bibliography is printed in Lucy, 34–8.
19 For essentially the same stance, see Greenblatt, "Shakespeare Bewitched", but see also Leimberg's response.
20 Madox Hueffer, 2, 3.
21 "Superstition in London", "The Belief in Charms" (all articles are cited from *The Times Digital Archive* at http://gale.cengage.co.uk/times-digital-archive/times-digital-archive-17852006.aspx); Lovett; his collection is now at the Pitt Rivers Museum (whose webpage includes a bibliography of his articles), and was recently the subject of an app game developed by the Wellcome Trust: http://england.prm. ox.ac.uk/englishness-Edward-Lovett.html and www.theguardian.com/culture-professionals-network/culture-professionals-blog/2014/feb/07/magic-modern-london-app-wellcome-collection.

22 "Superstition in Essex".
23 "Threatening Letters and Witchcraft"; see also reports of historical lectures such as "The Trial of Joan of Arc".
24 Favret-Saada, 4.
25 Davies, *America Bewitched*.
26 Buell, 245–52; Gould, 172–208.
27 See, for example, Owen, *Darkened* and *Place*, and Hutton, *Triumph,* for the ubiquity, diversity and thriving nature of supernatural beliefs among modern metropolitan elites.
28 On Celtic antiquarianism, see Gibson, *Imagining*, especially chapters 2 and 3; Bourke.
29 Lynn Linton, 1, 2.
30 Hutchison, "Scottish Issues".
31 As Toye points out, Lloyd-George – a Welsh speaker born of Welsh parents in Manchester – embraced the label (222, 346); on devolution in the period see Rembold.
32 Arnold, 344, 345; Knox, 27.
33 Halliday, 224–30; L'Estrange Ewen, *Witchcraft Criticisms* 1, 2. Ewen is usually said to have called Murray's idea on the witch-cult "vapid balderdash" but actually this phrase refers to her criticisms of his own work (5).
34 On Murray's influence see Oates and Wood, Simpson and Mallowan (although revised in 2004 this simply describes the witch-cult theory as "controversial"). For modern rebuttals, among many others, Cohn, 109; Hutton, *Triumph* 195.
35 Winick, 570. Winick usefully defines "fantastic scholarship" as "non-fictional prose that adopts a rational frame through which it interprets a collection of odd or unusual facts. The interpretation offers a strange yet plausible theory that allows the reader to see history, science, even the universe itself, in terms of meaningful patterns instead of meaningless chaos" (573).
36 Winick, 571, 572.
37 "Battle of the Aisne" and succeeding items in *The Times* on 18 April 1917 and "First Meatless Day in Hotels".
38 Murray, *Witch-Cult* 85, 133–6, 51–9.
39 Wickwar, 14–19, 24, 27.
40 Summers, *History* xiv, xvi, 1, 6, 7, 32.
41 Waters, especially 219–20; Summers, *Antinous*, especially "Antinous" (33–9).
42 Landy and Saler, eds; on the debate about (dis)enchantment see also Jenkins.
43 Summers, x–xiv. His *History* was followed by *The Geography of Witchcraft*. There were other similar books in this witchcraft boom: for example, Lowe Thompson's, which leans heavily on Murray
44 Summers, *Galanty* 155.
45 "Witchcraft and Non-conformity".
46 Joyce, 196 – Stephen Dedalus referring to James VI and I.
47 Buchan, *Witch* 271–7, 289; Murray, *Witch Cult* 16, 50–60, 171. Murray also published an article ("The 'Devil' of North Berwick") making the same case in a Scottish-specific journal.
48 Murray, *Witch Cult* 12–15, 61, 124–6, 129, 130, 136, 152–63; Buchan, *Witch* 114, 117, 118, 172–5; Summers, 32; Hutton, *Triumph* 199. Murray's influence is also noted in Greig, iv–xvii; a further debt to her is that the old religion is portrayed as perverted by Calvinist inversions, as argued by Harvie, x, xi. As far as I can see, Buchan left little reflection on his choices in *Witch Wood* (see for example Edinburgh University Library, John Buchan Papers, Gen. 1728/B/14/111–131 for more practical considerations).

49 Garrity (151, 161) is right to identify English ruralist impulses and discuss them in relation to the nation, but that nation is sometimes Britain rather than England, and the two terms might be better separated (e.g. in the discussion of Murray's work as focused on "English pre-history" and "the British rehabilitation of the witch" by Edith Lees Ellis (163).

50 Sylvia Townsend Warner archive MS F (right)/66/2 and diary, 1 December 1963, Dorset County Museum, Dorchester, cited in Harman, 59. All material quoted by kind permission of Tanya Stobbs, Sylvia Townsend Warner Estate and Dorset County Museum.

51 Townsend Warner, *Lolly* 75; Arnot, 155, 349 (Arnot's sources for the phrase were Sanderson, *A Compleat History of . . . Mary Queen of Scotland and . . . James* (London, 1656) and/or Spottiswoode, *History of the Church of Scotland* (London, 1665); Murray, *Witch-Cult* 50; Townsend Warner, *Lolly* 198; Murray, *Witch-Cult* 55.

52 Townsend Warner, *Lolly* 23, 95, 150, 156 (references to Glanvill, and other English works).

53 Garrity, 147, 150; Townsend Warner, *Lolly* 159; Murray, *Witch-Cult* 31, 180; Townsend Warner, *Lolly* 165; Garrity, 173-4.

54 Garrity, 152; Harker; Poulos Nesbitt, 461; Knoll discusses it as a feminist negotiation between passivity and aggression.

55 Townsend Warner, *Lolly* 118, 141–50, 155, 162, 166, 170, 187, 192–4. Mitchell is right to be concerned that Laura remains in the "ownership" of Satan, and her freedom is conditional on "her Master's immunity" (202, 203) but this is an advance on the fate on the North Berwick witches.

56 Pitcairn, Volume 1 Part 2, 191; Silberrad, *Sanchia* 131, 135, 163, 164, 249–52, 282, 283. Silberrad might have referred to Scott's account too, but he omits the barn location for the image magic and voices disquiet about the parties' guilt: "Lady Fowlis, if the indictment had a syllable of truth . . ." (156). There is little work on Silberrad, but see Macdonald, "Edwardian Transitions". Silberrad also dealt rationally with magic/science themes in other novels, for example, *Keren of Lowbole* (1913).

57 Townsend Warner, *Lolly* 181.

58 His own political interests – he became a Conservative MP in 1927 – also led him to write about *Witch Wood*'s Marquis of Montrose elsewhere in 1913 and 1928. The latter book, *Montrose*, drew on research for *Witch Wood* and described Montrose as a hero who "did his best to curb the appetite of the Kirk for witch-finding" (383).

59 Ewing; Macdonald "Witchcraft".

60 Macdonald, "Witchcraft"; 1 Samuel 15:23.

4   "We have started a new spell"[1]
Witchcraft in wartime

In the last chapter, we saw how in the 1920s some central themes of modern witchcraft fiction were defined and how dependent these were upon Renaissance stereotypes and imagery, often refracted through Romantic discourses of sublimity and rebellion. As the chapter showed, much of this imagery was specifically Scottish, rather than English: I argued that Scotland came to represent revolutionary, Celticising tendencies in the period's witchcraft fiction. This does not mean that Englishness in the witchcraft novel is equated with conservatism or safety, although it draws attention to the ways that England is often figured as idyllic.[2] But, of course, in focusing on identity politics, the chapter skirted the event for which the early twentieth century is best known in Europe: the First World War, with the horrors that it brought to England and Scotland alike. This chapter now moves backwards from the late 1920s to examine some of the most prominent impacts of the War on witchcraft fiction and how magical fictions arose in response to the sublime trauma of modern warfare. Without the War, I argue that the Renaissance witch may not have been rediscovered in modernity at all.

The rediscovery, and with it, reinvention, was partly prompted by a new interest in gender, specifically femininity, and in youth – issues that came to the foreground during the First World War. These have rightly been addressed in the small amount of criticism already devoted to the chosen novels and they are sketched at the end of Chapter 3. Gendered and generational aspects of the newly rediscovered witch were also noticed by commentators in the period, as this chapter explores. But it concludes by suggesting that these are only two of several important factors in a much broader readjustment of the image of the witch. The rediscovery of the Renaissance witch not only recapitulates Romantic themes of empowerment – as we saw in Chapter 3 – but addresses the very basics of the human condition, epistemology, philosophy and ontology, as well as foregrounding a pervasive early twentieth-century interest in technology and change. In this breadth and depth, the rediscovery is truly sublime, interacting with every aspect of the self, and especially the self in crisis and fragmentation. It was facilitated by a self-conscious medievalism and Tudorism across the arts in the 1920s and 1930s that dwelt nostalgically on an imagined past wholeness – as Alan Powers notes, "the rediscovery of early English Renaissance culture was in progress simultaneously in music, literature and the stage". Writers returned to medieval romance, Renaissance epic and drama with renewed creative impetus and the witch played an important role in that newly Romantic movement.[3]

In this way, witches are part of what Landy, Saler and others have called "the re-enchantment of the world", a phrase that responds in different ways to Max Weber's 1913 insight that "Progress" towards modernity was a process of "the disenchantment of the world" and, in the field of witchcraft studies, to Keith Thomas' 1971 perception of an eighteenth-century "decline of magic".[4] This chapter argues that the re-enchanting engagement with modernity was crucial to the survival of the witch-figure as it appears in culture today. Inserting witches into the world of tinned food, dynamos, Gotha bombers and Daimler automobiles allowed them to become modern, at times modernist – ironically, as Weber was rolling out his theory of disenchantment, others were working to reinstate witchcraft. And if the Anglo-Scottish frontier examined in Chapter 3 was the right place, the First World War was the right time. Once reinvented, witches could evolve beyond the traditional representations of wise-women, witch-trials, custom and superstition that we saw still in place at the end of Chapter 2, and that continued through Victorian and Edwardian fictions. The Celticising tendencies highlighted in Chapter 3 were also important, but without the simultaneous transition from early modern to modern contexts and meanings, it is hard to see how the witch could have become the prominent figure that we see today.

Wallowing in witchcraft: a new novelistic trend

In 1929, the *Punch* satirist E.V. Knox described:

> a recent tendency in English literature . . . [N]ot so much a frank, open-minded tolerance of witchcraft, voodooism, magical rites, incantations and heathen sacrifice such as might be expected from persons of intellect and culture. It is more than that. It is a desire to plunge into these things and wallow in their midst.

Knox felt that "young girls" might be particularly susceptible. One, he imagined, might decide to embrace Mayan religion and be sacrificed on a stone altar. Another might announce at breakfast "by the way, Dad, I have decided to become a witch", adding:

> I thought of getting a few toads together today and buying some simples and a one-eyed cat. I've seen a heavenly little cottage down in Hertfordshire that would be just the thing and I want you to buy it for me, please . . . I shall make little wax images for people who want to put evil spells on their neighbours, and I shall brew hell-broths and love-philtres, and cure people's rheumatism by making ointment from mouse-fat for them.

The doting father has doubts but agrees: "Wilkins will take you down in the Daimler".[5]

Knox's satire makes evident several facets of the contemporary "desire to plunge into" witchcraft and paganism. As he sees it, the phenomenon has a generational and gender bias towards "young girls". It also has an element of social stratification. Both the imagined "girls" of his review are of upper-middle-class or upper-class backgrounds. The first young woman's mother wonders plaintively if her daughter might put off her pilgrimage for a day, because "the Smiths are coming to-night, and I hoped you would arrange the flowers for dinner". The guests' artisanal name suggests a middling status and the girl will arrange the flowers herself, yet the notion of entertaining guests over evening dinner suggests aspiration. The second young woman's family can afford a plush car and a chauffeur. Her father has only to write a cheque to guarantee the Home Counties cottage.

Both "girls" are thus actually privileged women asserting new freedoms: to travel alone and abroad, to go into business providing social and medical services, to die for a cause, to practise religious freedom and, most basic of all, to live alone away from their parental home. As Knox observes, stories of this kind suggest "there is a distinct change here between our present attitude and that of Victorian literature", and the change is a very broad one, covering social and gendered expectations as well as attitudes to witchcraft. It is clearly informed by suffragism and feminism, for example: the self-sacrifice of the suffragette Emily Wilding Davison, the pioneering botany and social services of Marie Stopes. But alongside the social change is a central religious change: "Victorian literature, on the whole, was inclined to censure the heathen" Knox sums up. Now:

> in these modern books [s]omething very deep and innate and primitive and holy stirs in the heart of the watcher as soon as the knife-slashing and yelling and eyeball rolling begin . . . I suppose it is a kind of return to Nature, comparable to the feeling which inspired the poets of the Lake School. But Wordsworth never lapped blood.[6]

Knox rightly identifies the witchcraft novel as an outgrowth of a new post-Victorian Romanticism, as I argued in the Introduction. In fact, he sees it as a more sublime version, surpassing Wordsworth in its search for authentic emotion and genuinely disturbing.

He was also in part right about the portrayal of witches and pagans in Victorian literature. Censuring the heathen was important in many fictions of prehistory and colonial conquest, emphasising the benefits of reason and progress. There are exceptions, however, drawing on Romantic (indeed, Wordsworthian) notions. Esther Le Hardy's 1851 poem *Agabus* focuses on gentle Druids worshipping light, Algernon Swinburne's "Hymn to Proserpine" and "Hertha" (1860s to 1870s) revel in classical and Anglo-Saxon goddesses and so on. Margot Louis, Ronald Hutton and I have all explored Victorian paganism in literature.[7] Even in scientific writings, paganism flourished. In the 1880s the theorist of "intermediate" sexuality Edward Carpenter welcomed back Astarte as personifying "all the yearnings and dreams and the wonderment of the generations of mankind", whilst J.G. Frazer preferred Diana and Isis in his anthropological study, orthodox by the 1890s.[8] Like the Romantics, then, a number of late-Victorian writers who wished to explore the boundaries of Christianity and escape its confines turned to paganism to achieve that. Knox's insight stands, but requires refining: some Victorians were very heathenishly inclined, although they were a minority. They paved the way for the revival of occultism and the Romanticism of the new century.

However, it is true that witchcraft, as a subset of pagan possibility, was not favoured by Victorian novelists. It had not yet been reimagined *as* a religion in a way acceptable to the mainstream. Historians such as Jules Michelet, Karl Ernst Jarcke and Franz Josef Mone, anticipating Murray in some respects, had suggested that witches practised either Satanism or ancient paganism. But each theory was unsuitable for fiction – particularly Michelet's Priapic orgies.[9] And only a few authors, such as George Egerton (Mary Dunne), used imagery of witchcraft to explore dissatisfaction with Victorian constraint. In Egerton's "The Cross Line" (1894), for example, the female speaker comes to own "woman's witchcraft and woman's strength" as well as having it attributed to her by an admirer with "I believe you are half a witch!"[10] But in most Victorian and Edwardian fictions, witchcraft featured in traditional non-pagan ways, familiar to writers such as Arnot, Scott, Baillie, Samuel Taylor Coleridge (*Christabel*, 1816) or the novelist Thomas Gaspey (*The Witch-finder*, 1824). It appeared in Gothic mode as a psychological threat (favoured by poets such as Alfred Tennyson and occultists such as J.W. Brodie Innes) or in realism as a scapegoating error. This latter approach animates such diverse fictions as William Harrison Ainsworth's *The Lancashire Witches* (1848), J.G Holland's *The Bay Path* (1857), Elizabeth Gaskell's "Lois the Witch" (1859), Thomas Hardy's "The Withered Arm" (1888), Allen Raine's *A Welsh Witch* (1902), Edward Tylee's *The Witch Ladder* (1911) and Mary Johnston's *The Witch* (1914).[11] Witchcraft did not become an important part of Victorian or Edwardian flirtations with paganism.

As we saw in the last chapter, it was sometimes Murray's work that transformed understanding of Renaissance witchcraft, sometimes material from Pitcairn, Scott and others; Summers assisted, although, at times, his books achieved the opposite of their anti-Satanic aim. In 1952, for example, the historian C. J. Pennethorne Hughes described how he and a group of "extremely childish" fellow Oxford students had "founded a witch-group" in 1928. At the inaugural meeting, a paper was read amid black candles and specially painted "obscene" murals; later, a "puppet" representing the President of the Dramatic Society and Editor of *Isis*, was burned and it was ironically proposed that Summers be invited to join. Although the Oxford witch-group was "silly", Hughes comments that its witchcraft "vogue" was widely shared, and he suggests that "perhaps [it] dates from the publication, in 1921, of *The Witch-Cult in Western Europe*". As Hughes' testimony suggests, once Murray's and Summers' notions were accepted, witches were available as role-models for modern would-be pagans both serious and frivolous. Acutely, Hughes also draws attention to the way that Murray's ideas released "the repressed romanticism" of "war survivors", a claim that this chapter will further explore.[12]

Knox thus correctly identified a new post-Great War movement in his "Witches and Whatnot", as he titled his essay. And he was right in his sketch of some of the central themes of the new literary trend: shifts in power relationships and attitudes between men and women, age and youth, the powerful and the submissive, the Christian and the non-Christian. These are central to an understanding of what witches represent in fiction after the First World War. As Macdonald has noted, there was a "fashion . . . a concentrated witchcraft zeit-geist" during which "fantasy and the occult were used . . . to make important sociological points on topical subjects", in particular "non-conformity to society's norms".[13] But the post-War glut of new novels about witchcraft also dealt with deeper philosophical themes. Knox's word "whatnot" obliterates but also marks the epistemological and linguistic trauma of that War, in its refusal to speak clearly about the underlying causes of the social changes that Knox high-lights. Witchcraft novels were an amusing new trend, but they also responded to the traumatic paradigm shifts in human experience that were caused by the War, and from which the epiphenomena of social changes grew.

This chapter uncovers what Knox did not discuss. It complements Chapter 3, setting the social effects of the War alongside the identity politics discussed there. It amplifies, too, Chapter 3's contention that whilst the rediscovery of witches in the 1920s incorporated a response to Murray's work, it actually began before her the-ories were widely known and contains elements demonstrably not implanted by Murray. Macdonald agrees that the post-War witchcraft boom is not just slavish Murrayism, noting of Townsend Warner, for example, that she "borrowed judi-ciously, not wholesale" from Murray. But, even more strikingly, there is at least one example of witches being rediscovered before the author in question knew anything of Murray's witch-cult. There is thus more to the post-War witchcraft vogue than reference to *The Witch-Cult in Western Europe* can explain, and what cannot be attributed to Murray and her Scottish sources can persuasively be traced to the social transformation and trauma of the First World War.

What these women believed: witches and femininity

We can start our discussion where Chapter 3 finished, with the recognition that whilst *Lolly Willowes* demonstrates Murray's influence, novels of the period also drew on other inspirations for their witchcraft material. Indeed, Townsend Warner signalled her distance from Murray in a note responding to *The Witch-Cult*. She wrote that when she had finished reading it, her first question was "what was it these . . . women had believed and had had to die for?" Yet Murray's book had purported to tell its reader something of that: crucially, her formulation did not satisfy Townsend Warner. In part, this was because her novelistic interest lay in the female witches of the "cult", their emotions and needs. Townsend Warner saw the witch-cult as "the romance of their hard lives, their release from dull futures".[14] *Lolly Willowes* attempts to answer the question Townsend Warner asked about witches' beliefs because she felt Murray had not answered it. In this important sense, *Lolly Willowes* is not a Murrayite novel. Indeed, Murray herself recognised Townsend Warner's departure from her ideas: whilst she called *Lolly Willowes* "one of the finest and most human presentations of a witch that I know", she found a "false note" in the witch's relationship with Satan. "Your devil is not the devil of the witches but the devil of the Christians", she stated.[15]

It is no wonder that Murray found the novel's devil wanting. Her own Bothwell-derived devil has a limited role. Laura goes to a Murrayite sabbath as part of her refusal to be constrained by patriarchal norms, not because she wishes to join a tightly controlled fertility cult. She finds the sabbath disappointing – for her, the coven-members are misguided, responding enthusiastically to an "offensive young man", a masked celebrity author who licks his followers. Laura feels "furious ... insulted and made a mock of", and storms off to find the real Satan, refusing to accept his substitute human agent. Miriam Wallraven suggests that Murray's Horned God is "ridiculed", which seems too strong, but Warner's rejection of Murrayite paganism is certainly clear.[16] Laura becomes a solitary witch, uninterested in heterosexual sex, sabbaths or submission. Instead, she is the sort of witch that Knox described, but even more subversive: she rents her cottage herself and hers is a distinctly Sapphic wallowing in witchcraft. It is interesting in this context that Townsend Warner's Satan is an author: in many ways, she is her own transsexual Satan, authoress and masked creatrix of her other avatar, Laura. Little of this subversive play with concepts of authority, fixity and gender can be said to stem from *The Witch-Cult*, whose constraints *Lolly Willowes* transcends.[17]

Laura's rebellion comes instead from Townsend Warner's own sense that witches were women who stood out, and often possessed a compelling, queer energy. A witch "can do what she wants and have what she wants", she wrote in "Modern Witches" (1926), with a hint of satire – "they grow the largest sweet peas ... everyone enjoys their dinner parties".[18] Witches brought a frisson of passion: in a poem, Townsend Warner described the regrets of a bewitched king when his enchantment is lifted following the execution of the witches. "I was at peace there ... why have you snatched me back ... ?" he weeps, recalling feasting with poets and philosophers. Townsend Warner's partner, Valentine Ackland, seems to have shared a similar understanding of witchcraft. In her 1949 *West Country Magazine* article "The Village Witch", she describes traditional wise women who were independent and powerful. Ackland's Old Allie or Old Bessie, Lucy Blandamer, Fanny Way and Granny Moxon are poorer but no less potent versions of Laura Willowes. They are valued, and celebrated: when Old Allie, the "last of the official witches" dies, "to this day someone puts flowers on her grave".[19] Surely there is an echo of Virginia Woolf's *A Room of One's Own* here, with its call to "let flowers fall on the tomb of Aphra Behn" as a pioneer of female empowerment: Behn is replaced by the village witch.[20]

These witches go well beyond Murray's *Witch-Cult*, and so do a number of other witchcraft novels of the 1920s. For example, in Catherine Isabella Dodd's *Three Silences* (1927), magic is also viewed as empowering women, in a way both like and unlike *Lolly Willowes*. Dodd's novel draws knowingly on early modern witch stories, yet changes their terms significantly as her "witches" enter modernity. The Silences of the title are three women whose words and deeds are noisily celebrated as creating opportunities for future generations. The first, Silence Cass, is a Scottish woman whipped in 1646 for being a "white witch" (note, in passing, the Scottish origin again). Silence "followeth the craft of her mother and maketh healing ointments", yet her neighbours say she is bewitching them. She escapes to the Isle of Man and lives by dispensing medicines and charms from her mother's handmade book. The book passes to a second Silence in the mid-eighteenth century and another in the 1820s. This third, Silence Quaife, is a girl of ten who passionately wants an education but whose family cannot afford it. The "talisman" or "lucky buk", as a local wisewoman calls it, transforms her life.[21] The third Silence's story is thus paralleled and contrasted with that of her "witch" ancestress.

Both women empower themselves against the odds by magical means. Yet, magic is not really the cause of their transformation. As a folklorist, Dodd was interested in folk beliefs about luck and fate: she included hand-drawn illustrations in her manuscript of the symbols used by cunning folk in charms. But she was also a rationalist: instead of magic, it is Silence's intelligence that prevails, even as a child. For instance, noting the brisk trade of village charm-maker Phoebe, young Silence offers to draw magical symbols for her. She improves Phoebe's range by adding bags and gets the contract. The lesson is repeated for adults, when after a disastrous elopement, Silence salvages her fortune by turning to the medicinal knowledge in her witch book, updating it for the industrial age:

> There was a brewhouse in the backyard and here they [Silence and her aunt] started to make ointment and pills . . . Very soon Silence had to engage a man with a horse and gig to take the pills to the chemists' shops and to deliver to customers. Each week the sales increased. There was a boom.[22]

Like Dodd, a pioneering educationalist at the University of Manchester, witches are women who wield the magics of education, enterprise, strength of character and intelligence, embracing modern opportunities. This has nothing to do with a witch-cult or with magic as a real force.

It is also important to note that sometimes the witchcraft metaphor is not deployed in a positive way in 1920s fiction: it dramatises conservative unease about social change and the empowered woman. In Anthony Richardson's *The Barbury Witch* (1927) the "witch", Henriette de Fevel, is not magical but simply a scandalous and possessive older woman. She lives impoverished in a cottage, shunned because of her illegitimate children, she has attempted in her past to practise abortion, and she dies accidentally by hanging, but there the metaphor of witchcraft ends. Nevertheless, the themes of women's rights and wrongs, the freedom of younger women – Henriette's daughter Margaret and her wish to leave home and marry – and the politics of generation and authority are invoked, associated with the notion of witchcraft in a way that relates the novel to the others discussed here.[23] Other examples of novels with a witchcraft element related to gender – and there are many – include Louise Gerard's *The Witch Child* (1928), Esther Forbes' *A Mirror for Witchcraft* (1928), H.G. De Lisser's *The White*

Witch of Rosehall (1929) and Durward Grinstead's *Elva* (1929). These British and American works continue the pre-War model where witchcraft dramatised the Woman Question, as, for example, in the suffragist Mary Johnston's 1914 *The Witch*.[24] But where earlier fictions looked back to early modernity without much change to the image of the traditional witch-figure, the War changed all that.[25]

"Magic rose again"

The post-War witchcraft novel is profoundly influenced – indeed, I would argue it was created – by the trauma of the First World War. To begin with, the War sharpened the existing Woman Question: women took new roles in industry, commerce and public life, replacing men drafted to fight. The novels reflect this. Youth is another important context, as Knox noted – young women's opportunities are a particular focus, and youth is to some extent redefined so that even Laura Willowes, in her forties, is able to begin her life anew. But much more pointedly, the War's trauma enters the witchcraft novel in the form of overt commentary on the period's challenges to the very concept of humanity – scientific, ontological, moral, epistemological and social – interweaving with the story of magic. The ways in which the trauma of the War saturated literature, transforming the representation of gender in particular, has often been examined – for example, by Margaret Higonnet *et al.*, Trudi Tate, Joanna Bourke and Santanu Das – and it is widely recognised that surreal and magical realist arts and literatures such as Dadaism drew on the trauma of the First World War for some of their energies.[26] But the relationship between witchcraft and the War in fiction has not been explored before.

A "renaissance" or "revival" of witchcraft in fiction was provocatively encouraged as early as 1908 by Oliver Madox Hueffer in his not-entirely-serious *The Book of Witches*. As we saw in Chapter 3, Madox Hueffer documented contemporary interest in magic. But he also suggested the need for new literary responses to witchcraft, denouncing "the scientist" who "has robbed us of Romance" and adding that "perhaps the greater share of human happiness is based upon 'make believe'". He thought the witch had special political relevance for "the right and wrongs of women", and was prescient in his declaration that "there could be no more appropriate or deserving figure to be chosen as Patroness of the great fight for freedom than the much-libelled, much-martyrised, long-enduring, eternally misunderstood Witch".[27] His novelist brother, Ford Madox Ford, was at the same time writing *The Half Moon*, whose witch Anne Jeal is rightly accused of image magic and ill-wishing, and there is clearly a symbiosis between the brothers' interests. But *The Half Moon* is a traditional historical novel of the seventeenth century: Ford did not respond to Oliver's challenge to bring back the witch in modernity.[28] Instead, it was a relatively unknown young novelist, Stella Benson, and her book *Living Alone* (1919) that transformed the witch from an early modern into a modern Romantic icon. The new ingredient – not present for Hueffer's suggested revival of 1908 – was the War.

Living Alone offers an explanation of the trend for "Witches and Whatnot" in fiction that both trumps and complements Knox's article, and it pre-dates Murray's *Witch-Cult* by two years. As its title suggests, it is concerned with independent women, and it is also about a new humanist spirituality, thus fitting Knox's model to some extent. But it devotes much of its energy to exploring wider philosophical ideas in the light of the War. Class conflicts, issues of charity and commercial ethics, social responsibility and freedom and technology and nationalist ideology are all considered in the light of an epistemological crisis that Benson traces unequivocally back to the War. The conflict frames and permeates the novel. It begins with a committee running War Savings and social work organisations as part of general mobilisation. As Joy Grant suggests, this reflects Benson's own war-work with the Charity Organisation Society.[29] Committee-members Lady Arabel and Miss Ford are satirised as they rebuff the "undeserving" poor, and further satire concerns the Mayor, a war-profiteer. These characters are transformed when a witch enters their committee room and shows them how to allow magic into their lives. Like Macbeth and Banquo meeting the weird sisters, the authority-figures are transformed by contact with witchcraft.

By "witchcraft" Benson means a fluid combination of humanity, imagination and joy. As Debra Rae Cohen suggests, in psychoanalytic terms "magic is pre-sented . . . as the antithesis of the law, as everything the abjection of which makes the law possible".[30] Benson's witch is like Shakespeare's or Middleton's witches, opening up a heterotopic space in which corrupt authority may be questioned magically and wishes come true. In Benson's own life, magic was represented by mysterious "Secret Friends", whom she imagined curing what she called "war disease" or "war crises" of depression and sickness. The Secret Friends are perhaps delusional voices, perhaps spirits, never explained despite repeated diary entries about them. However, what they responded to is clear: Benson experienced a "feeling of outraged impotence" in the face of wartime atrocity – such as the bombing that destroyed homes in the areas where she worked – yet also that sense of sublimity so usefully delineated by Siegel, which she found both beautiful and terrible. "All this suffering and wonder . . ." she wrote in her diary, "the splendour and the greatness of it all. And yet I am coming quickly to the moment when I cannot bear it I cannot bear it [Benson's punctuation]".[31] The witch of *Living Alone* incarnates this eruption of the sublime into the everyday, just as the book grew from Benson's "war disease" breakdown in mid-1917. She was transformed, leaving Britain for a new bohemian lifestyle in America. Her characters are also transformed. Until the witch shows him magic, the profit-eering Mayor is so materialistic that he considers her broom "hardware".[32] In fact, it is a sentient creature named Harold, hiding in plain sight like a Secret Friend. Once the Mayor can see this magic, he is reformed.

Harold is not just a companion to his witch, however. He also flies with her against German witches attacking London from the air. Magic is thus in part a challenge to militarism and its technologies, although also growing out of, and parodying, them. The broomsticks recall the Gotha bombers whose attacks on London traumatised Benson in 1917, as if the novel is helping her deal with her terror and grief at the destruction in neighbourhoods where she worked. The witches debate other issues that distressed her too, including war-guilt. The German witch repeats "England is the World Enemy . . . Throughout the ages she has been the Robber State . . . forcing this war of aggression upon her peace-loving neighbours". The English witch, who has no fixed name but in this section suddenly becomes "our witch" rather than "the witch", scoffs "you've been reading the *Daily Mail* and misunderstanding it. The whole of that quotation applied to Germany". Both sides are thus blamed, with Lord Northcliffe's *Mail* implicated in creating mutual hatred, and the book espouses pacifist and inter-nationalist sentiments. The witch says that she was "born a conscientious objector", so when the German witch advocates bombing civilians at home, she retorts:

> It is at home that people are kindly and think what they will have for supper, and bathe their babies. Men come home when they are hurt or hungry, and women when they are lonely or tired . . . Nobody feels scourged or instructed by a bomb in their parlour, they just feel dead, and dead without a reason . . . ah, what are we about, what are we about? We are neither of us killing Evil, we are killing youth.

The German witch is moved: "I know", she weeps. "My wizard fell at Vimy Ridge". To post-Potter readers, the episode is like a game of quidditch between the lines, where magic brings a moment of sanity to the War.[33]

The presence of the War in Benson's novel might be dismissed as historical coincidence – could a satirical novel written in 1917 to 1919 have avoided it? But it is actually vital to understanding witches in post-War fiction: the War is specifically identified as the source of the book's fantastical element. Read alongside Benson's diary, *Living Alone* explains clearly why she chose witchcraft as a narrative device – indeed, it was so important to her that the novel was originally titled *Witches and Wizards*. We learn why when the non-witch heroine Sarah Brown (an avatar of Benson, who called herself SB) debates magic with the wizard Richard Higgins, and having accepted the existence of witches and wizards in her world, enquires about their role in political affairs. "I suppose the War was made by black magic", she hypothesises:

> "Good Lord, no" replied Richard. "The worst of this war is that it has nothing whatever to do with magic of any sort. It was made and supported by men who had forgotten magic, it is the result of the coming to an end of a spell. Haven't you noticed that a spell came to an end at the beginning of the last century? Why, doesn't almost every one see something lacking about the Victorian age?" "Something certainly died with Keats and Shelley", sighed Sarah Brown. "Oh well", said Richard, "I don't know about books . . . But obviously what was wrong with the last century was that it just didn't believe in fairies". "Does this century believe in fairies? If the spell came to an end, how is it that we are so magic now?" "This century knows that it doesn't

know everything" said Richard. "And as for spells – we have started a new spell. That's the curious part of this War. So gross and so impossible and so unmagic was its cause, that magic, which had been virtually dead, rose again to meet it. The worse a world grows, the greater will magic grow to save it".[34]

Here is a key statement of how Benson came to select witchcraft as a remedy for the War. Her witches reject nationalism, economic motivation and violence – all the key themes of History 1, in Chakrabarty's terms. Instead, Benson offers a version of History 2 in fictional form, where in suffering through the War, and hating its atrocity, reasonable people living quiet lives – eating supper and bathing babies – are aligned with magical creatures such as fairies and witches.[35]

The specific nature of wartime crisis becomes clear in Richard and Sarah's conversation. First, Richard, a serving soldier, differentiates himself from those who "made and supported" the war. The active monosyllable "made" further suggests the war may have been manufactured deliberately. This relates to the satire against the *Daily Mail*, viewing the war as a conspiracy.[36] Then, Richard's commentary together with Sarah's interjections suggest that factors such as "Victorian" religiosity and morality, the industrial revolution and the end of Romantic radicalism meant that even pre-war life was "lacking". The War has, in Richard's opinion, broken the self-confident grip of Victorian epistemology, allowing a humbler open-mindedness to return. The new century may be one in which people are experiencing doubt and self-accusation, but it is portrayed as more honest in this. It is the acceptance of ignorance and regrowth of the ability to wonder and question that has readmitted magic to the world, beginning "a new spell". Finally, Sarah's reference to Keats and Shelley situates the Great War generation as heirs of the Romantics a century earlier, inheritors of the protest and passion associated with the witchcraft sublime.

Benson spoke more about Romantic witches than Renaissance ones, despite echoing the Renaissance association between witches and heterotopia. She also rediscovered witchcraft without knowledge of Murray's witch-cult, as her diaries show. She was part way through writing "Witches and Wizards" in April 1917 and spent the day of Murray's Folklore Society talk in Marlow: so we know she did not attend it. Then, on 24 May 1917, she was visiting a relation when Mrs Benson "perturbed" her:

with facts about the real meaning of witches, and witch marks, and witches' Sabbaths. All physical: a witch mark is a survival of animal days – one or two extra nipples, and all witch habits and festivals are survival of unthinkably old Bacchanalian "Fertility Rites". The Devil was the father of all witch children, witches went forth in great parties with high holiday on their "sabbaths" to meet him . . . My innocent witches are historically unfounded . . . I must think more than twice about my book now.

It's interesting that these Murrayite "facts" were circulating in conversation a month after Murray's lecture – some were more commonplace ideas, but did her talk stimulate chatter? Nevertheless, the ideas made little impression on Benson's novel: she remained true to her original "innocent" vision.

She also recorded, but does not seem to have responded to, another chance conversation in August 1917 when she visited her cousin Marion Ward, who:

> told us an odd story of how she was once accused of witchcraft by a man and wife with whom she was staying, and had to leave so as to take the spell off the wife, as the husband was so indignant at Marion's dark practices.

Ward's anecdote related to a traditionally demonic understanding of witchcraft, but *Living Alone* was part of Benson's notion to turn negative into positive, demonic into near-angelic. It could have been a negative book about the War – which, revealingly, she referred to in her diary as "the Devil" – but instead it became a book about a happy, empowering witch.[37] Benson appears as a kind of witch herself, given power by her war-Devil that she then used to heal and re-create herself.

The empowering link between the First World War and the resurgence of witchcraft is represented in *Lolly Willowes* too, although less overtly. Here, again, the War is metaphorically demonic: it is described as Satan's "latest organised Flanders battue" (a hunting term for driving prey towards guns). It is a bad thing, but paradoxically frees Laura from her pre-War "moorings" and from "old times".[38] And the Satanic War recurs in Norman Matson's *Flecker's Magic* (1926), when the world's last witch is briefly suspected of having started it. A Parisienne shopworker, Marie, explains how she questioned the witch:

> "You say you have great Power. Why don't you use it? You say you decided years ago to change the world. It has not been changed, unless ..." A great suspicion opened in me and I could not go on. "No", said the old witch after a minute, although I had not spoken further. "No, I didn't make the War. It was a logical, reasonable war!" She smiled her ugly, wistful smile.[39]

Matson's witch – who remains nameless, like Benson's – is perfectly capable of having "made" a war (and note the use of the same verb).[40] She possesses a magic ring that grants any wish to its wearer: she gives it to the hero, Spike Flecker, and he is awed by its force. Yet instead, like Richard, she tells us firmly that the war was a logical event, not a magical one. And if the war was brought about by over-confident trust in the sole power of reason, she suggests, then what is needed is the return to "the plural world in which we witches could live". The kind of change that she wished to bring about was one that answered logic with something better. The witch of *Flecker's Magic* wants to re-enchant the world in just the heterotopic way that Richard thought had been done in *Living Alone*, and that happens in *Lolly Willowes*.

However, Matson's witch's status as the "last witch" means that Matson takes further than Benson the idea that the Victorian century did irreparable damage to humanity. For Matson, the world cannot be re-enchanted, there is no "other place" to go and the last witch will have to leave the world to logic and reason. She explains to Marie that witchcraft has died out in response to scientific understandings of politics, industry and human life more generally. "It was not too well with us on the eve of the French Revolution; when the industrial revolution got its stride we perished as men perished in the Black Plague". Some witches fled to Africa, Ireland, the American frontier or remote Norwegian mountains. "But the greatest number magically killed themselves. What else was there for them to do? Men paid less and less attention to us, and we live by human attention". All are now dead, except herself. Her fellow-witches could not bear to exist in the same world as mathematics, physics, electricity and suburbia. Physics appears to be especially toxic, for the witch sees in it an assertion of uniformity. As she puts it, to the physicist the universe is "fundamentally, eternally the same". If everything can be reduced to atoms, then the multiplicity of explanation on which notions of witchcraft depended is lost.[41]

Matson's novel turns on the witch's last stand against this flawed, uniform epistemology. At its opening, she believes that she has found a way to reinsert magic into scientific discourse. She tells Marie that because it cannot be determined what atoms are made of, or for that matter how the universe began, scientists are forced to invent new, subatomic particles and processes that are just that – inventions. The witch gloats:

> If you divide a thing into the things that make it, and then divide them into the things that make them, and so on, and so on, you find that whenever you want to stop you've got down to Nothing! At the centre of a thing sleeps a word. And what is a word? . . . A word is the spirit of a witch.

With this linguist's insight, the witch thus corrects the claim that everything can be reduced to atoms. In fact, everything can be reduced to nothing, she argues, and therefore, nothing in the universe can be said to really exist. "The world isn't real . . . it is based on nothing". Her conclusion is a simple one:

> the world rests upon magic, plain, old-fashioned, my kind of Magic – upon Just-Suppose, Error, Contradiction, on the As-If . . . Without my unreasonable magic, the reasonable world can't go on!

Having argued herself back into ontological necessity, the witch embarks on her plan to change the world. She chooses Spike Flecker to help: young, American, atheist and filled with imaginations about the mysteries of existence and the need for social reform and gives him her ring.[42] But, consumed by self-doubt, Flecker does not know what to wish for: the epistemological crisis of the War has disempowered him beyond the help of magic. He fails the witch and destroys her ring.

Meanwhile, however, the witch has made a powerful case for the continued relevance of magic in the world and the novel shows indubitably that it was of renewed importance in fiction. In the post-War novel, witchcraft is reinvented to assist in discussions about profiteering, mechanised warfare and atomic theory, among other modern issues. To reassert witchcraft is, paradoxically, to engage with the new technologies and possibilities of modernity. Whether witchcraft survives this engagement is dependent on the mood of the author, but Benson's choice was to be the popular one in the 1920s. For her, witchcraft not only survived the War, it was reborn during and because of it. Her type of magic – where magic represents not just a heterotopian alternative but within that a eutopic one in a "good place" where life, poetry, romance, peace and youthful idealism flourish – is essential to modernity. And although writers repeatedly juxtaposed witchcraft and technology, fearful that the latter would kill the former, new technologies actually strengthened the presence of magic in culture. It was not modern technology that witchcraft opposed, but the reductive conclusions to which science could lead and the evil uses to which machinery could be put.

Witches and aeroplanes, in fact, belonged in the same sublime category, as Benson saw: in 1908, Madox Hueffer had also pointed out that witches "flew through the air upon a broomstick" just as "Mr. Henry Farman and Mr. Wilbur Wright . . . are doing". Why, he asked, was "the Devil" less credible than "the Dynamo"? In the same comparative vein, Holt Marvell's *The Passionate Clowns* (1927) regretted that the last witch was being driven to extinction by "Movies and Television, Airships and Radio". Children had "no time to believe in witches", he suggested, when these new technologies "already make so large a demand upon their credulity" – both witches and the very new technology of television lived on fiction and demanded belief.[43] The technologies Marvell chose to replace witches were those of entertainment, and in real life, he approved of them, for he was a pseudonymous creation of Eric Maschwitz, a BBC executive and Editor of the *Radio Times,* who went on to become Head of Television Light Entertainment. Here, he did indeed produce marvels. Fascinatingly, despite their preoccupation with the "last witch" in their 1920s fictions, both Matson and Maschwitz actually recreated their interest in the fantastical in the world of cinema and television. Matson, returning home to the United States, cowrote the novel on which the landmark film *I Married a Witch* (1942) was based (see also Chapter 6), and in the 1960s, Maschwitz steered the BBC to produce science fiction programming such as *Doctor Who.*[44] For these writers, the post-War magical mood created opportunity – commercial and aesthetic – and so it did for many contemporaries. Magic was ideally suited to translation into new visual technologies, as *The Tempest* in 1908 had first suggested (see Chapter 3).

It was also ideally suited to the literary experiments of modernism and its related genres. Novels such as *Living Alone* and *Flecker's Magic* are filled with modernist and imagist fragments. Disillusionment with realism as a genre is important to an understanding of why fictions about witchcraft flourished in the 1920s, although perhaps not as important as their historical context. The writers discussed here were often not self-consciously or overtly modernist, or linked by any other school of literary production – some were wholly traditional and middlebrow in their chosen form. Yet, several of them made oblique reference to their movement away from realism or linked their work slyly to more flagrantly challenging books. Benson, for example, commented implicitly on the relationship between the content and form of her witch story in her preface to *Living Alone*:

> This is not a real book. It does not deal with real people, nor should it be read by real people. But there are in the world so many real books already written for the benefit of real people . . . that I cannot believe that a little alien book such as this, written for the magically-inclined minority, can be considered too assertive a trespasser.[45]

In similarly whimsical tone, Matson teases his readers with Joycean echoes. Flecker's dinner one day consists of a self-consciously Ulyssean image:

> One shirred egg in a little frying pan of its own. Its Cyclopean regard, yellow as a sunset, fixed him steadily. He sprinkled it with black pepper, stuck it with the sharp edge of bread crust.

Flecker also imagines headlines about himself like Joyce's Stephen Dedalus: "AMERICAN ART STUDENT MAKES COMPACT WITH WITCH; OFFICIALS MOVE TO DEPORT".[46] Indeed, Matson was compared favourably with Joyce by E.M. Forster in his *Aspects of the Novel* (1927). For Forster, Joyce raged in a "superfetation of fantasies", whilst Matson was "happier or calmer", "a true fantasist" who "merges the kingdoms of magic and common sense by using words that apply to both . . . the mixture he has created comes alive".[47]

The post-War witchcraft novel can thus be seen as part of a trend towards a new fantasy, a magical realism that incorporated elements of the sublime and surreal alongside traditional narration. Benson was the trail-blazer but, perhaps because her work is, as Grant puts it "highly idiosyncratic" (Cohen prefers "arch, wild and hectic"), it was Townsend Warner whose less peculiar and more realistic novel drew sustained attention seven years later to the theme of "Witches and What-not" as an important new trend in fiction.[48] As this chapter has shown, this trend was a response not only to the assertion of personal freedoms, but also to a deep wartime and post-War anxiety about the nature of knowledge and of the human being itself. What if everything could be reduced to atoms? To paraphrase Theodor Adorno, was poetry possible after the Somme, Passchendaele, Vimy Ridge? What was "real" in such a world? Post-First World War witchcraft fiction deals with these ideas in the wake of the trauma of the conflict, and similar claims have been made generally for fantasy, in particular, J.R.R. Tolkien's *Lord of the Rings* cycle. Witchcraft in fiction has not, however, been subjected to the same analysis.[49] And unlike many High Fantasy fictions, the witchcraft novels examined here and in Chapter 3 seldom surrender to generic conservatism and nostalgia, however radical.[50] Instead, they retain a remarkable diversity of generic forms and remain constantly inventive.

In responding to the dislocations of epistemology caused by the First World War, the witchcraft novel is a truly modern form – surprisingly, because one might expect it to be always historical, always early modern and never modern. If the fictions were all based on Murray's *Witch-Cult*, perhaps that is how they might have felt – more like Buchan's *Witch Wood* than Benson's *Living Alone*. But, in fact, the pre-Murrayite, Romantic forcing together of the Renaissance idea of the witch with the concerns of modernity produced a subgenre of post-War fiction in which writers could reflect extremely creatively on the challenges of their era. Murray reinforced an existing trend with her stimulating ideas, but few writers were wholly happy with her demystification of Satan into Bothwell or high-flying, spell-casting witches into orderly pagan churchgoers. What they wanted were the sublime passions that had animated the original Scottish sources and those who first rediscovered them. So instead of confining witchcraft to historical fiction, introducing magic into the novel freed up form and defeated conventional expectation whenever required. Some of the novels discussed in this chapter have obviously modernist elements; others do not. But it is notable how many of them resist pigeonholing. In doing so, they bequeathed to the contemporary witchcraft novel a generic freedom, an interest in experimental literary form, a magical realism, and relatedly, as I have suggested here, an ambitious engagement with political and scientific discourses and philosophies. From the First World War onward, witchcraft fiction embodied a new, and – as Pennethorne Hughes put it – hitherto repressed, Romanticism.

Witchcraft, war, Romanticism: summary

This chapter has argued that the trauma of the First World War released a Romantic impulse into contemporary fiction, during which reference to witchcraft helped to transform terrible realities into empowering magics. Writers moved away from the historicist novelistic form, with its witch who was often a hapless scapegoat, and turned her instead into a new kind of heroine. Transforming the sublime terrors of trench warfare, bombed cities and the dawning of the atomic age into stories of witchcraft, they also experimented with new literary forms to express their wartime sense that – as Favret-Saada said of witchcraft events – there was "*something in this cannot be coped with*".[51] The era dealt with in this chapter also created the filmic and televisual witch, who will also be explored further in Chapters 6 and 7: thus, new technologies, despite their destructive potential, actually aided the rebirth of the witch.

Notes

1 Benson, chapter VII.
2 For example, in Jacobs, where England is "liminal" and its inhabitants are resistant colonised subjects of the conservative, Baldwinesque, vision of the nation (82); see also Chapter 5.
3 Powers, 12.
4 See Introduction, and Jenkins, especially 13, 18 and 29; Weber spoke of "disenchantment" first in "The Social Psychology of the World Religions", 1913 (published 1915), "Religious Rejections of the World and Their Directions"

(November 1915) and "Science as a Vocation" (1919) – see Gerth and Wright Mills, eds, 139, 290, 350; Thomas, *Religion and the Decline of Magic*.

5 Knox, *Eden* 16, 18, 19. A regular contributor, Knox became editor of *Punch* in 1932.

6 Knox, 21, 22.

7 Louis' work focuses on Hellenism, Hutton on broader paganisms from the Golden Dawn to Druidry and my *Imagining* examines paganisms linked to Celtic and Anglo-Saxon ethnicities.

8 Carpenter, 47; Frazer, 11, 13, 18.

9 Speculations on the matter were risky: for example, Wright's *Narratives of Sorcery and Magic* (1851) suppressed his views on Priapic religion, which were based on discussion with Michelet and published anonymously as *The Worship of the Generative Powers* (1865) 154–95.

10 Egerton, 30, 31;

11 Ainsworth's novel was serialised in 1848, and published complete in 1849 (see Richards), with Gaskell's serialised 1859 and published in 1861 (see Pettitt, Wynne and Krueger, chapter 1, the latter on realism and scapegoating as feminist legal advocacy in Victorian work more generally); Brodie Innes was a Golden Dawn initiate who explored magic in both real-life and fictive settings – for example, his *For the Soul of a Witch* (1910), *Scottish Witchcraft Trials* (1891) and *The Devil's Mistress* (1915) a novel about Isobel Gowdie that later appeared in Dennis Wheatley's *Library of the Occult* (see also Chapter 5).

12 Hughes, *Witchcraft* 11, 12, 218. The President was Peter Fleming, brother of the more famous Ian.

13 Macdonald, "Witchcraft".

14 Sylvia Townsend Warner archive MS F (right)/66/2, Dorset County Museum, Dorchester; Harman, 59.

15 Murray, letter to Townsend Warner, 13 February 1926, Sylvia Townsend Warner archive MS Q (LBL) 1/M/26.

16 Townsend Warner, *Lolly* 166, 167, 198; Wallraven, 69.

17 See also Wallraven's excellent discussion of unfixity and "becoming-witch" (62, 74–8), although I prefer to stress queering aspects of Laura's identity rather than "becoming-woman".

18 Townsend Warner, "Modern Witches".

19 Townsend Warner, untitled poem "When all the witches were haled to the stake" (draft, Sylvia Townsend Warner archive MS N (lower left)/1/24 and published as "King Duffus" in *King Duffus*). See also an unfinished story beginning "The witch's daughter" MS N (lower middle)/14/5); Ackland, "The Village Witch" *West Country Magazine* and Sylvia Townsend Warner archive MS R (SCL)/4/133, B cupboard periodical and R (SCL)/4/108.

20 Woolf, 69.

21 Dodd, 15, 16, 47, 49.

22 Dodd, 52, 144, 145, 241, 242.

23 Richardson, *Barbury*; the novel does refer to sarsen stones and ancient Britons living around Barbury (e.g. 10, 92, 93) but does not make use of these pagan remnants. Richardson wrote mainly thrillers and romances, although interests in social and philosophical reflection are evident from his first publication, *Word of the Earth* (1923).

24 Gerard's novel is an African romance: see also https://only2rs.wordpress.com/2006/05/14/louise-gerard/ and Hapgood, Chapter 6; De Lisser's novel is set in Jamaica, where he was a journalist for the *Daily Gleaner*. For Forbes and Grinstead see Chapter 6. On Johnston: www.encyclopediavirginia.org/Johnston_Mary_1870-1936.

25 I have capitalised references to the First and Second World Wars in line with the practice of many of the writers I discuss, for whom the War often assumed a persona.

26 Higonnet, Jenson, Michel and Weitz, eds; Tate, *Women, Modernism* and ed., with Raitt, *Women's Fiction*; Bourke, *Dismembering*; Das; Hämmerle, Überegger and Bader Zaar, eds; Bowers, 12.

27 Madox Hueffer, 7, 17, 18.

28 Madox Ford, *Half Moon* (1909) vii, xi–xiii, 77, 176–8, 224, 254–8, 335, 336, 344; see also *Young Lovell* (1913) 1–8, 64, 65, 68. Madox Ford's influences include *The Alchemist, Macbeth, Richard III* and *Doctor Faustus*.

29 Grant, *Stella Benson* 60–3.

30 Cohen, 60.

31 Benson's diary 23 April 1917, 17 June 1917, 8 November 1917, Cambridge University Library MJ MF 11391. All material quoted by kind permission of the Syndics of Cambridge University Library.

32 Benson, chapters I, II, VIII.

33 Benson, chapters I, VI, VIII. The description "English" rather than "British" is Benson's choice.

34 Benson, chapter VII. Note the intersection with Barrie's *Peter Pan* (first published as *Peter and Wendy*, 1911) 118.

35 Grant explores *Living Alone* briefly as "a fairy tale of wartime London", which Benson afterwards thought the product of an illusory belief in the marvellous (139, 140).

36 This later became the "merchants of death" theory, after the 1934 conservative isolationist exposé of the "war machine" by Engelbrecht and Hanighen.

37 Benson, diary, 24 May 1917, 25 July 1917, 16 August 1917, 4 August 1917 and *passim*. Ward also wrote supernatural fiction, listed here: http://desturmobed.blogspot.co. uk/2012/01/marion-fox.html.

38 Townsend Warner, *Lolly* 148, 60, 61.

39 Matson, *Flecker's* 154.

40 Writing at the same time as Benson, Aleister Crowley embraced the shocking idea that magicians had "made" the War, attributing it to his adept Simon Iff and explaining that it was intended to create a new social and sexual aeon, *Moonchild* (1929, written 1917) 299 – see also Chapter 5.

41 Matson, *Flecker's* 141, 142, 149.

42 Matson, *Flecker's* 143–50.

43 Madox Hueffer, 12, 14; Marvell, 8.

44 On Matson and the film, see Gibson, *Witchcraft Myths* 195–8. Biographies by Took and Simkin, and Maschwitz's autobiography document his decisive shaping of the Corporation.

45 Benson, preface.

46 Matson, *Flecker's* 69, 92.

47 Forster, 107–14. Knight makes a similarly laudatory point in his second chapter.

48 Grant, xv; Cohen, 60.

49 Adorno, 34, "to write poetry after Auschwitz is barbaric . . . it has become impossible to write poetry today", although this is often misquoted and misunderstood (see Tiedemann, ed., xv–xvii). On Tolkien and warfare see especially Garth (the First World War) and Veldman (nuclear weapons).

50 A controversial debate: for contrasting views, see Newsinger, James and Mendlesohn, eds, (especially Butler's chapter 224–35), and Jackson *Fantasy* on fantasy and subversion.

51 Favret-Saada, 22.

5 Strange conflict

Witch-hunters and witches in Britain, c.1930 to 1980

The preceding two chapters have dealt primarily with witchcraft in novels whose authors either treated the figure of the witch with sympathy or approved of witches outright. But the reader will have noted that some fictions represented witches with more traditional disapproval (Buchan, Richardson, Silberrad and others). This chapter continues the discussion of works hostile to witchcraft, moving away from Romantic radicalism towards reactionary conservatism: the witch did not have an unchallenged passage into modernity. This chapter examines the conflict between the conservative version of the witch, which often saw a witch-hunter as the hero, and versions of the witch that continued the post-First World War vogue for celebrating witchcraft. A mid-twentieth century shift away from the "new spell" (Benson's term for the positive portrayal of magic) towards a reaction in favour of witch-hunters, and then back towards the witch, helps to chart twentieth-century attitudes towards other phenomena as well. These include sexual and religious freedoms, women's liberation, race and empire, political and other passions, age and notions of the Other more generally: all the "minorities" for which the minoritarian witch made a suitable proxy. Looking at the other side of the witch/witch-hunter coin shows us the witch-hunter in a number of positive lights, as a defender of public order, moral guardian, anti-communist, anti-fascist, even love interest, hero or heroine.

As such, the witch-hunter usually represents an anti-Romantic authoritarianism, excited by the sublimity of witchcraft but believing it to be a real crime and committed to containing it. A conservative backlash set in during the middle years of the twentieth century against the automatic assumption that witches were innocent victims or harmless pagans, and the witch-hunter was part of this, seeking and punishing "real" witches in various forms. The focus on witch-hunters was partly a response to the growth of communism and Nazism, partly about fears of immigration and the end of empire and sometimes relating to intra-British tensions: thus, it dealt with a desire to persecute and kill a political enemy. In this sense, some witchcraft fictions began to be party-political in the 1930s in a way that anticipated developments in American fiction in the late 1940s (see Chapter 6). Post-1945, British works also drew attention to a more general authoritarianism, deference and conservatism in British society after the Second World War. In this climate, fictionalised witch-hunters helped readers consider what was a reasonable level of control and conformity in a greatly changed world, decide which innovations were acceptable and which were not. But in the 1960s came a further challenge to the conservative norms implied by the witch-hunter novels and this included their appearance as villains (a discussion that will be continued in Chapter 7).

Witches divided

To pick up where Chapter 3 left off, therefore, we can see elements of conservatism even in some fictions of the post-War "new spell". For example, Silberrad's *Sanchia Stapleton* (1927) can be seen in some ways as a riposte to Townsend Warner's *Lolly Willowes*, published the preceding year, as I suggested earlier. Sanchia is a figure analogous to Laura Willowes in many respects, and to some of the other witch-figures of her period, such as Dodd's Silence Quaife. Her intelligence, independence and bravery lifts her out of the circumstances of her birth, as we have seen, so that although she comes to Ravensrigg as a servant, she ends the novel as its mistress. But instead of aligning with witches, despite her similarities with Catherine Renwick, Sanchia is instead a witch-hunter – not by choice, for it is made clear that her Protestantism is not of a persecuting kind, but because she finds herself in circumstances where people she loves are being attacked by magic. Witchcraft is perceived by Silberrad to be an ineffective means of attack unless accompanied by poison, but nevertheless, Sanchia tackles and defeats the witches, ensuring that they are punished. Thus, even at a time when witches were frequently celebrated in fiction, as Knox noted, it was still possible to portray them as villainous.

This choice is even more likely if an author believes magic to be a real, rather than a metaphorical, force. In particular, Ronald Hutton draws attention to the role of practising occultists in producing witchcraft fiction in the early twentieth century. Some occultist-novelists portrayed some of their witches as evil in order to define their own chosen magic as good by contrast. For instance, the Golden Dawn member J.W. Brodie-Innes' *For the Soul of a Witch* (1910) features a witch who is a werewolf-like monster, and the Thelemic pagan Aleister Crowley's witchcraft fiction pitted an avatar of himself against a "Black Lodge" of witches. In his novel *Moonchild* (1929), these villains attack their Dianic rivals through acts of murder, abortion, "filth" and "fiendish violence" dedicated to Hecate, accompanied by "the gratification of sensuality in abnormal and extra-human channels". Gleefully, Crowley modelled his witch-villains on former Golden Dawn mentors and Ordo Templi Orientis ex-associates with whom he had quarrelled: people such as Annie Besant and Samuel Liddell MacGregor Mathers. As Hutton suggests, writings like this created the impression that mainstream members of pagan, Masonic-derived or theosophical cults might be demonic witches, a view that was easily absorbed into fiction by non-occultists.

Some novels also dramatised an internal struggle between good and bad magic in key characters, and had done for some time before the post-War witchcraft vogue. For instance, the theosophist medium Mabel Collins' *The Blossom and the*

Fruit (1889) is subtitled *The True Story of a Black Magician*. It shows Collins' heroine Fleta struggling through numerous incarnations "to reach toward the White Brotherhood" of benign adepts, and repeatedly tempted back into witchcraft by pride. Likewise, Dion Fortune, an occultist who hovered between Christian and pagan magics, dramatised the conflict between good and evil in her ambiguous hero, Justin Lucas. Her 1927 novel, *The Demon Lover*, follows Lucas, a pagan and witch in former lives, through death to redemption with the saintly heroine Veronica. Thus, even as they strove to revive magic in modernity, some occultists helped to embed the notion that witches could be a real threat in *fin de siècle* and Edwardian society. Ironically, Crowley was the chief victim of this process, featuring in both W. Somerset Maugham's *The Magician* (1908) and Dennis Wheatley's *The Devil Rides Out* (1934) as a Satanic villain, an image of him still current in popular culture.

When in the 1930s a definite reaction set in against the witch-friendly "new spell", it focused on this supposed threat. There were two elements to this reaction: a conservative religious impulse and the metaphorical linkage of witches with subversive forces, communism in particular. Summers' work was influential in both contexts. As we saw in Chapter 3, Summers recanted his Edwardian decadence, converted to Catholicism, and by the 1920s was denouncing witches as social, political and sexual outcasts. Even Murray's *Witch-Cult* (1921) suggested that witches had been a real secret organisation analogous with communist cells. Spurred on by "factual" books such as Theda Kenyon's *Witches Still Live* (1929) and Elliott O'Donnell's *Strange Cults and Secret Societies of Modern London* (1934), the threat of the witch was accordingly updated in fiction by conservative writers. And in *The Devil Rides Out*, and its sequels, a London wine-merchant, Dennis Wheatley, began celebrating witch-hunting.

Wheatley conducted some research to reach his conclusion that witches were a real-life threat. He read works by Summers and Crowley, and met both. But he then conflated their views to conclude that modern paganism was simply Satanic witchcraft. He proceeded to publicise this new demonology assiduously, reinventing the witch-hunter as a mid-twentieth-century hero of espionage fiction.[1] The choice of genre was not accidental – Wheatley began writing in a popular vein to make money – and it helped to shape his stories of binary good and evil. Witchcraft was also on his mind for specific reasons: he routinely read books on occult subjects, and in 1926, he read *Lolly Willowes*, under its alternative title *The Loving Huntsman*. However, whilst Wheatley may have written romances, he was no latter-day Romantic. His war service had given him an interest in intelligence work and derring-do, rather than scarring him as it had more sensitive souls like Benson. Instead, by his own account, he had had a lucky escape, training in England until August 1917 before spending a year in France. Highlights included joining the officer class, learning about aestheticism and philosophy and visiting the brothels of Amiens.[2] Wheatley did not therefore find himself drawn by trauma to the witchcraft sublime. For him, witchcraft was a hateful evil practised by enemies of God, Britain and her allies, and he intended readers to understand this as clearly as he did.

Forbidden territories: Wheatley and Satanism

Wheatley's first supernatural novel, *The Devil Rides Out* (1934), was widely read and discussed. It concerns a group of socialites (the Duke de Richleau, Rex van Ryn and Richard and Marie Lou Eaton) who combat witches because the cult has bewitched their friend Simon Aron. Wheatley distributed over 21,000 promotional leaflets about it, it was serialised in the *Daily Mail*, recommended by the Crime Book Society and Book Guild and reviewed worldwide as "a weird, fascinating, splendidly exciting story of devil-worship in contemporary society" and "an accelerando of horrid excitement".[3] After 1934, Wheatley wrote over fifty more novels, along with short story collections, essays and journalism, which often referred to what he called "Black Magic". He also selected another forty-five books for the publishers Sphere to form the "Dennis Wheatley Library of the Occult", and wrote introductions for them reiterating his own views. Several of his books were adapted for the cinema.[4]

Because of this prolific output, Wheatley came to be considered an expert on occult matters. He received letters requesting help against supernatural entities, advice on depicting Black Masses in fiction, sharing views on Satanic conspiracies, and invitations to speak on Satanism to organisations as diverse as Brockenhurst Grammar School, the London Ghost Club, Putney Conservative Party, Harrods Book Department and Swinton and Pendlebury Public Libraries.[5] In 1934, he was asked to write a non-fiction account of magic for the publisher John Long, but declined, passing the task to his occultist advisor Rollo Ahmed. Finally, by then confident of his knowledge, in 1971, he produced a "factual" book for Hutchinson, *The Devil and All His Works*, which claimed to be the "findings and conclusions" of "a lifetime of reading and research".[6] However, whilst wide-ranging, the book is not a reliable history: it is full of errors and unsubstantiated assertions. For example, it presents Americans as unique in hanging and not burning witches. As we saw in Chapter 1, witches were hanged rather than burnt in England and Wales, among many other polities.

Wheatley relied on sources that were often themselves inaccurate: for instance, Ahmed's 1934 *The Black Art*, which refers to James VI as marrying a "Norwegian Princess" and to Fiene as Fane, ascribing the cat-christening to him.[7] In Wheatley's 1974 *Satanism and Witches*, we see more of the nature of his research. *Satanism and Witches* is an anthology, presented in Wheatley's introduction as consisting "mainly of essays that contain so much valuable information upon supernatural happenings, and historical records of witchcraft" that he has added it to his Library. But the "information" and "records" are excerpts from popular texts, among which fiction and non-fiction are not differentiated. Authorship ranges from demonologists (Cotton Mather), through academics whose views were by then long-discredited (Murray), novelists and poets (Nathaniel Hawthorne, Robert Graves), to showmen and occultists (P.T. Barnum, Crowley). The result is a hotchpotch: worthless as a history book, but fascinating as an insight into Wheatley's magpie intelligence. For instance, Wheatley presents an excerpt from *Moonchild* detailing a rite of the Black Lodge as a factual event in Crowley's life. On this basis, Wheatley's authority was built.[8] Yet it strongly flavoured mid-twentieth century British culture, helping to stimulate literary witch-hunting over the course of four decades.

This was wholly intentional. In *The Devil and All His Works*, Wheatley stated that after "in 1951 Parliament repealed the ancient Act that made witchcraft a crime", Satanism had flourished and a real-life witch-hunt was needed:

> To fight this evil, which is now a principal breeding-ground for dope-addicts, anarchists and lawlessness, new legislation should be introduced. Psychic investigation should be encouraged, but only under licence; and persons participating in occult ceremonies other than those approved by a responsible body should be liable to prosecution.

It was, in fact, a Witchcraft Act of 1736 that in essence decriminalised witchcraft. The 1951 Fraudulent Mediums Act decriminalised the *claim* that aspects of magic and the supernatural existed: it meant that fortune-tellers and mediums were no longer prosecuted under a "Witchcraft" Act. This fact, however, did not stand in the way of Wheatley's political and social concerns, which included promiscuity, rebellious youth, hotel-style prisons, socialism and the loss of Britain's empire.[9] Wheatley returned to these themes consistently throughout his writing career in both non-fiction and fiction. Linking all of them together through Black Magic helped him categorise what he saw as evil and to create a personal demonology.

For Wheatley, Black Magic embodied a spectrum of threats to civilisation. Civilisation meant boundaries, hierarchies, self-restraint, strong government, private property, reverence for a benign force in the universe, manliness/womanliness and what Wheatley saw as the superior experience and character of white Europeans. Other identities and choices were usually "forbidden territories" (the title of his first novel, a spy adventure set in Soviet Russia): fearful but fascinating, and Satanic. Recalling the notion – see also Chapter 4 – that Satan caused the First World War, he thus deplored the Devil's "sabotage [of] peace, prosperity and good stable government" by "luring individuals into sin [to] . . . break up families", "fostering trade disputes" and "arousing the passions of nations".[10] Like Renaissance demonologists, Wheatley saw Satan as representing everything he disliked. This is especially clear in *The Haunting of Toby Jugg* (1948) and *The Satanist* (1960), where devil-worshipping witches fund communists, commit murder, drug and rape women and blackmail public men in an attempt to destroy the British economy and, eventually, cause World War Three. *The Satanist* in particular includes opinionated reference to contemporary politics: the Trades Union Congress, the right-wing Industrial Research and Information Service and the BOAC strike of 1958.[11]

Wheatley's Satanists also attack the British Empire and American WASPs. It is no coincidence that whilst he believed magic could be "white" – that is, good – his focus was on "Black Magic", which he linked with Afro-Caribbean magical religion. Many of his villains are imagined in racially derogatory terms: for example, the Haitian Doctor Saturday, Indian Mr Ratnadatta and Native

American Henrik G. Washington. In *Strange Conflict* (1941), Haitian magicians join Nazis in attacking convoys. In *The Satanist*, Native American religion is conflated with Black Magic. In 1973's *The Irish Witch*, followers of Wolfe Tone (seen as precursors of the IRA) combine Egyptian and Satanic rites. Most disturbingly, in *Gateway to Hell* (1970), Nazis support Black Power, a Satanist front. The rape and murder of a Jewish activist by a Moroccan and a "Jamaican mulatto" acting for an SS fugitive conflates non-white rapists with fascists and witches.[12] As here with civil rights, Wheatley thus drew on contemporary events to fuel his demonology. In the *Sunday Graphic* in 1956, he linked the discussion of "Black Magic" to the Kenyan "Mau Mau" insurgency that contested British rule from 1952.[13] Wheatley also routinely stripped the phrase "practitioners of Black Magic" down to "Blacks". Although he was friendly with individual black and Asian people – Ahmed, a black Guyanan, and the Thai prince Chula Chakrabongse – he also listed "anti-apartheid demonstrations" as potentially Satanic.[14]

Wheatley's depiction of witchcraft was thus self-evidently shaped by changes to mid-twentieth-century British life. Britain became multi-cultural and more egalitarian, with the first large West Indian migrant group arriving in 1948 and the gains of socialist parties from 1945 permitting the creation of the welfare state and the increased role of trade unions in political life. Britain introduced legislation and other measures intended to promote equality of sex, race and class.[15] In this progressive climate, it is interesting that traditional fears of witchcraft returned to the public mind. It is true that some neo-pagans such as Gerald Gardner began to self-identify as witches (so there actually *were* witches in post-War Britain) but in Wheatley's works, the furore over supposed Black Masses and "Satanic orgies" appears to be a reaction to social anxieties: racial, political and sexual.[16] The shock generated by his articles was documented by Gardner and others.[17] In fiction, Wheatley continued his campaigns, through the Duke de Richleau, C.B. Verney, Gregory Sallust and Roger Brook: all doughty conservatives combatting witchcraft. The liberal subversives of Chapters 3 and 4 who explored their aspirations through the "new spell" of witchcraft fiction appear in Wheatley's fiction as likely Satanists.

It would be a mistake to dismiss Wheatley as simply reactionary, however. His personal explorations were much wider than this would suggest. Although a demonologist and witch-hunter, he was no conventional Christian. He was fascinated by Jewish, Buddhist and Muslim cultures. He credited the recall of past lives, and was a disciple of the reincarnationist Joan Grant and her husband, the mystic Charles Beatty.[18] His friends included prominent gay men, such as the MP Tom Driberg. He loathed any religion that demonised sex and he spoke openly about his own sex life. And Wheatley found himself seduced by the narrative possibilities of magic too. In *Strange Conflict*, for example, Satanic Nazis are invading the minds of naval officers on the astral plane. The Duke – an Ipsissimus on the scale of benign magical initiations devised by MacGregor Mathers – flies out of his body to investigate, hovering over London during the Blitz. This reprise of Benson's 1919 witch-dogfight leads on to flights over China, Liverpool, Spain and into a dream world where he and Marie transform into insects, birds and animals. *Strange Conflict* also reveals the Duke's previous lives: he meets a priest, noting that "at one time the two of them had been twin sisters . . . they were devoted to each other".[19] This species-changing, sex-changing fantasy, in which good witches fight bad ones, is a long way from the them-and-us simplicity of Wheatley's more strident passages.

Nevertheless, Wheatley's portrayal of witches as a menace to sexual morality, political stability and national security is essential background for understanding the witch-hunting mentality of much post-Second World War British fiction. It was widely believed to be an accurate picture. Wheatley's authoritative, earnest tone was also echoed by the journalist Peter Haining, who wrote investigative books, including on Satanism, and the retired policeman Robert Fabian, who attributed a number of gruesome murders to Satanists.[20] Following Murray and Summers, and through them their Renaissance sources, Wheatley and his fellow witch-hunters depicted witches as literally and incessantly defiling the Host, kissing the Devil's anus, participating in orgies and human sacrifice and cursing and seducing the innocent and good. Their witch-villains are latter-day Dr Fienes, Ewfame Macalʒeans, Ericthos and Hecates, depicted by a new generation of demonologists as obsessed by sex and power. And during the post-War period, there were many similar, although usually milder, versions of these portrayals. Many were based on more accurate research, and thus incorporated Renaissance models and sources quite self-consciously.

Historicism and social conservatism in the 1950s witchcraft novel

Often these stories are a response to the historicism of the mid-century period, a "Tudorism" in fact veering from medievalism through to Stuartism, which recalled the nostalgia of the 1920s. In the new Elizabethan era (Elizabeth II was crowned in 1952), and an age of post-War reconstruction, there was a renewed emphasis on continuities with the first Elizabethan era and those preceding and following it. The overtly modern literary experiments in witchcraft fiction that followed the First World War were not recapitulated post-1945: instead, conservatism of literary form and cultural content dominated. The period's most celebrated literary works – the kitchen-sink drama and novels of so-called Angry Young Men – tended away from the supernatural, focusing instead on a combination of realist materialism and a rejection of the past. Therefore, it was often left to popular novelists and genre fictions to rediscover witchcraft histories. These fictions have received little attention from scholars, but a growing interest in middlebrow fiction (see also Chapters 3 and 4) has meant that they are now being recovered and discussed.

The best-known witchcraft novel of the period was Robert Neill's *Mist over Pendle* (1951). As we would expect from the tone set by Wheatley, it portrays its witch-hunter, Roger Nowell, in flattering terms. Nowell is taken directly from Potts' *Wonderfull Discoverie* and Neill dedicated his novel to Potts, demonstrating his historical credentials. But Potts' Nowell – described only as "a very religious honest Gentleman, painefull in the service of his Countrey" – becomes in Neill's novel, a Tudorist poster-boy: "full six feet . . . broad of shoulder and slim of hip", radiating "authority" and "vigour", an "impish" opponent of Puritan rigour, favouring "wine-red velvet, with arabesques of gold". He is a swashbuckling hero and his ward, Margery, a spirited heroine. Accordingly, the novel sold well, described by reviewers as a "detective" story, "thriller", "murder mystery" and "film material". C.P. Snow called it "entertaining and exciting", Marghanita Laski promised "excellent entertainment".[21] *Mist over Pendle* was the first historical novel chosen as a *Daily Graphic* Book Find, and its publisher Hutchinson – also Wheatley's publisher – described it in publicity material as receiving "instant acclaim". Neill was even invited to appear in a TV broadcast at the 1951 Festival of Britain's Telecinema.[22] Witches continued their association with sublime excitement and new technology, but had reverted to being the demonised Other. Instead of the witch, the witch-hunter took the heroic central role.

Yet Neill's hero Nowell is an ill-match for the Renaissance realities of Potts' Nowell, who committed for trial at least two families of beggars, several poor widows, teenaged children, a victim of (at best) sexual harassment and two infirm grandmothers, one blind. All died for a crime that *Mist over Pendle* suggests does not exist. This makes its approval of witch-hunting difficult to explain and creates a plotting problem.[23] Neill represents Nowell's witchcraft charges as the convenient containment of Alice Nutter, here imagined as a sociopathic poisoner, and her accomplices. Yet most of these co-accused are guilty of little more than anti-social behaviour. We see nothing of the trials or hangings. Even some reviewers were concerned that Nowell's actions were "not very ethical by modern legal standards".[24] Indeed, the book ends by acknowledging its inability to represent the execution of witches. On the last page, Margery burns the quill that has written Nutter's mittimus: "almost she could see blood on the thing, and she ran to the hearth and thrust it into the fire". Her qualms about "the assizes" and, euphemistically, "what must follow on a windy moorland" are also Neill's, and the burnt quill points to his unwillingness to write a frank conclusion.

Avoiding that allows him to support unequivocally Nowell's actions. His targets – the Demdike-Device and Chattox-Redferne families – are portrayed as "venomous", "hideous", "a picture of malice and savage temper", "sly" and so on. The reader is asked to accept that Nowell's suspects may be beaten, punched and whipped, because "one could not have a world in which girls [Alizon Device] were free to fling dung at churchwardens". In an interview with the *Burnley Express and News*, Neill confirmed his dislike of Alizon, arguing (although without citing evidence) that "she was just the slut I have made her".[25] Meanwhile, the witches' victims are portrayed as largely blameless. The uncharitable pedlar John Law becomes Falstaffian "Fat Jack" and Robert Nutter, the would-be seducer or rapist of Anne Redferne, is excused: she "was sweet seventeen then, and sweet she was to look on" but with "a tongue like a sewer . . . that angered him, and he threatened". The *Saturday Review* remarked that "at times even the kind hearts and noble motives of Roger and Margery seem doubtful" in this context.[26]

The novel is thus strikingly traditional in demonising witches – less modern, more early modern. Even their poverty brings the Demdike-Device family little sympathy. Elizabeth Demdike tells Nowell: "I'm old and poor, and none to find for me, and there's been no bite in the house since yestere'en, and the cold's colder when your belly clings", whilst her children and grandchildren steal, poach and eat scraps gleaned from the mud floor of their hovel, with its broken windows and straw beds. Yet what Roger and Margery notice primarily about the Devices is that they swear, drink, fight and scream abuse at authority figures.[27] *Mist over Pendle* chimes with a complacency about inequality that was characteristic of its time: to be young and poor was seen to be especially unusual now that the welfare state existed. The Rowntree and Lavers report (1951) suggested that only 1.5 per cent of the population was now absolutely poor, and that the most explicable cause was old age. Young people had less excuse, since after 1945 there was near-full employment.[28]

In the context of Neill's own times, the younger members of the Demdike-Device family and their counterpart, Anne Redferne, thus appear wilfully idle and maladjusted, echoing contemporary concerns about teenage delinquency. The young witches are rebels without a cause. Conservative concern about this kind of youthful malaise was highlighted in the period both by sociological studies and fiction such as *The Blue Lamp* (1950) in which a popular policeman is murdered by a young gunman.[29] More generally, *Mist over Pendle* favours an authoritarian model of society, *pace* Wheatley, Haining and Fabian. Witches are a real threat to this, and must be rooted out, especially female witches. Nowell's fellow-magistrate, Nicholas Banister, sums up:

> [Witches are] an evil sisterhood, Roger, and dangerous. They think they can kill, and, believing that, they sometimes do kill.

This auto-suggestive explanation for the apparent success of some curses recurs in Neill's later fiction, and it allows witch-hunters, such as Nowell and Banister, to be heroes because they stand against a genuine, if not magical, threat.

The same is true in Dorothy Macardle's *Dark Enchantment* (1953). Although set in modernity, it follows Neill's depiction of the witch-hunter and it is partly a retelling of *The Witch of Edmonton* and Goodcole's *Wonderfull Discovery*. Macardle was an early modernist teacher, editor of Philip Sidney's *Defence of Poesy* and biographer of Shakespeare.[30] As in Goodcole's pamphlet, her novel's villagers (here French) suspect a one-eyed broomseller, Terka Fontana, of witchcraft. Like Sawyer, no-one wants Terka's brooms: "I couldn't persuade you to buy a broom?" the hero asks, "it's that poor woman over there. Nobody buys from her." We see Terka assailed by the innkeeper René, with "harsh exclamation" from which she "shrink[s] . . . as from blows". Yet like his prototype Old Banks, René is "friendly and . . . kind and fair and patient" to others. When he shoots and lames Terka, his neighbours applaud him. Like *The Witch of Edmonton*'s audience, the novel's protagonists, Michael Faulkner and Juliet Cunningham, see the witch-suspect initially as a victim.[31] But in investigating René's crime, they unexpectedly find she really is a witch, in intent at least. Whilst the reader may be appalled that René has "lamed her and beggared her", living as she is in "horrible, sordid poverty", Terka is dismissed even by gentle Juliet as a "wicked, smarmy, disgusting hypocrite" falsely pretending innocence. At last, the reader sees her malice, and the novel ends with her committal to a "clinic for mental cases".

Unlike *Mist over Pendle*, where heroes and villains are labelled from the outset, *Dark Enchantment* is sophisticated in its manipulation of our sympathies, like *The Witch of Edmonton*, making us guess which way the scales of justice will tip. Terka's identity is deliberately blurred too. She is a "gypsy" or "Romany", but Juliet initially thinks her Italian, then wonders if her name is Hungarian and alternatively suggests she looks Greek.[32] The novel also coyly refuses to explain her "magic". Perhaps she is a devil-worshipper, as the village's cunning man believes. Did she poison René's goat, picking the lock on its stable using skills learned in the Resistance? Or did she bewitch it? Did she start a fire with a timed explosive? Or call down lightning? How did she paralyse René's wife – through auto-suggestion? Macardle believed in ghosts and poltergeists and explored spiritualism and psychical research. Once, she remarked that she thought a former friend was bewitching her by sticking pins in a wax image – how seriously she took this idea, it is impossible to say.[33] But several of her novels deal with occult themes in a way that combines ambiguity with an ultimate endorsement of the idea of a spiritual otherworld.

Perceptively, Nadia Smith suggests that Macardle's refusal to decide upon the witch's guilt can be explained by her identification with both accuser and witch. In particular, she suggests, Terka echoes Macardle's own fears about ageing, mental illness and childlessness, and more specifically, the forgetting of a political legacy. Terka's role in the Resistance counts for nothing with her former comrade René, recalling Macardle's belief that her legacy as a pioneering Irish nationalist had been discarded.[34] Therefore, whilst like Juliet she rejects Terka, Macardle also gives her a fair hearing. This balancing act is repeated from Macardle's play *Witches' Brew* (1931) in which the mind of a Spenserian allegorical character, Una, is battled over by a "witch-girl", Blanid, and a Christian minister. As in the play, Terka/Blanid's evil is eventually made clear, and as in the play, the clinching evidence is provided by a priest. Despite shooting the unarmed, fleeing "witch" with a submachine gun, René is judged to have had a reasonable fear of her because it is revealed that she had also tried to kill the village *curé*. Witchcraft may or may not be real, Macardle suggests, but the witch-hunters of community, state and finally church were right to pursue their suspect.[35]

The "exoticke" witch-cult in the mid-twentieth century

A similar sympathy for the witch-hunter shapes Hilda Lewis' *The Witch and the Priest* (1956), drawing on *The Wonderfull Discoverie of the Witchcrafts of Margaret and Phillip Flower*. Here, Samuel Fleming, who questioned the witches, is the prot-agonist and he is vindicated: "Samuel, they were witches" his sister insists, "nothing could be clearer" and so it proves. As with Macardle's reliance on church teaching, Lewis' stance was influenced by her contact, Canon Alfred Blackmore, during her research. Lewis' letter to Blackmore – Fleming's successor as Rector of Bottesford (1943 to 1958) – has not survived, but his reply suggests she may have intended a more critical portrayal of Fleming than eventually emerged.[36] Blackmore wrote:

> I feel I must drop you a line to say I cannot agree with you when you suggest that possibly Samuel Fleming's bequest [of monies for a widows' almshouse] might indicate a feeling of remorse. After all "witches" were a menace in those days and it was only right that their practices should be stopped. I admit the law was cruelly rigorous; and the punishments imposed were, to our way of thinking, quite barbaric. Still, one cannot blame my good predecessor for that. I consider he was only doing his duty as a magistrate, if he helped to suppress the "witches", especially when the noble Earl believed that the "witches" had caused the death of his little sons ... It seems unduly hard to me if you attach any stigma to Samuel Fleming, even by way of "speculation".

So concerned was Blackmore for the reputation of his fellow churchman that he went on to suggest:

> If you must have someone to blame, why not introduce some imaginary "cruel High Sheriff", or, safer still, some purely fictitious person who had a special interest (say a large bet!) in having so many witches brought to the gallows that year.[37]

Although Lewis resisted, she did portray the witches as guilty, even a "menace" as Blackmore had seen them.

Lewis was also influenced by her readings in R. Trevor Davies, John Hale, Cotton Mather, and particularly Summers and Murray, from whose work she took copious notes. Indeed, she wrote to Murray, receiving a reply about coven maidens and admission ceremonies that left her in no doubt about "how powerful the Old Religion still was" (Murray's words). Against this assured authoritativeness, Lewis' reading of C. L'Estrange Ewen, G.L. Kittredge, Wallace Notestein and earlier witch-defenders, such as Francis Hutchinson, had no effect.[38] The novel documents the confession of Joan Flower's ghost of her membership of a Murrayite witch-cult. Joan is given a backstory as the child of a "foreign gentleman", and is "a bad woman, a bad wife ... *that foreigner*" (Lewis took the pamphlet's description of Flower as "exoticke" to mean foreign rather than its early modern meaning, strange). Her "bad" sexuality is what sends her to the devil: when she realises that her lover Peate (in the pamphlet, a man who had displeased her) is attracted to her daughter, she fears "soon no man would want me ... I remembered women I'd seen ... old women ... beards. And *witch* the children would call them". The devil offers to let her "never grow old ... and that's how he caught me". Lewis' reference to beards recalls the pamphlet's woodcut as well as *Macbeth*.[39]

Joan progresses from this early sinfulness towards a particular hatred of the local nobility: thus, the novel reproduces the pamphlet's disdain for witches' ingratitude. Joan's dislike of the Earl of Rutland's family begins after an interview with the Countess, requesting employment. The Countess responds charitably, but assumes the wildflowers Joan has gathered are a gift for her, takes them, and does not in return offer Joan the fruit she is carrying: "I hated her because she was good", Joan confesses, "and most of all I hated her because she had not thought to offer me an apricot". Joan's envy recalls the pamphlet, like Blackmore's reference to the "noble Earl": the 1619 pattern of moral indignation and social deference was repeated in the 1950s. As the countess exclaims, "these are . . . women who have eaten our food, taken our wages". Also drawn from the pamphlet is the bewitching of the Earl's children using their gloves and the familiar Rutterkin. Lewis explains Margaret Flower's dismissal from service at the castle, and the gift of a pillow and mattress with it, by telling us that Margaret was found with a lover – Mr Vavasour, the other man whom in real life displeased Joan Flower – in the Countess' own bed.[40]

Yet, despite her historicist adherence to her source, Lewis' witches' sabbaths are not taken from the pamphlet – instead, Murray's *Witch-Cult* provides these, along with Madox Hueffer's first chapter from *The Book of Witches*, titled "A Sabbath-General". Lewis mentions both in her research notes, along with sabbath material from Michelet, the demonologists Pierre de Lancre, Jean Bodin, Reginald Scot and Henry Holland and *Macbeth*.[41] Following Murray, Lewis describes sabbaths as "festivals of the Old Religion, older by far than . . . Christ". The Flower family and their fellow-witches fly to the festivals like Isobel Gowdie, meet a masked devil, the "Horned One", for initiations and celebrations, feasting, sex and the sacrifice of "infants as yet unbaptized". Philippa Flower bears the devil's child whilst Margaret offends him and is raped. Unlike their historical originals, both sisters are devil-worshippers. Indeed, Philippa dies a martyr to her god: "I serve the Master whom I adore . . . My God is the Devil". For her, almost quoting Murray, "ours is a joyous faith", although the Christian frame of the book shows the devil betraying his followers.[42] Yet despite its Murrayite innovations, *The Witch and the Priest* makes the same point as any witchcraft pamphlet: Satan is untrustworthy.

The breadth of Lewis' research demonstrates her concern, and the concern of 1950s historical novels in general, for authenticity. She wrote to Canon George Addleshaw, high church historian, to check rites and festivals, and to librarians and archivists at Nottingham University and the City of Lincoln Public Libraries. Through them she accessed items in Lincoln Cathedral library, in Lord Monson's collection and at Belvoir Castle. She read English witchcraft pamphlets from *The Examination and Confession of Certaine Wytches* (1566) to *The Full Tryals, Examination and Condemnation of Four Notorious Witches* (1690), *Newes from Scotland* and other Scottish sources in *A Collection of Rare and Curious Tracts*, as well as a range of early modern contextual sources.[43] This research peppers her text with references to other pamphlets: villagers consider swimming the witches, tied crosswise thumbs to toes as in *Witches Apprehended* (1613); Sir George Manners, like the prefacer of *A True and Just Recorde*, opines "we are too merciful in this country of ours. We should do as they do elsewhere . . . burn"; and the witches are starved, walked, watched and deprived of sleep as were Hopkins' suspects.[44] But it was for its Murrayite Sabbaths that Wheatley chose *The Witch and the Priest* for reprint in his "Library of the Occult". He saw Lewis' novel as supporting his contention that witches were Satanists, a subversive threat in post-War life exactly as they were during the Renaissance.

That the witches of 1950s fiction really are witches (rather than innocent victims) appears related to the anti-communism that motivated Wheatley, and led to the McCarthy "witch-hunts" (see Chapter 6).[45] Such paranoia manifests partly as xenophobia. Macardle's witch Terka is Romany, Greek, Italian or Hungarian. Lewis' "exoticke" Joan Flower is part-Spanish or Italian. Neill's Alice Nutter, Elizabeth and Alizon Device are English but their "raven hair", "black hair" and "dark eyes" contrasts with the Nowell clan's red-gold-brown curls and the accuser Jennet's "golden" hair: it echoes the "dark" and "glossy black hair" of the two others. These dark witch-women constitute a colour-coded threat, related to the racial rhetoric of Wheatley, and foregrounded in Macardle's title *Dark Enchantment*. At times, this "foreign" darkness relates directly to secrecy and spying, again linked to communism. Terka is the most reminiscent of a secret agent, with her *maquis* training to "fiddle locks; set a time-fuse and start fires; [and] mix drugs".[46] She resembles the Irish nationalists that Macardle knew, reconfiguring the traditionally subversive Celtic witch as a Republican terrorist. Alice Nutter's poisoning and involvement in a treasonous gunpowder-plot explore the same concerns. But whilst 1950s British witches share some characteristics with terrorists, spies and subversives, their most obvious threat appears to be crudely racial.

An obvious context is the collapse of Britain's African and Asian empire after the Second World War. Norah Lofts' *The Devil's Own* (1960) hints at the forces at work here. Lofts – a Conservative borough councillor and wife of a Suffolk sugar-refiner – wrote the novel under her pseudonym Peter Curtis. *The Devil's Own* shows the Essex village of Walwyk harbouring a witch-cult led by an archaeologist who returns traumatised from a dig near Carthage. Her cult curses, kills and intimidates villagers. When one of them flees, she warns the school-teacher Deborah Mayfield *"be careful . . .* I've broken with them, on account of the filth and the wrong ideas" and Miss Mayfield, formerly a missionary in Kenya, draws an analogy:

> It was the letter of a Kikuyu, forced to take the Mau Mau oath and aware of its potency, who yet felt that he owed a little allegiance to some European who had been kind.

Witchcraft is imagined twice-over as an African threat: something that came from Carthage and a Mau Mau revolt. The Kenyan uprising in particular coincided with the British mood of national impotence following the 1956 Suez crisis, when the formerly British-controlled Suez Canal zone was ceded to Egypt. Fighters known by colonists as "Mau Mau" were said to swear to kill Europeans, oaths accompanied by drinking body fluids, orgies and so on. This "filth" is what the Essex villagers have fallen into, in response to invasion by foreign ideas. Walwyk has become effectively African, suggesting that fears about both decolonisation and immigration lie behind Lofts' depiction of witchcraft. This became even more evident when *The Devil's Own* was filmed by Hammer as *The Witches* in 1966, prompting greater emphasis on African art and artefacts as a visually interesting source of evil and increasing the focus on imperial anxiety.[47]

Defending witches: the decline of the witch-hunter

Whilst some fictions responded to the conservative social politics of the time by lionising witch-hunters and demonising the poor, teenaged and foreign, a minority took a more liberal line. Christopher Fry's *The Lady's Not for Burning* (1948) is more akin to Benson's 1919 fantasy (see Chapter 4) than the conservative realism of Neill, Macardle, Lewis and Lofts. Fry, a Quaker medievalist, wrote "metaphysical plays", "whimsy" to counteract war, "an escape . . . from despair" and "the exhaustion . . . of the post-Second-World-War period". Kenneth Tynan said he created "worlds in which rationing and the rest of austerity's paraphernalia could be forgotten". In this spirit, Fry produced what Ben Redman calls the best poetic drama "since Elizabethan days", inaugurating "a new Elizabethan age" in response to "the Holocaust and the Atom bomb".[48] Part of this historicism was a rediscovery of witchcraft as risible, wicked persecution:

> The hunters, having washed the dinner things,
> Are now toiling up and down the blind alleys
> Which they think are their immortal souls,
> To scour themselves in the blood of a grandmother.
> They, of course, will feel all the better for it.
> But she?

The hunters are endorsed by their mayor, Hebble Tyson, when they accuse Jennet Jourdemayne – named after Shakespeare's Witch of Eye from *2 Henry VI* – of *Macbeth*ian "supernatural soliciting". But Jennet escapes and the world of the play is redeemed. In this optimistic ending, *The Lady's Not for Burning* prefigures a number of gentle, Christian witch-fictions such as Elizabeth Goudge's *The White Witch* (1958) where the good witch is a romanticised healer, and even the evil witch Mother Skipton is saved by returning to church.[49]

Alongside an enlightened modern Christianity, science is also seen as coming to the aid of the accused witch in the post-War period. The Sexton Blake mystery

Witch-Hunt! (1960) replaces the Renaissance magistrate with a detective who soon dismisses "superstitious idiots" seeking "jiggery-pokery-witchery rubbish". But in other ways, the mystery echoes the conservative themes discussed so far in this chapter. The "witch" Yvonne has no magical ability, but she recalls Alice Nutter, the Device women, Joan Flower and Terka Fontana in her colouring, ethnicity, morality and independent-mindedness. Yvonne is the French-Algerian wife of an English war hero: a "foreigner" with "raven hair", radiating an "aura of sexuality" and with several lovers. She is even associated with manifestations of youthful rebellion: she reads novels by the teenage sensation Françoise Sagan and is blamed for overturning of headstones in the churchyard, in reality the work of "Teddy Boys". However, when the "witch" is murdered, Blake works hard to find her killer and she is remembered warmly by several characters as well-loved and "thoughtful and easy-going".[50] *Witch-hunt!* has its cake and eats it, allowing readers to retain conservative prejudices but asserting the primacy of reason and justice once the witch is safely dead.

From the late 1960s, a softening of attitudes to witches can be traced, in line with increasing social liberalisation. Chapter 7 will look at the case study of the "Witch Finder Generall" story of Matthew Hopkins and its translation into film, but the trend was a wider one. For example, the later works of Robert Neill offer a fascinating progression from witch-hunting to its reverse. Following his success with *Mist over Pendle*, Neill returned to witchcraft in three different historical periods: the Civil War in *Witch Bane* (1967), the Georgian in *Witchfire at Lammas* (1977) and the Restoration in *The Devil's Door* (1979). But by the 1960s and 1970s novels, his witch-hunters have become villainous or credulous: the dashing Roger Nowell gives way to the cruel witch-pricker John Seton (perhaps named after Geillis Duncane's torturer) and the deluded ministers Mr Soames, Mr Heron and Richard Loveday. Relatedly, none of the witches in Neill's later novels is as evil as Alice Nutter or Elizabeth Device. Responding to the counter-cultural spirit of the times, Neill had become convinced that Murray's witch-cult existed and that witches might have been misunderstood pagans. As part of this new insight, he further hypothesised that auto-suggestion rather than poisoning could explain their power. Thus, in *Witch Bane*, the accuser Isobel Grimshaw becomes rheumatic after a wetting, but it is her conviction that she is bewitched that brings on paralysis. Once her fear is assuaged, she recovers. Isobel is in fact being attacked magically – by a cult-member soaking and crumbling a clay image in revenge for Isobel's role in the fatal ducking of her mother – but Neill excuses and pardons the "witch", because she does no actual harm and is merely responding to an attack on her religion.[51]

As he moved beyond the Lancashire trials of 1612 to new historical sources, Neill also tried to distinguish Murrayite pagans from Christians falsely accused, whilst extending tolerance to both. *Witch Bane* opens with the pricking of its Presbyterian heroine, Mary Standen, who is only saved from execution by a chance intervention. Neill based this incident on a story from Ralph Gardiner's *England's Grievance Discovered* (1655), a post-Hopkins attack on the credulity of local officialdom.[52] Yet blameless Mary is contrasted with a member of the village's pagan coven, who is also pricked and, ironically, cleared of witchcraft. This woman, Judith Hay, is later seen at a sabbath. Echoing *Newes from Scotland*, Neill depicts Judith and her witches dancing, drinking and playing instruments, worshipping a supposed devil, kissing his "posteriors", reporting their mischief to him and having sex with him in the churchyard, where Judith is chosen as a Murrayite Coven Maiden. Mirroring Neill's vacillation, Mary's feelings about the witches fluctuate from "fear" to "disgust", but her own experience of accusation means that she does not betray them to the authorities. We learn that Judith is only seventeen, and when she is threatened with burning without trial by ignorant neighbours, the readers' expected response becomes clear: we are to pity Judith and hope for her deliverance. The novel ends with both women safe from the opposite coercions of pricker and coven.

Sixteen years after *Mist over Pendle*, Neill's version of witchcraft is thus as much a lifestyle choice as a religion or crime. Mary's maid, Betty, explains her conversion to it as the result of boredom: "you have to do something", she states, pointing out that under Presbyterian rule "there isn't anything for anyone now, if you aren't wed. What can you do on Sundays now?" For Neill, witchcraft is more forgivable in the age of Hopkins than it was in Nowell's day, as an outlet for frustrated women and disenfranchised youth. The sceptical demonologist John Webster is brought in to make just that point.[53] And by 1977's *Witchfire at Lammas*, witchcraft is even an admirable choice. Celia Bancroft, a sensible, kindly gentlewoman, is proudly a witch. She divines using tea-leaves and a familiar-like pet cat, leads sabbaths – reduced in the eighteenth-century setting to feasting and dancing – and argues that these are only occasions where people "enjoy themselves. And why not?" Like a 1970s New Ager, Celia blends Christianity with herbalism and humanism. Witches are no longer "wicked and more or less mad":

> Perhaps they were, in the old days. Think how they were treated – cursed and kicked by everyone, beaten, swum in ponds, pricked with pins, and on the least excuse hanged ... It was every hand against them ... Do you wonder they turned near mad and hit back ...?

Witch-hunters are clearly to blame for witchcraft here, not the other way round. And in Neill's fictions, including his final novel *The Devil's Door* (1979), they are always Puritans. In moving beyond Thomas Potts' Pendle to the more critical literature of the Hopkins cases and their aftermath, Neill discovered the horror of witchcraft prosecution from the point of view of the accused witch.[54]

Witch-hunters and witches: summary

This chapter has examined the return of the witch-hunter as a hero in the literature of the mid-twentieth century, a depiction typified by the "Black Magic" novels of Dennis Wheatley. But the approving rediscovery of the witch-hunter extended across a wide range of fictions, particularly those written in the

1950s. As the 1960s arrived, the conservative mood waned, and by the 1970s, a strong tradition of presenting the witch as usually an innocent woman had grown up, returning to the largely pro-witch sentiment of the 1920s. Later, this partial portrayal would animate feminist, magical realist and postmodern fiction and move towards the possibility of witchcraft romances, which would come to fruition in the 1990s and the new millennium. These texts will be addressed in Chapter 7. But before resuming the story of the rediscovery of Renaissance witchcraft in British culture, Chapter 6 will examine the transatlantic dialogue about witchcraft that contributed so much to that story from the 1950s onwards and it will also look at the debt American fictions owe to British Renaissance witches.

Notes

1 Crowley, 268–74; Collins, 5, 95, 123, 130, 131, 182–5, 261, 284; Fortune (Violet Mary Firth); Maugham embodies Crowley in the character of Oliver Haddo, whilst Wheatley depicts him in Damien Mocata; Hutton, *Triumph* 253–9, 261, 262; Wheatley, *Gunmen* 235.

2 Leeds University Library, Wheatley MS 1942 Box 9/Part 2, "Books Read during the Year of Our Lord Nineteen Hundred and Twenty Six" and 1923 (note the Christian phrasing). For 1925's list, Box 15/ii; Baker, 97–153. All LUL material quoted by kind permission of Leeds University Library.

3 LUL MS 1942 Box 15/ii, Box 1/ii (the *Scotsman* and the *Daily Telegraph* quoted in promotional material); *Daily Mail* advertisements in the Dennis Wheatley Museum at www.denniswheatley.info/museum/room.asp?id=7&exhib=10. Wheatley Museum material quoted by kind permission of Charles Beck.

4 Among them *The Devil Rides Out* (1968) and *To the Devil a Daughter* (1976) – see below and Hunt 88, 89.

5 Wheatley MS 1942 Box 1/iii, Box 2/ivA, Box 5/iPart1, Box 10/i, Box 13/iv, Box 17/v, Box 19/iii. The contents are not individually numbered; Christopher Lee, quoted in Cabell, *Dennis Wheatley*, n.p.; poster for Pendleton talk in the Dennis Wheatley Museum (www.denniswheatley.info/museum/room.asp?id=7&exhib=14) and Baker, *Devil* 315. At the Ghost Club, he followed witchcraft historian Christina Hole and Wiccan Gerald Gardner as a speaker.

6 Wheatley, "Introduction" to Ahmed, *Black Art* 7.

7 Ahmed, *Black Art* 223, 224, see also note 8.

8 Wheatley, "Introduction" and Crowley, "The Black Lodge" in Wheatley, ed., *Satanism* 10, 74–82. The Dennis Wheatley Museum lists some of his sources, including Crowley, Summers, Ahmed and Maugham (www.denniswheatley.info/museum/room.asp?id=7&exhib=1) and exhibits 2–8. Murray is also mentioned by Wheatley in exhibit 6.

9 Wheatley, *Devil* 257, 285, 291; assorted targets listed 289–92 and *passim*.

10 Wheatley, *Gunmen* 236.

11 Wheatley, *Toby Jugg* 55, 56, 204–6, 301–3, *Satanist* 12–16; Jenkins, "B.O.A.C" 30–4; Fishman.

12 For example, *Satanist* 349, 350; *Irish Witch* 54, 55; *Gateway* 340, 417–28, 523–30; *Strange* 45, and *passim*. For a contrasting view of Native American religion as "white" magic, see *Irish Witch* 153–7, 440, 441. Wheatley's views on anti-Semitism are confusing: Simon Aron is a positive Jewish character on the whole, one of Wheatley's heroes, but for a troubling representation of another Jew as a Communist subversive see Deborah Kain, *Toby Jugg* 124–7, etc.

13 Reprinted in *Gunmen* 191, 192. "Mau Mau" is a contested term – see below for further discussion. Wheatley gained much of his information from sources within the British colonial establishment in Kenya, with some of whom he corresponded regularly (e.g. LUL MS 1942 Box 2/ivA, 4/iiiPart 2, etc.)

14 Wheatley, *Devil* 290; Rollo (born Abdul Said) Ahmed usually described himself as Egyptian, although he was born in Guyana (see *I Rise*, subtitled *The Life Story of a Negro*, an autobiographical novel, and Josiffe); on Chakrabongse, LUL MS 1942 Box 2/ivA.

15 For example, the Race Relations Acts (1965, 1968, 1976), moves towards a comprehensive school system under Tony Crosland as Education Secretary in the mid-1960s, and the Sex Discrimination Act (1975).

16 Wheatley, *Gunmen* 191, 192, 238.

17 Gardner, 219–29.

18 LUL MS 1942 Box 19/iii and 20/iv, correspondence from Beatty about *Gate of Dreams*; Wheatley, *Devil* 98; Grant, *Winged* and *Carola*; see also www.joangrant.net.

19 Wheatley, *Strange* 59, 67, 68, 72, 79, 80, 97–102.

20 These had authoritative and eye-catching titles: for example, Haining's *Anatomy of Witchcraft* and Fabian's *Fabian of the Yard* and *London after Dark*.

21 Potts B2; Neill, *Mist* 24, 25, 34, 37; reviews: anonymous, *Newcastle Journal*, *Bristol Evening World*, *TLS* and *Preston Guardian* (19 May 1951), Pomfret, Raymond, Match, Snow and Laski all in Neill's Cuttings Book, Lancashire Archives DDX177/acc7655 Box 5. All material quoted by kind permission of Lancashire Archives.

22 Advertisement features: *Daily Graphic* (30 April 1951, Cuttings Book) and *TLS* (25 May 1951) 317; *WH Smith Trade Circular* (23 June 1951, Cuttings Book). It was also spelt Telekinema.

23 Although Neill himself is said to have believed in witchcraft's powers and been "fascinated by the unknown quality of the occult" (Bourne).

24 Anonymous review, *Burton Daily News* (Cuttings Book).

25 Neill, 24, 25, 34, 58–63, 81, 105, 182, 328; anonymous interview, *Burnley Express and News* (Cuttings Book).

26 Neill, 35, 43; anonymous review, *Saturday Review* (Cuttings Book).

27 Neill, 59, 63, 56, 112.

28 Rowntree and Lavers; Gazeley, 173; Hatton and Bailey re-evaluated the data, finding significant underestimation of social deprivation. Galbraith's *The Affluent Society* (1958) coined the title phrase, and documented continuing, overlooked inequality in the US. See also Quinault, and Carter, 8 – in 1951 a third of Britons had no bath or shower and 14 per cent had no flushing toilet.

29 Jackson and Bartie, 12.

30 Macardle, ed., *Defence* and Macardle, *Shakespeare*.

31 Is Juliet named after Dr Fiene/Cunningham, or is the similarity coincidence?

32 Macardle, *Dark* 7, 47, 48.

33 Smith, 60. See also Macardle, *Uneasy*.

34 Smith, 128–30, 56, 57.

35 Macardle, *Dark* 28, 47, 48, 78, 99–101, 121, 122, 136, 199, 205, 206, 239, 243; Macardle, *Brew* 9; Leeney, 117–25.

36 Lewis, 14. Fortey and Blackmore.

37 University of Nottingham Library, Manuscripts and Special Collections LWH3/1/11 8 February 1954. All material quoted by kind permission of Manuscripts and Special Collections, University of Nottingham.

38 LWH3/1/12 16 December 1954; LWH3//2/13, 14, 16, 1720, LWH3/3/21–39 and 40–59, 60–78 and 79–93 *passim*.

39 Lewis, 29, 32–6.

40 Lewis, 45, 74–6, 209.

41 Madox Hueffer 19–44, 46, 88, 89, 94, 99–102, 106–13.

42 Lewis, 54–60, 129, 180, 233, 234, 298; Murray, *Witch-Cult* 15.

43 LWH3/1/1, 5; "George William Outram Addleshaw"; LWH3/1/3, 4, 7, 10. On the *Collection* see Chapter 3.

44 Lewis 212, 213, 243, 245, 277, 278.

45 A linkage of witches and spies is alluring. It has been suggested for both the wartime prosecution under the Witchcraft Act of the spiritualist Helen Duncan, said to have discussed classified information, and the "Bella" case (the murder of an alleged Dutch spy and/or a ritual sacrifice?) But in no case is there compelling evidence that official secrets and witchcraft were linked. On Duncan see Cassirer, Gaskill, *Hellish* and Mantel. On "Bella", McCormick, Vale, and Punt. On Nazi occultism, see Goodrick-Clarke, *Occult* and *Black*.

46 Neill, *Mist* 11, 23, 24, 57, 60, 61, 68; Lewis, 28; Macardle, *Dark* 7, 181, 203.

47 Curtis, *Devil's Own* (1960; retitled *The Witches*, after the story was filmed by Hammer under that title, 1966) 186, 187, 246; Elkins, 26–8; Hunt, 90–2.

48 Anonymous "Obituary"; Bemrose, 51; Tynan, n.p.; Redman, 1.

49 Fry, *Lady's* 14, 16, 52, 41.

50 Reid, *Witch* 8, 13, 15, 17, 19, 22, 31, 35; see Hutton 268 on this kind of "Satanist" vandalism. For another example of mid-twentieth-century changes in the representation of witches see my "Kissing the Medium".

51 Neill, *Witch Bane* 122, 123, 134, 135, 138, 139, 142–4, 154–8, 165, 166, 176, 177.

52 Gardiner, 169, 170.

53 Neill, *Witch Bane* 18, 41–8, 52, 80–4, 130.

54 Neill, *Witchfire* 32, 34–6, 72, 73 and *The Devil's Door*.

6 American influences

It may seem surprising that a chapter on America is included in a book otherwise focused on the rediscovery of early modernity and the witch as a Renaissance figure. After all, the early modern period is usually defined as stretching from around the end of the Wars of the Roses (1485) to, at most, the British Commonwealth and Protectorate (1642–1660), with the Renaissance starting in Italy at least a century earlier. Using this definition, the Salem trials of 1692 cannot well be described as "early modern", much less "Renaissance". Only the witchcraft trials of Joan Wright (Virginia, 1626), Alse Young (Connecticut, 1647) and those of the 1650s, such as Hugh and Mary Parsons' trials at Springfield, Massachusetts, might be regarded as qualifying.[1] However, witchcraft prosecution persisted well into the eighteenth century, and a book discussing British representations of witchcraft in the twentieth and twenty-first centuries would be incomplete if it did not discuss the close relationship of American history and its literature with British literature. The "Salem" trials have always been a major theme in American literature and that has repeatedly influenced British depictions of earlier, Renaissance witchcraft as well as American works that also draw – sometimes to a surprising extent – on British sources.

The British trial accounts that most shaped the culture surrounding the Salem trials were the Hopkins texts of 1645 to 1648, *A Tryal of Witches* (1682, documenting the Bury St Edmunds case of 1662) and the pamphlets about the Bideford witches: *A True and Impartial Relation of the Informations against Three Witches* and *The Tryal, Condemnation, and Execution of Three Witches* (1682).[2] Transatlantic dialogue has continued in representing Salem (for example, British authors, such as Elizabeth Gaskell and Celia Rees, have written Salem-based fictions) and the figure of the witch more generally.[3] I have already discussed some texts that crossed and recrossed the Atlantic (Matson's *Flecker's Magic*, set in Paris, and Benson's *Living Alone*, completed in California) including in my *Witchcraft Myths in American Culture*. Apart from this general historic closeness, however, it is also important to note specific connections between British and American witchcraft fictions. This chapter thus examines several key fictions of witchcraft produced in America from the end of the Second World War, focusing primarily on their rediscovery of early modern British witchcraft tropes and their influence, in turn, on British fictions that also rediscover those tropes.

In the chapter's last section, I focus in particular on John Updike and his witches of Eastwick as an exemplar.

A new spell in the United States?

American creative writers usually chose the Salem trials as the background for their witchcraft fiction, often flagging up their New England historicity in their title or subtitle, even when they had invented substantial additions to real events. A reviewer for the *Michigan Alumnus* in 1929 joked that when "our Puritan ancestors at Salem launched in upon their wholesale persecution of witches, they should have considered" that they were also creating a literary phenomenon: "all the hysterical and melodramatic books that have been written about them".[4] Some writers did choose other colonial witchcraft trials – for example, J.G. Holland's *The Bay Path* (New York, 1857) focused on the 1651 Springfield witches. But Salem became particularly popular as an educative parable: over forty young adult English language books about it can today be found without effort.[5]

Older works drawing on the 1692 to 1693 events include the anonymous *Salem: An Eastern Tale* (1820), Lydia Maria Child's *The Rebels* (1825), John Neal's *Rachel Dyer* (1829), Nathaniel Hawthorne's "Young Goodman Brown" (1835) and *The House of the Seven Gables* (1851), *The Salem Belle: A Tale of Love and Witchcraft* (1842), Henry William Herbert's *The Fair Puritan: An Historical Romance of the Days of Witchcraft* (1844–5), John W. De Forest's *Witching Times* (1856–7), D.R. Castleton's *Salem: A Tale of the Seventeenth Century* (1874), Pauline Mackie's *Ye Lyttle Salem Maide* (1898), Marvin Dana's *The Puritan Witch* (1903), Amelia Barr's *The Black Shilling* (1903), Lucy Foster Madison's *A Maid of Salem Towne* (1906) and Henry Peterson's *Dulcibel: A Tale of Old Salem* (1907). As a result of this literary interest, witchcraft was a major theme in early American cinema too: in 1911, Pathé Freres released *A Puritan Courtship* ("a beautiful story of the days of witchcraft and the witchery of love") and it was followed in 1913 by the homegrown Mutual Film's *The Witch of Salem*, *The Judgment* and *The Curse*, and in 1916, Paramount's *Witchcraft*. All were based on "Salem"-related stories.[6] But despite some distinctive American voices, such as Hawthorne's, the vast majority of these texts are comparable to British witchcraft fiction of the Victorian and Edwardian periods in their narrative arcs and themes.

As in Britain, the late 1920s produced several witchcraft novels that challenged established binaries of innocent/guilty and rationalist/magical, notably Esther Forbes' *A Mirror for Witches* (1928) and Durward Grinstead's *Elva* (1929). In the former, an unconventional young woman known as Doll Bilby believes (rightly or wrongly, the reader must decide) that she has taken a demonic lover, and thus accepts the identity of a witch. In the latter, the eponymous Elva Pope is a faithless, shallow but pitiable person who accuses others out of delusion and malice. Both these novels used the notion of witchcraft to explore female sexuality and rebellion in inventive ways, setting the nuances and ambiguities of magical belief alongside their protagonists' other complexities. Bernard Rosenthal notes the role of Freudian thought in *Elva*, suggesting that the novel is unjustly "neglected". In comparison with *A Mirror for Witches*, it certainly was: Forbes' Doll Bilby reappeared as the heroine of both a ballet (Britain, 1952) and an opera (US, 1974).[7]

Its stage afterlife may result in part from the striking appearance of Forbes' novel. She, her publisher, Houghton Mifflin, and the British illustrator Robert Gibbings, attempted to mimic early modern witchcraft pamphlets. *A Mirror for Witches'* title page thus features a lengthy, sectional title in different cases and fonts and each chapter has an italicised Argument. To complement this pastiche, Gibbings produced "dramatic woodcuts". These illustrations, part of his revival of woodcut art for his Golden Cockerel Press in London, give the book both a traditional and modern appearance – woodcuts are an archaic medium, with contemporary, Art Deco styling. They are the most modern feature of the book and the most European: colonial American books were not illustrated with nearly the same frequency as British ones. Likewise, the plot of *A Mirror for Witches* begins with the European roots of witchcraft prosecution, with reference to fictitious cases in Northumberland and Oxfordshire. Doll herself is a Breton, brought to the New World by a sea captain. These exotic touches interested readers: the *Spectator's* reviewer called Doll a "creature of hunted foreign grace in that cruel New England". Meanwhile, Grinstead's Elva Pope was named after Agnes Sampson's familiar.[8] But despite its flirtation with European materials, American witchcraft fiction of the 1920s did not witness the radical literary experiments of British witchcraft fiction. American fictions were almost always historical and realist, perhaps because the First World War did not have the same traumatic effects in America as in Britain (see Chapters 3 and 4): no War, no witchcraft sublime.[9]

There were flickerings of interest in a more imaginative rediscovery, however, that would later bear fruit. L. Frank Baum's *The Wonderful Wizard of Oz* (1900, with sequels until 1919) does not draw on witchcraft history in any overt way. Nor does it feature the same sharp juxtaposition of realist and magical genres as Benson or Townsend Warner's fantasy. But it does place the witch-rich Land of Oz in a space alongside the mundane twentieth-century world to make satirical, political and, at times, feminist points, as they did. The 1939 film of the book replicated this strategy, although less pointedly. In the same vein is the feminist-socialist Charlotte Perkins Gilman's 1910 "When I was a Witch". Here, a New York working woman acquires magical powers, attributed to an unspoken "one-sided contract with Satan". Echoing Gilman's utopian radicalism, the witch's wishes punish "corporations and officials", "stockholders" and "directors" who cheat the public with rotten food and dysfunctional transport. "In mills and mines and rail-roads, things began to mend", she rejoices. The witch curses preachers with honesty and colour-codes the lies, malice and product placement in newspapers. Her last wish is that "women, all women, might realize Womanhood at last; its power and pride and place in life", as mothers and wives shaping humanity's course. But this is too much for Satan: the wish is too benign, and the witch loses her power.[10]

Gilman's blending of humour, satire and idealism anticipates both *Living Alone* and *Lolly Willowes*, although "When I was a Witch" is a six-page skit, not a fully developed narrative. It was published in *The Forerunner*, Gilman's own radical ten-cent paper, which had a tiny circulation in New York, so that it is unlikely that Benson or Townsend Warner ever read it. But the story's placement in Gilman's pioneering journal suggests that, like them, she was thinking of magic as a transformative metaphor that might inspire change. Gilbert and Gubar speak of the story's "New Womanly fantasy", and Gilman said that *The Forerunner*'s aim was to "arouse hope, courage and impatience". But since Gilman had to write all the content herself, the paper has a hurried off-the-cuff air.[11] Further, Gilman was a forcefully unmystical thinker, and did not return to the idea of witchcraft as empowerment: her idea did not progress as it deserved. The heyday of the witch as empowered American woman would have to wait until the middle years of the century, with *Bell, Book and Candle* and *Bewitched*.[12] Whilst it has a place in this long-term, developing context, "When I was a Witch" is thus most readily understood within the contemporary context of pulp American humour, where a light version of magical realism flourished in the 1920s and 1930s.

In 1926, for instance, James Thorne Smith began a highly successful series of comic stories in which American men discover another side to their mundane lives through encounters with ghosts and gods. In each adventure, a mild, unsuccessful man, often married to a dull or unfaithful wife, finds new love and courage. Sexual politics was a central theme, this time empowering men rather than women. Smith shared a masculinist outlook with his friend James Thurber, who was exploring similar comic territory, eventually with "The Secret Life of Walter Mitty" (1939). Beyond the amusement of these stories is a desire for escape from social constraint, which echoes that found in both *Living Alone* and *Lolly Willowes*. Smith lived a bohemian life as a poet in Greenwich Village after the First World War and then, despite conforming to the extent of taking a job in advertising, at the experimental socialist commune Free Acres, New Jersey. He had begun a story about witches, *The Passionate Witch*, when he died in 1934. His book was taken over by Norman Matson, whose *Flecker's Magic* (see Chapter 4) was a work in a similar bohemian vein.

Matson finished *The Passionate Witch* in 1941, and, in 1942, it was adapted to become the film *I Married a Witch*. It was in this film that a large American and worldwide audience first saw the full potential of the witch in modernity: a sparkling, glamorous role model for newly empowered wartime workers.[13] The film removes the book's unpleasant satire on wives and girlfriends, as well as the savage execution of the titular witch. Instead, it allows the libertarian and libertine impulses of the hero, Wallace Wooley, to be shared by the witch, played by the established star Veronica Lake. Lake's character – Jennifer – is presented broadly sympathetically. She outlives her Puritan persecutors to wreak revenge on their descendants, demonstrating ruthless, powerful resourcefulness as a *femme fatale*. But she is also endearingly vulnerable, and falls in love and marries her target instead of ruining him. Some of the radical energies of Smith's and Matson's previous fiction thus found their way into the film, but they created a narrative of only partial female empowerment. *I Married a Witch* is very evidently the ancestor of more firmly feministic works such as *Bewitched* and *Charmed*.[14]

American fiction thus took a decade and a half longer than its British counterpart to reach the point where witchcraft became strongly associated with the exploration of modern femininity in a positive, experimental way. It took the Second, rather than the First, World War to unleash this energy, and the fusion took place in film. Not coincidentally, this renewed focus on witchcraft in popular culture preceded and accompanied the well-known McCarthy "witch-hunts": investigations by Senator Joseph McCarthy and the House Un-American Activities Committee into the political and entertainment sectors that saw witches associated metaphorically with communists and subversion of other kinds. This national agony of suspicion and purging continued throughout the 1950s when, as M.J. Heale has argued, McCarthyism was only one aspect of a toxic culture of right-wing paranoia. In particular, Robbie Lieberman and Clarence Lang have explored its interconnections with the contemporary racial politics of division and exclusion.[15] In mid-twentieth-century America, there-fore, witches were positioned as a proxy for otherness – especially sexual, political and racial, together or in combination – in the conservative cultures of Truman's and Eisenhower's America. It was this era that produced the most influential statements about what witchcraft meant in American modernity. These were not sublime fantasies motivated by ontological crisis, but they were texts dealing with sublime emotions: guilt, self-sacrifice, terror and hatred of the Other.

Witches as others

The association between witchcraft and alterity has always been strong in American culture. Witchcraft has been a cause of sharp division, too. Suspects, the supposedly bewitched and those who questioned the motives of accusers, frequently formed camps or "sides" as Cotton Mather called them in *Wonders of the Invisible World* (1693), regretting "alas, my Pen, must thou write the word, *Side*, in this Business?". Because most American witches were prosecuted in the latter half of the seventeenth century, by which time the existence and nature of witchcraft evidence was suspect, and because the trials culminated in events involving hundreds of colonists, American witchcraft was often controversial. From the Hartford trials of the 1660s onwards (a confused proceeding that saw some convicted suspects hanged but others pardoned), colonists fought over standards of proof, the veracity of accusers and the culpability of parti-cular individuals. The earliest accounts of the Salem crisis were violently poli-ticised between Congregationalists (the Mathers, Cotton and Increase, who also differed to some extent from one another) and the Baptist Robert Calef. In the eighteenth, nineteenth and twentieth centuries, historians and creative writers continued to take politicised positions.[16] The debate about witchcraft in America has thus been more uniformly angry than comparable British discourse. Marc Mappen labels its historiography simply "Fixing the Blame", perfectly conveying its adversarial tone.[17]

Blame for witch-hunting was diversely and pointedly attributed. In the mid-nineteenth century, for example, the historian and Member of the House of

Representatives, Charles Wentworth Upham, and novelist and journalist, Josiah Gilbert Holland, both targeted theocracy from a (respectively) Whig and Republican standpoint, blaming ministers such as George Moxon of Springfield and Cotton Mather of Boston personally for witches' deaths. Upham then engaged in "spirited debate" over Mather's culpability with the *North American Review*'s book critic William Frederick Poole, librarian of the Boston Athenaeum. He also intrigued against the Democrat Nathaniel Hawthorne, who responded by caricaturing him in *The House of the Seven Gables* as the corrupt descendant of witch-hunters – which was Hawthorne's own background as the descendant of witch-trial magistrate John Hathorne. In the early twentieth century, George Lincoln Burr blamed elite groups and their governance for witch-trials across America and Europe, whilst George Lyman Kittredge spoke out in their defence and focused instead on fear of the "mob". As Gould and Buell have discussed, the "people" and their capacity for anarchic disorder had become a favourite theme by the later nineteenth century. But Kittredge's argument also blamed European culture for infecting the American colonies with witchcraft beliefs. His 1929 title, *Witchcraft in Old and New England*, was designed to make exactly that point.[18]

Kittredge's stance highlights a tendency in one strand of American writing to regard both the practice of witchcraft and its persecution as diseases brought from somewhere else, by outsiders. This tendency appears across both scholarship and fiction. The easiest equation is a simple one, between witches and all kinds of Others: for example, H.P. Lovecraft conflated witches, African-Americans, Italian-Americans, Polish-Americans, foreigners, people of mixed race and non-human entities in his short stories, portraying witchcraft as a cultic religion worshipping alien gods. Murray was a key influence: in "The Call of Cthulhu" (1926) among the notes of Professor Gammell Angell appear "comments on long-surviving secret societies and hidden cults, with reference to passages in . . . Miss Murray's *Witch-Cult in Western Europe*". Lovecraft also drew on "non-Euclidean calculus and quantum physics" for his demonology. In "The Dreams in the Witch House" (1932), the student Walter Gilman combines these with folklore, concluding that one of the Salem witches had contacted non-human entities. This woman, the fictional Keziah Mason, "had told Judge Hathorne of lines and curves . . . leading through the walls of space", of "midnight meetings" and the "Black Man". Then, "she had drawn those devices on the walls of her cell and vanished". Gilman eventually follows her into a fourth dimension, meeting a bloody end. The "Outer Gods" of Lovecraft's fiction, with their spaces beyond reason and civility, are the ultimate outsiders, representing all the rest.[19]

From the outset of the American trials, such outside spaces and persons were associated with witchcraft. As we saw in Chapter 1 with "Indyen" Tituba, colonists' suspicion of Native Americans created tension. But in a revealing historiographical slippage, by the time Arthur Miller began to research his Salem play *The Crucible* in the 1940s, the debate about what had caused the Salem trials had refocused on the poorly understood notion of Caribbean "voodoo", and especially its black practitioners, just as in Wheatley's fiction. In histories of

"Salem", Tituba was appearing as an African-American conjuror, although the historical Tituba was almost certainly a Native American, and there is no evidence that she practised magic. Historians had concluded that she had been brought by Samuel Parris as a slave from the West Indies, and that therefore she was of African descent: the first assertion seems to be accurate, the second inaccurate.[20] But following histories such as Upham's *Salem Witchcraft* (1867) and Marion Starkey's *The Devil in Massachusetts* (1947), many post-War creative writers portrayed her as a "negro", without complication. Others, such as William Carlos Williams, referred to her as both "a black slave" and "half-Carib, half-Negro". As Chadwick Hansen and Bernard Rosenthal later pointed out, this confused depiction reflected contemporary unease about the early civil rights movement, racism, and more generally, the place of formerly enslaved African-Americans in a WASP-centred and deeply divided society.[21]

Miller's *The Crucible* continued the tradition of depicting Tituba as a "Negro" woman, apparently unaware that there was any other choice. He also followed earlier writers in suggesting that her Barbadian activities led to the Salem accusations: "Tituba knows how to speak to the dead" and "conjured Ruth's sisters to come out of the grave", it is asserted, while Parris tells us that he saw her singing "Barbados songs" and dancing around a fire in the forest with naked village girls, "screeching and gibberish coming from her mouth". The girls accuse her rather than face accusation themselves. But Miller's main concern was with McCarthy as an analogue of Puritan persecutors rather than with magic: he wrote that "there was a new religiosity in the air . . . an official piety which my reading of American history could not reconcile with the free-wheeling iconoclasm of the country's past". In this context, he condemned witch-hunters of all kinds, speaking of "the unrelieved, straight-forward, and absolute dedication to evil displayed by the judges of these trials and the prosecutors", whom he accused of "sadism". In this radicalism, *The Crucible* has more in common with *The Lady's Not for Burning* than with the British texts of its own decade, which favour witch-hunters. Nevertheless, Miller praised the British for refusing "contemporary diabolism". In contrast, "in America any man who is not reactionary in his views is open to the charge of alliance with the Red hell".[22]

Despite its complex racial and gendered politics, this brave, clear rejection of witch-hunting continued to influence American writing throughout the mid- and late twentieth century. Echoes can be seen throughout popular culture: an episode of *Sabrina the Teenage Witch* (1997) is titled "The Crucible" and focuses on a false accusation; repeated reference occurs in *The Simpsons*, as in "Easy Bake Coven" (1997) and "Rednecks and Broomsticks" (2009).[23] These references have scholarly roots wherein Miller's version of Salem is subtly conflated with the historical event. For instance, Rossell Hope Robbins, in his 1959 *Encyclopaedia of Witchcraft*, discusses "the accused, named as well as nameless, who fought back against the mania, and who by their courage in dying laid a seed of doubt in the validity and honesty of witch believers and witch trials". Miller's John Proctor, with his concern to be "named" and to end the prosecutions by his death, seems to be the inspiration here.[24] Hope Robbins summed up his motivation for producing an encyclopaedia of witchcraft prosecutions in his "Introduction":

> If the cries and shrieks of these martyrs for humanity – for such the "witches" and their defenders were – and the protests of writers can be taken from the steel-doored vaults of libraries to show the present-day reader the dangers of bigotry and rigidity of thought, and the prerequisite of the inquiring mind in all phases of man's activity, this work will hold more than antiquarian or sensational values.[25]

The modern relevance of witchcraft was thus strongly stated in American culture, by Miller, his contemporaries and those influenced by his work.

In this American reading of witch-hunting, witches were positioned as victims of tyranny and folly, just as they had been in eighteenth-century Scotland, although they also retained a parallel (and sometimes contradictory) role as the threatening Other in some fictions. In mid-twentieth-century America, the chosen forms for protesting modern witch-hunts were primarily dramatic and filmic, and in the late 1960s in Britain, this tradition was continued when Michael Reeves' film *Witchfinder General* (1968) reproduced a bleaker version of the Crucible's central tropes. A few years later, Caryl Churchill's *Vinegar Tom* (1976) is perhaps the British work that is most like *The Crucible* in its use of witchcraft for contemporary political ends, although it departs radically from Miller's broadly realistic model. British writers' debt to Miller will be further explored in Chapter 7, but meanwhile, the more recent politics of American witchcraft fiction is the subject of the final section of this chapter. With *The Witches of Eastwick*, we move back to a focus on magical realism, as in Chapters 3 and 4, and – surprisingly – also to a focus on Scottish witchcraft.

"Where the place?": Scottish witchcraft rediscovered in Eastwick

Like *The Crucible*, John Updike's novel *The Witches of Eastwick* (1984) was conceived by its author as a politicised text – in this case, an intervention in the long-running American battle over the association of witchcraft with gender. In 1984, publicising the novel, Updike said that it was an attempt to respond to criticism that his previous female characters were "subsidiary to men". Again, when interviewed in 2008, he said that he thought of *The Witches of Eastwick* as an attempt to address women's concerns by imagining the world from a female viewpoint. The world of the 1980s was "full of feminism", Updike explained, which demanded a serious engagement from creative writers. However, whilst he gave his new female characters, Alexandra Spofford, Jane Smart and Sukie Rougemont, "freedom of a sort, acquired power, the power that witches would have if there were witches", he also made them murderesses, as well as flawed in milder ways. This represented for him the insight that women would "behave no better with their power than men do. That was my chauvinistic thought".[26]

It is not, in fact, a chauvinistic thought, although it is a misanthropic one – perhaps shaped by Updike's Christianity, with its belief that unless redeemed by divine grace humans are irretrievably fallen.[27] Nevertheless, by 2008, Updike had accepted that misogyny might have moulded his witches. A number of reviewers certainly thought so.

As we have seen, venomous controversy is a keynote of American witchcraft discourse, and Updike's readers responded in the traditional way. Nina Baym dismissed the book's witchcraft as a "gimmick", regarding it as "obsessive, joyless pornography" in which "women are *always* trouble for men". Merle Rubin agreed: "cheap" and "ponderous", the novel left an "aftertaste of misogyny". Yet, Baym drew attention to praise from other reviewers, "women reviewers too", she commented in irritation. These included Margaret Atwood, who took Updike's "weird sisters" literally as witches, and called the novel "strange and marvellous". She especially liked the fact that it "redefine[d] magic realism". Diane Johnson praised Updike's "tact and detachment", despite noting that "the lesson is perhaps that women make trouble when left on their own". In a review of Updike's sequel, *The Widows of Eastwick*, written in 2009, Alison Lurie discussed readers' earlier divisions: for some, *The Witches of Eastwick* "proved that Updike hated women. Others . . . claimed that on the contrary Updike loved women, but did not always like them very much. Also he did not trust them". The controversy raged and continues today.[28]

As an intervention in the identity politics of gender, "wondering what it's like to be a woman" as Atwood puts it, *The Witches of Eastwick* is very well known. It is also, however, a book about the identity politics of witches and about Renaissance witchcraft. Updike's fantasy of witch-hood turns out to be just as revealing as his fantasy of woman-hood, particularly as it is often a specific fantasy about what it was like to be an early modern Scottish witch. Whilst American works clearly influence British witchcraft fictions of the 1960s onward, Updike's novel is an example of influence crossing the Atlantic westwards. It is based almost entirely on European, largely British, often Scottish source material – an insight that has not previously been discussed, and that contributes to the book's sense of alienation. Readers often experience an uneasy sense that Updike is playing with or mocking them and that the book is neither satisfactorily one thing nor the other. Even more tantalisingly, it might be two different (and incompatible?) things at once: as, for instance, in Emily Nussbaum's suggestion that it is "a genuinely great misogynistic novel". Uneasy readers are right: *Witches* is concealing beneath an American, urbane and jokey exterior an exotic origin, a Celtic passion – even sublimity – and a surprising depth of scholarship. Fuelled by this wide reading and careful thought, it is seriously subversive: it refuses to be pinned down politically, generically or even magically. In this elusiveness it is, among the books we have examined so far in this study, most reminiscent of Townsend Warner's "bi-location" in *Lolly Willowes*.

It is significant therefore that *Lolly Willowes* was one of Updike's chief inspirations. Like *Lolly*, *The Witches of Eastwick* is a book poised between two geographical locations: in Updike's case, usually Scotland and New England.

A few of his sources were also French, the most important being Michelet's *La Sorcière*, which Updike read at university. But from Michelet he progressed to *Lolly Willowes*, absorbing from Townsend Warner, he wrote, the notion that it was possible "respectfully [to] construe the word 'witch' as 'free woman'" – the genesis of his own project. Updike followed the "refined witchery" of Townsend Warner's work thereafter with admiration, and echoes in *The Witches of Eastwick* all the elements of *Lolly Willowes* that he itemised in an affectionate review in 1978. Laura, he said, "makes a pact with Satan, acquires a 'familiar', attends a sabbat, joins a coven, and holds lengthy discourse with the Devil".[29] As James Schiff, James Plath and Kim Loudermilk agree, Updike's interest in witchcraft peaked during his reworking of Hawthorne in *A Month of Sundays* (1975) but, whilst contextually important, that does not account for Updike's transatlantic focus in *Witches*. *Witches* is "Hawthornesque", to quote Schiff, but it is also Townsend Warneresque.[30] And of the seventeen printed sources of inspiration listed by Updike in a "Special Message" prefacing the Franklin Library edition, thirteen are British (including Scott, Townsend Warner, Murray, Summers, Hughes and Haining).[31] To understand *The Witches of Eastwick* fully, in fact, it is necessary to recognise Updike's debt to Townsend Warner, and beyond that to the Scottish witches of the Renaissance.

The Witches of Eastwick begins, literally and metaphorically, with not one but two epigraphs drawn from Scottish witchcraft trials. The first is from Isobel Gowdie via Pitcairn, describing the devil as "a meikle blak roch man". The second cites Agnes Sampson, describing the devil making the witches "kiss his ers" and touch his body, cold like "yce" and "hard lyk yrn". This material is not from Sampson's dittay but from Melville's *Memoirs* as quoted by Pitcairn.[32] It is interesting how carefully Updike read Pitcairn's materials in his sources, although he had also encountered the same material in Murray. Perhaps he checked his sources because – as he confirmed in the "Special Message" – he had read attacks on Murray's scholarship. For example, Murray includes the Gowdie material on page 37 but splits the Sampson material between pages 62 and 128, making it hard to reconstruct.[33] This attention to detail shows how seriously Updike took his sources, as does his decision to quote the texts in early modern Scots; he thought Murray was "Scots" too.[34] Although Updike calls one of his characters Abigail, apparently in a reference to *The Crucible*, and briefly mentions Cotton Mather and a bird familiar like *The Crucible*'s yellow bird, he seems barely interested in the standard motifs of Salem.[35] Instead, the reader is transported to early modern Scotland.

The choice of exotic sources is the more striking because Updike was living at Beverley, only seven miles from Salem, when he wrote *The Witches of Eastwick*. Beverley was the home of John Hale, the minister who in *The Crucible*, as in real life, participated in, and later deplored, the witch-hunt in his *Modest Inquiry* into its origin. And whilst Eastwick is like Ipswich – Updike's former Massachusetts home, eleven miles from Salem – it is also unlike Ipswich in the ingredients of its witchcraft.[36] It would have been easy for Updike to write yet another Salem novel, specific to New England. Instead, building his witches from European materials, as well as locating them physically in Rhode Island, distances them decisively. Only Jane is a New Englander: Sukie is from upstate New York, Alexandra from Colorado. The Rhode Island setting allows Updike to refer to the state's history offering sanctuary to what he calls "outcasts", naming Quakers, antinomians, Anne Hutchinson and Roger Williams – people fleeing from both England and Massachusetts.[37] Sukie, Jane and Alexandra are among these out-casts, deliberately not-local. The novel thus engages with the American tradition of blaming the outsider for bringing witchcraft into the community.

Several of the other Eastwick witches – Rose Hallybread, Dawn Polanski, Greta Neff – also recall European models. Rose's name comes from one of Hopkins' witch-hunts, in Essex in 1645, likely via Murray. Dawn's surname might suggest Roman Polanski, director of *Rosemary's Baby* (1968) and *Macbeth* (1971). Greta's German accent is described as "un-American", which seems a nod to Miller, but in its Germanic origin is also a nod to middle-European demonologies – Updike mentions *Malleus Maleficarum* in particular.[38] With European witches in mind, he also suggested that the novel's first inspiration might have been the "Dutch" (Deutsch, German) pow-wow and hexerei of his Pennsylvanian youth where "the presiding spirit of the land was certainly German".[39] Eastwick's devil, Darryl Van Horne, is certainly preoccupied with German witch-hunts: "you know what they used to do to witches in Germany?" he asks, answering "sit them on an iron chair and light a fire underneath . . . the good old *Hexestuhl*". But the novel ends as it began, with Scotland, for Darryl is moralising on this theme during a sermon, delivered from Eastwick's pulpit. Trailed in the novel's second epigraph, Van Horne's "admonitions" rewrite *Newes from Scotland*.[40]

Their European origin influences the portrayal of the Eastwick witches strongly, as well as that of their devil. For example, their sex-lives are those of sabbath-attending European witches, not their chaster American cousins. The epigraphs by Gowdie and Sampson point us towards recognition of these transplanted sexual elements: Darryl is cold-bodied, so that Alexandra feels a "chilly tingle" when he touches her; he has cold semen; as at North Berwick, the witches kiss his "ass", and so on. Other elements are also European in inspiration: Alexandra causes a sea-storm like Sampson, uttering "forbidden names" taken from MacGregor Mathers' *The Key of Solomon the King* via Haining.[41] There are other possible borrowings from Renaissance European witch-texts too. Alexandra's dog Coal sucks a "supernumerary pap" like English familiars, and in the same passage, he is referred to as "good Coal", so that I suspect a nod to Goodcole. Likewise, Clyde Gabriel, who kills his wife Felicia under the influence of witchcraft, is a version of *The Witch of Edmonton*'s Frank Thorney. Updike's witchcraft, then, is part of world history and literature, especially western European, and within that especially Scottish. It teases as it crosses the sea by refusing to settle itself in Salem. Instead, Eastwick is a legendary, liminal, Atlantean place where witchcraft traditions meet.[42]

All this directly echoes the Renaissance demonological understanding of witchcraft as real and the different-but-linked reality of Murray's witch-cult.

Are Updike's witches really witches, as the section title "Guilt" suggests we conclude? We are told repeatedly that they kill Jenny Gabriel, and in his 2008 sequel *The Widows of Eastwick*, Updike confirms this murder offhandedly: "thirty years ago, Alexandra had slain a sister witch: she and Sukie Rougemont and Jane Smart had killed little Jenny Gabriel".[43] Yet, he also teases with apparently metaphorical types of magic. For example, the three women do come between husbands and wives, but not by the "disruptive ligature" the world suspects. Instead, they are just ordinary adulterers. When Updike begins to say they accept that "the world not merely accused but burned them alive . . ." we assume at first that he is referring to historical executions. But, teasingly, the sentence ends ". . . in the tongues of indignant opinion". Alexandra's curtain pattern looks like devils, but it is only peonies. What are we to think? Did Sukie really turn her husband into a place mat? Do the women kill Jenny by wax image-magic, giving her cancer, or is her job as an X-ray technician to blame?[44] Critics dispute: de Bellis thinks "their spell kills Jenny" and Ra'ad finds their "powers limited".[45] Are the witches just harmless Wiccans, raising a cone of power occasionally in what *Widows* calls "a half-baked suburban variety of witchcraft"?[46]

Eastwick and *Widows'* cover art summarises neatly how the women both are and are not potent Renaissance European witches. On the 1984 cover, Dürer's *Four Witches* (1497) suggests that the witches depicted might be Jane, Alexandra and Sukie – and perhaps Jenny? The use of Dürer's engraving allows Updike to quote the quintessential Renaissance notion of the witch, placed before the reader even before s/he reaches the epigraphs. But Updike was a proud art historian and would know that there are problems even with this image of witches as a real threat. Dürer's "witches" are not necessarily witches at all – the title assigned on the back flap of the novel is one of several and the four women could be goddesses or allegorical figures instead. Updike's choice of the image and caption push the reader towards seeing Renaissance witchcraft in the novel, as does his comment on the colour of the dustjacket as "diabolic purple".[47] But like so much else in the book, the image both affirms and undermines the historicity and reality of its witchcraft. For *Widows*, Updike chose equally contradictory images of guilt and innocence, linked by collaborating artists: Masaccio's weeping Eve, cast out of paradise, but also Masolino's unfallen Eve, smirking serenely, both from the Brancacci Chapel, Florence, c.1424 to 1425.[48]

Shakespearean literary echoes add to this playful complexity. Updike first read *Macbeth* in high school, and over thirty years later it saturates *The Witches of Eastwick*.[49] But as so often, the recollection is ironic, expressed in echoes that might or might not be indications of serious purpose. Offered Mexican food by Van Horne, Jane recites "tamale and tamale and tamale", which is Macbeth's "To morrow and to morrow and to morrow", but parodied and vulgarised. When the witches play tennis, they tease each other with transformations (or illusions?): the ball becomes a bat, a toad; later, Alexandra mourns her babies, grown up now, but whom she imagines "sliced into bits" by time. Yet, these ingredients do not go into the cauldron – instead, the witches enter Van Horne's hot tub and are boiled and bubbled. Alexandra's storm recalls both *Macbeth* as well as the

North Berwick witches.[50] Meanwhile, the *Hamlet* epigraph of the sequel speaks of blessed times when "No Faiery talkes, nor Witch hath power to Charme" – which quotes the First Folio directly to establish its closeness to Shakespeare and Renaissance England, and affirms the powers of witches, but in a negative context, at times when it does not apply. Updike's playfulness situates his witches both inside and outside the stereotype of the early modern European witch, which is enjoyed but also ridiculed as "medieval nonsense". As de Bellis notes, his love of Spenser emerges too: for instance, in the witches' ability to use love magic and to create ideal partners, as the witch of Book Three creates the false Florimell for her son.[51]

The book is well aware of its literary, and filmic, heritage. We saw how it echoes Hawthorne and other American Gothic fictions, so much so that one of its characters is named Lovecraft. Avril Horner and Sue Zlosnik see *Witches* as "comic Gothic". Others, like Algis Valiunas, see it as a response to the 1980s magical realism boom, a tribute to Gabriel García Márquez. Atwood found the novel magical realist but also "satire", a "puff pastry" political fantasy revisiting *The Wizard of Oz*.[52] And, as she suggests, the novel is populist in its frame of reference, not confining itself to a particular literary-critical model. Updike's treatment of witches recapitulates that of films such as *Bell, Book and Candle* (1958, to which Updike refers in his 1960 *Rabbit, Run*) and TV shows like *Bewitched*.[53] However, the novel's underpinning of deep research, its engagement with questions of ontology, theology, science and art, its Vietnam-era setting and its poetic prose make it a serious, delicately crafted novel aligned with Benson's and Townsend Warner's magical realist fantasies.

If it is magical realist, *Witches* is also a very personal version of magical realism. Notably, Updike's mother, Linda Grace Hoyer, also conceptualised herself as both a victim of witchcraft and a witch in her fiction. In *Enchantment*, she begins with a child's tale of a "Bad Witch" and recounts her own "bewitched" life story where "the natural and the supernatural were indistinguishable". Hoyer's heroine is a girl "possessed" with a spark that even "the most indifferent student of Jules Michelet (*Satanism and Witchcraft*)" would notice. By her old age she "seemed to have become a witch" completely.[54] Michelet is where Updike started reading about witches, and in this shared frame of reference, it can be seen that his relationship with witches is linked to his relationship with his mother. Whilst it is decisively set far away, *Witches* is also close to home for Updike – at Salem, but also at Shillington and Plowville, Pennsylvania, where he grew up in the shadow of his mother's literary ambition.[55] The novel is thus heartfelt. It is haunted by war and death, sublime in its ambitious questions of human purpose and nature, and at least partly about Updike's own family history.

The story of *The Witches of Eastwick*, however, does not end with Updike, as, in 1987, the novel was adapted for the cinema under the same title. While it retained elements of the book's malice and violence, the film transferred blame from the witches to the devil. Van Horne (Jack Nicholson) is a traditionally monstrous Satan, growling and grotesque, whilst the witches (Cher, Susan Sarandon and Michelle Pfeiffer) are transformed into aspirational figures.

The ageing, adulterous murderesses of the book become lonely and frustrated, but young and gorgeous, innocents. These women inadvertently summon Van Horne as they resist belittling and harassment by the school principal, "a liar and a lecher". Like the North Berwick witches, they summon a storm: it rains harmlessly but satisfyingly on the school speech day. The newly empowered women fail to realise that their power can actually kill their enemies, and are appalled when it leads to the murder of Felicia. The far more problematic killing of Jenny is omitted from the film's plot, and it then develops into a slapstick battle between witches and devil when they reject his further help. At last, the witches use magic to defeat the devil, emerging broadly triumphant.

That the witches are portrayed as strong, articulate, justifiably angry with their society and the epitome of 1980s glamour, helped the film's success. The novel was thus tamed: the film had more in common with *I Married a Witch* or *Bell, Book and Candle* than with the unsettling meditation on female evil that Updike had concocted from the same materials. As with *Bewitched*, in the Eastwick film, witchcraft was domesticated, whilst retaining its sexualised appeal. Optimistically, Loudermilk describes the film as "feminism reclaimed", suggesting that it breaks out of the strait-jacket of witchcraft-related misogyny that, for her, marred Updike's novel. Other viewers, such as Paul McInnes and Janet Maslin, have felt more unease with the film's politics, noting that the witches spend the film "fawning over a man, just like [their] oppressed forebears" and that they "are conceived here only in the sketchiest way", primarily as "a hairdresser's delight". Either way, the transformation from text to screen was hard to forget: a number of TV pilots and series and a musical resulted. In 2008, James Wolcott suggested that Updike's sequel, *The Widows of Eastwick*, had needed twenty years to efface the memory of the film and resume the story of the novel's witches, but, in 2009, a TV series, *Eastwick*, essentially reprised the action and characters of the film rather than dramatising either Updike's first or second novel.[56] Most people will thus have encountered Alex, Jane and Sukie through George Miller's filmic version of them or its descendants, and their influence has been the establishment in contemporary culture of the witch as a mainstream more-or-less feminist icon.[57]

American witches: summary

This chapter has examined some aspects of the relationship between British and American witchcraft fictions and their legacy. Initially working in distinct cultural spheres, the two traditions grew closer over time and the interchange between them became strong and two-way. Updike's novel, in particular, blends a few images from the Salem stories with a much greater mass of Scottish witchcraft material. *The Witches of Eastwick* surprisingly returns, therefore, to the sources with which the rediscovery of witches began after the First World War, in delicate tribute to Sylvia Townsend Warner's works. Meanwhile the anger and division – sexual, racial and social – that permeates the American historiography and creative response is much less frequent in British fictions until the late 1960s. At that point, it emerges strongly, partly as a result of the radical feminist embrace of the figure of the witch and partly because of the growth of the horror genre in British cinema and literature. Both these trends had American roots. The last chapter will look at all these elements in British witchcraft fiction since the 1960s, as the British literary scene that produced *Lolly Willowes* grows into one that could produce *Witchfinder General* and *Vinegar Tom*.

Notes

1 See Gibson, *Witchcraft Myths* chapter one for further discussion.
2 For Hopkins see Chapter 1; Geis and Bunn; Gent.
3 On Gaskell see Chapter 3; Rees, *Witch Child* and *Sorceress*.
4 Anonymous review, *Michigan Alumnus*.
5 www.goodreads.com/list/show/75414.YA_Middle_Grade_Salem_Witch_Trials.
6 Advertisements: *Moving Picture World* (October–December 1911) 98, 150, 380; *Reel Life* (1 November 1913) 14, 15, (November 1913) 9, (13 December 1913); *Motion Picture News* 14:15 (14 October 1916) 2281; see also 14:16 (21 October 1916) 2523, 2551.
7 Rosenthal, *Salem Story* 149; ApIvor and Howard; Floyd.
8 Forbes left seven boxes of research notes on witchcraft to the American Antiquarian Society (MSS Boxes F); on Gibbings see Andrews and Empson; anonymous, review, "A Mirror for Witches", *Spectator*; reviews in Bates, 25–7.
9 America did not enter the War until 1917.
10 Gilman's heroine's wishes prefigure Gilman's utopia *Herland* (1915) and echo her earlier treatises.
11 Gilbert and Gubar, 88; Gilman, *The Forerunner* 1:1 (1909) 32.
12 See Gibson, *Witchcraft Myths* chapter five for further discussion.
13 For example, Thorne Smith, *Topper* and Walker. On later sparkling witches, see Moseley.
14 See Gibson, *Witchcraft Myths* chapter five for further discussion.
15 For contexts, see Heale; Lieberman and Lang, eds; Weigand; and on the more contemporary significance of witch-hunts in US politics, Madsen; the figurative use of the term "witch-hunt" is dated by *OED* to 1915, but saw a peak relating to political contexts during the 1930s to 1950s (*OED* "witch-hunt" n. [1986]).
16 See Gibson, *Witchcraft Myths* chapters one and two for further discussion.
17 Mappen, 36.
18 See also Hawthorne, "The Custom House" prefacing *The Scarlet Letter*; Upham, *Salem Witchcraft* and "Prefatory Note" to *Salem Witchcraft and Cotton Mather*; Poole, "Cotton Mather"; on the historiography see especially Weisman, chapter two and Mappen.
19 Lovecraft, 204, 209, 210, 212, 213, 301; Murray is also referred to in "The Horror at Red Hook" and "The Whisperer in Darkness", and on this see Waugh.
20 Breslaw found reference to someone who may have been Tituba in slave records, but also suggested that her name was of South American origin, confirming contemporary identification of her as "Indyen".
21 Starkey, 8–9; for example, Barker, 47–52; Williams, 226, 232, 239; on these, Rosenthal and Hansen, see also Gibson, *Witchcraft Myths* chapter three.
22 Miller, 40–3, 229, 231, 235, 237, 249.
23 For example, *The Simpsons* Halloween episodes, 1997, 2009; *Sabrina the Teenage Witch*, episode titled after Miller's play, 1997.
24 Hope Robbins was further influenced by his wife Helen Ann Mins, who had volunteered for the XV International Brigade in the Spanish Civil War and who spoke out

against McCarthyism in the 1950s: see "Rossell Hope Robbins" and "Helen Ann Mins Robbins".

25 Hope Robbins, 2.

26 Stevens, 1; Nussbaum.

27 Begley, 39, 108, 197, 223, etc.

28 As well as the quoted reviews, still circulating online, see Pollitt; Raine; Verduin; Campbell, 11; Newman, 1; Tayler; and Moore.

29 de Bellis, 468; Updike, "Lolly" 284, 285; Updike "Mastery" 234.

30 Schiff, quoted in Plath 211, 212; Loudermilk, 98; see also Schiff, and Coale, 143.

31 Also: Muriel Spark, Norman Cohn, Isabel Adam, Charles Williams, Richard Cavendish, Colin Wilson, Ronald Holmes; the non-British ones are Michelet, J.K. Huysmans and Robert Pinget (French) and Erica Jong (American).

32 Pitcairn: Sampson from Volume 1, Part 3 240, and Gowdie from Volume 3, Part 2 610. Updike does not mention Pitcairn, and probably gathered his quotations at second hand.

33 In the first edition of *Witches,* the "l" was omitted from "pulpit" (3); on Updike's epigraphs as keys to reading, or not, see de Bellis 161, 162; in particular, Updike had read Cohn – see "Special Message" 855.

34 Updike, "Special Message" 855; de Bellis 468; in an essay on his sources for *The Witches of Eastwick,* he especially notes Adam's *Witch Hunt;* Murray, *First Hundred Years* 11–16.

35 de Bellis, 300; Updike, *Eastwick* 4, 9; Miller, 224.

36 Begley, 411.

37 Updike, *Witches* 9, 10.

38 Murray, 30, 318, based on *The Full Trial* (1690); Ed(ward) Parsley also comes from the Hopkins trials, for example, H.F., 10; Updike, *Witches* 15, 25, 27.

39 Updike, "Special Message" 854.

40 Updike, *Witches* 295–302.

41 Updike, *Witches* 15–19, 39, 117, 123, 189; MacGregor Mathers, 90; Haining, 48.

42 See the novel's last lines, where the narrator looks westwards (316).

43 Updike, *Witches* 254, 303; *Widows* 11.

44 Updike, *Witches* 7, 69, 73, 76.

45 de Bellis, 386; Ra'ad, 31.

46 Updike, *Witches,* for example, 78, 85; *Widows* 6.

47 Brion, Updike, "Dürer"; de Bellis, 72. Isn't the cover dark blue?

48 The Eves may be before and after, but *Widows* is not a book about the witches' lives before their witchcraft; Updike, *Witches* front cover, back flap; Updike, *Widows* front cover, back flap, which states the common origin and features a photograph of Updike laughing.

49 Begley, 87.

50 Updike, *Witches* 101, 102, 106, 110, 120; *Macbeth* 5.5.18; Johnson, "Weird".

51 Updike, *Widows* epigraph (n.p.), 39; de Bellis 159.

52 Updike, *Witches* 49; Horner and Zlosnik, 136, 143.

53 Updike, *Rabbit,* 115. See also Haining 92, 93, which might have recalled it for him.

54 Hoyer, 1, 4, 23–5, 39, 158.

55 Begley, 2, 36, 54, 55, 118, etc.

56 Loudermilk, 110. Although popular with viewers, *Eastwick* was cancelled during its first season's run in 2010.

57 See Gibson, *Witchcraft Myths* chapter five for further discussion of televisual/feminist witches and their pitfalls.

7 Magical realism, magical romance

Witchcraft genres since the 1960s

This book's final chapter takes a step back in time to complete the story of transatlantic exchange begun in Chapter 6, whilst also returning to the end of Chapter 5 to investigate in more detail what happened to the figures of the witch and witch-hunter in the late 1960s and 1970s. With Updike's *Witches of Eastwick*, we reached 1984, but before moving on to the story of how Eastwick-inspired witches came eastwards to Britain, we also need to understand how 1960s and 1970s British writers had already moved westwards to meet them, towards an American-flavoured understanding of witchcraft as a politicised phenomenon. The association of witchcraft with unjust persecution that shaped *The Crucible* in the early 1950s is an important part of the transatlantic story, as well as the wish-fulfilment feminist fantasies that resulted from *Eastwick*, particularly from the 1987 film of Updike's book. Switching between genres as well as between continents, this chapter also makes the point that much of the transatlantic interchange of the period from 1960 to the present was, and is, filmic. It has a different audience and purpose from the novels that have been the focus of much of this book so far.

Because of the wealth and creativity of the Hollywood studios, and the comparative poverty of the British film industry, most of the filmic traffic is one-way. As Leon Hunt has demonstrated, therefore, the earliest British witchcraft-horror films, *Night of the Demon* (1957), *Night of the Eagle* (1962) and *Witchcraft* (1964) all drew on American tropes and talent. Their writers and stars – Jacques Tourneur, Richard Matheson, Charles Beaumont, Dana Andrews – were American, and the films strongly recall the American horror films by producer Val Lewton, such as *Cat People* (1942).[1] As well as knowing American cinema, British film-makers knew American horror fiction, and so older American Gothic influences can also be seen in their films. For example, *Witchcraft* (1964) focuses on the disturbed grave of a witch, property and family feud in a way recalling Hawthorne's *House of the Seven Gables*. Hammer's *Curse of the Crimson Altar* (1968), featuring a pagan cult hidden in an attic, is explicitly based on Lovecraft's "The Dreams in the Witch House".[2] Alongside dramatic experiments that recalled *The Crucible*, these filmic horror fictions shaped British understandings of witchcraft from the late 1950s, a trend continuing today. Meanwhile, since the late 1980s, many British and American witchcraft fictions have blurred the boundaries between real and unreal in a way more reminiscent of the novels of the "new spell". Together, these genres have created a popular magical realism that slips between horror, mystery, children's fiction, social realism and fantasy. But it is in children's fiction that the result has been most spectacular, with J.K. Rowling's *Harry Potter* stories[3] meaning that British witches are in fashion across the globe.

This closing chapter will thus address two areas of witchcraft fiction in the period from the late 1960s to today. One is the serious concern that stories of witchcraft, and especially witch-hunting, continue to embody – stronger in the earlier works than it is today, but still present. The second is the pleasure that fictions about witchcraft can bring to readers and viewers, now clearly in the ascendant in the witchcraft novel and film. As part of its exploration of essentially tragic and comic modes of representing witchcraft, it will also look at the interplay between different subgenres of witchcraft fiction: the horror novel and film, the Brechtian play, the social-realist and romantic novel.

Witchfinder general: from historical novel to "horror" film

One of the developments in the representation of witchcraft at the end of the twentieth century is that the portrayal of witch-hunters moves from approbation to repulsion. In part, this was due to wider cultural movements: a concern for social, gendered and racial justice, and distaste for arbitrary authority. The demonisation of the witch-hunter in this context follows the pattern defined by *The Crucible*. But a specific historical milestone was the rediscovery of the Hopkins trials of the 1640s in Ronald Bassett's 1966 novel *Witchfinder General*. Bassett was an ex-naval PR man who wrote historical novels exploring the seamier side of military and naval adventure. These are not obvious contexts for the rediscovery of the witchcraft sublime. But like the post-Great-War fictions that began this book, *Witchfinder General* is preoccupied with war and its trauma. Bassett thus creates a background for his Matthew Hopkins in Civil War military service. This ends in a breakdown after he witnesses the murder of Irish Catholics and is, he believes, "cursed by the dying breath of a witch". After this collapse, Hopkins becomes a witch-finder, driven by obscure fears and a desire to regain his self-possession, ranting about "spawn of the Devil . . . gather[ing] in packs" and constantly touching his lip because he believes the "witch" placed a sore there. Stearne, another ex-soldier, is a different type of wartime threat: an unabashed lecher and robber, exploiting the opportunities of anarchy and driving the action by his vices.

In this sense, *Witchfinder General* is not about witchcraft: like the film it became, it defines a new horror genre between *Peeping Tom*, *Psycho* and *Straw Dogs*, exploring damaged, psychopathic characters.[3] For instance, whilst the novel's first accusation (of Elizabeth Clarke) is genuine, after that, witchcraft is irrelevant as Stearne and a gaoler beat and rape Clarke and fabricate her confession. Hopkins and Stearne also abuse John Lowes' ward, Sara (a character without historical origin), coercing her sexually in return for sparing her adoptive uncle. An interlude when Hopkins discovers a suspected "Lammas Sabbat" – actually an orgy – is symptomatic of the novel's uninterest in witchcraft: despite the episode's origins in Murray and Wheatley, Hopkins does not consider it witch-related. Instead, it is an exploitation vignette. The witchcraft sublime thus began its return in the unpromising setting of mid-century pulp fiction, with a reprise of the linkage between witchcraft and war-trauma, and a commitment to noting that a witchcraft prosecution is an encounter with human evil. But the 1960s rediscovery of witchcraft is not characterised by either the bohemian experimentation or middlebrow security of earlier fictions. Instead, it dwells on violence and sex with a queasy fascination, so much so that Benjamin Halligan dismisses Bassett's novel with the damning labels "tedious" and "low-brow".[4]

Yet the novel caught the zeitgeist and was adapted to become Michael Reeves' film *Witchfinder General* (1968; also titled *The Conqueror Worm*). As in the book, Reeves' Hopkins (Vincent Price) and Stearne (Robert Russell) are sadistic predators. Stearne tortures and swims Lowes (Rupert Davies), hanging him without trial from a tree. The book's sexual violence moves from Clarke to Sara (Hilary Dwyer): in this version, she offers herself to Hopkins but is forcibly raped by Stearne. Meanwhile, Clarke is conflated with Mary Lakeland and burned by being lowered into a fire, Hopkins' "new method of execution". Horrified, the British Board of Film Classification's censor rejected the script's first draft, commenting: "there are few pages on which some helpless human being is not shown being hanged, burned, drowned, raped, beaten-up, dragged about or otherwise bullied and threatened". After redrafting, some reviewers, such as Alan Bennett, still found the film "sadistic and morally rotten . . . degrading". However, Reeves' response to Bennett shows that he had intended the film to be "entirely factual" in important respects, "a serious picture", both "anti-violence" and "moral". It was in the horror genre, he argued, because it was progressive, concerned about real-life horrors and had been researched accordingly rather than simply lifted from the novel.[5]

Reeves explained to Bennett that as well as reading Bassett he had based his film upon an "article about witchcraft in the Middle Ages" in the *New Statesman*. This claim relocated the film from pulp fiction into the discourse of scholarly left-wing politics. In fact, it was inaccurate, but Halligan suggests Reeves might have misremembered Hugh Trevor-Roper's "Witches and Witchcraft", a two-part piece for the similar magazine *Encounter* in 1967. Halligan's identification appears correct. Trevor-Roper anticipates Reeves' reading of witch-hunting as a relevant theme in modernity, arguing that persecution accompanied, rather than being overcome by, Renaissance "progress" and that in contemporary life, American anti-communism and Nazi anti-Semitism replicated it. Anti-Semitism was "a new witch-craze", whilst "the Red scare" in America was equally a "collective emotion" in "stereotyped form". The *Encounter* piece also seems to have shaped Reeves' film visually. It contains woodcuts of torture instruments and burnings and the title-page illustration of Hopkins' *Discovery* with its cloaked, hatted figure, and its text "Matthew Hopkins Witch Finder Generall" as a caption. This is, in fact, the full name of Reeves' film, according to its title-credit.[6] It is a filmic version of the pamphlet's woodcut in many ways. This may derive from Trevor-Roper's historical essay, itself inspired by recent, horrifying American and European events and by an understanding that witchcraft persecutions could be used, as in *The Crucible*, to explore these.

But whilst Reeves' *Witchfinder General* is often historically well-informed, and realist to some extent, it is also influenced by romantic genre fiction including pulp horror and pornography. Critics such as Marcus Harmes regard it therefore as surprisingly conservative in its politics. It is certainly more Bassett than Trevor-Roper in mood, and whilst it recalls *The Crucible* in its themes, it could not be further from Miller's stark simplicity and earnest commentary. Instead, it recalls cinematically the Lewtonesque films of the 1940s to 1960s. *Witchfinder General* is surprisingly beautiful, and it titillates, repulses and disturbs for unpredictable, deliberate shock value. Its landscapes are painterly and the film's music, by Paul Ferris, recalls Ralph Vaughan Williams' Tudorist compositions with its lush, folky strings. Its sweet "Love Theme" – released on 7" because of its appeal – introduces images of soon-to-be rape victim Sara with troubling ambiguity.[7] The film's American distributors rightly, if clumsily, drew attention to its traditional Gothic pleasures in retitling it after a poem by Edgar Allen Poe. And the film sits – albeit uneasily – within an emergent exploitation genre that included slashers and bodice-rippers. *Witchfinder General*'s producer, Tony Tenser, also made *Naked as Nature Intended* (1961), *My Bare Lady* (1962) and the stripper film *Secrets of a Windmill Girl* (1966).

Tenser's *A Study in Terror* (1965) perhaps best illustrates his interest in exploiting fear and desire without serious intent, and it anticipates *Witchfinder General* in its linking of historic horrors with cinematic pleasures. In *A Study in Terror*, the real Ripper murders are investigated by the fictional Sherlock Holmes, oddly combining Hammer-ish shocks with cosy Baker Street detection and exploitation visuals. In one sequence, the viewer occupies the murderer's viewpoint – as in *Peeping Tom* – as a prostitute strips for him. The fact that the film's cast includes "legitimate" theatre stars such as Anthony Quayle and Judi Dench, the *Carry On* actresses Barbara Windsor and Edina Ronay and the horror and exploitation actress Adrienne Corri suggests its generic uncertainty.[8] *Witchfinder General* too problematises genre: too legitimate to be exploitation, too exploitative to be legitimate, too romantic to be wholly realistic, too real to be comfortably romantic, it is sensation cinema, like a Victorian sensation novel. It even has comedy. Reeves told Bennett that humour was out-of-place in horror, but how then to explain the presence of Wilfrid Brambell? Brambell, best known for his role as a rag-and-bone man in a television sitcom, appears as a villager horse-trading with Hopkins.[9]

Part of *Witchfinder General*'s appeal, then, was based on the pulp, exploitation, "low brow" and comic genres that flavoured its narrative. Yet, as Reeves claimed, the film did also possess a genuine, *Crucible*-esque campaigning aspect, knowingly connecting past horrors with contemporary ones: racist lynch-mobs, the Vietnam War and Nazi genocide. The film begins as a woman is hanged by her neighbours and there are scenes showing troops massacred by forest guerrillas. Stearne describes the witchfinders' trade as "extermination". And despite being repelled by the "hero" Richard Marshall's murder of Hopkins at the film's end, audiences are invited to hate the witchfinder. Tenser described attending one screening where as he watched Hopkins die a viewer shouted "kill the bastard!... Smash him! Kill him!"[10] Gone is any sense that the witch-finder might be justified. However, even here is an element of camp and Gothic. Price was celebrated for his pantomimic villains, and was known to declare proudly "I have never been realistic". *Witchfinder General* thus revisits aspects of the Romantic interest in witches as victims of tyranny, but there is an undertow of sensationalism, artifice and generic self-awareness that problematises its representation of witch-finding as simply a reprehensible crime.

After *Witchfinder General*, it was uncommon to portray witch-hunting in anything other than a horrific context, however.[11] And during the 1970s, the seriousness of this endeavour became more evident. For example, the Scottish writer Stewart Conn's 1971 *The Burning* (begun in the late 1960s) dramatised the story of King James, "Effie McCalyan" and (in his version) her lover Bothwell, not because of "any predisposition on my part towards Scots historical drama" but because of its "theatrical potential", demanding a stage "as bare as possible – where practicable, completely bare", and resisting historical specificity to emphasise the universal relevance of the story. "The play wasn't triggered (compare *The Crucible* vis-à-vis the McCarthy trials) by any topical event or events" he told me. Instead, *The Burning* summed up "a general climate and an awareness, as James puts it, that in any struggle for dominance it tends to be 'those trappt in the middle, must pay the price'". Conn sees the ultimate arena of the play as being "the human heart", and so in pursuit of that emotional truth, he read Pitcairn, *Daemonologie*, Murray and histories of Scotland and Jacobean life. The burning of Effie for witchcraft – to which she is betrayed by both James and Bothwell – is then seen to be the horrific, predictable outcome of human conflict, whether as a result of the political strife of the 1590s, the Civil War (as in Hopkins' time), or in Conn's own time of the Vietnam War or the Irish Troubles.

Theatre: Brechtian witches

Although *The Burning* might have mid-century resonances, Conn does not see himself as a political writer. Other writers of the mid-twentieth century, however, often adopted explicitly political forms to make polemical points. Many used alienation techniques, jarring the audience out of their immersion in character and plot to consider wider issues. The notion of "alienation" is best known in the theatre of Bertolt Brecht, which relies on the *Verfremdungseffekt*, or the alienation effect. Aspects of Conn's play – its ritual tableaux "like a dream", its breaking into verse or song – do have a Brechtian feel.[12] But much more assertively, Caryl Churchill's *Vinegar Tom* (1976) draws attention to its own politicised theatricality with the aim of forcing audiences to connect witchcraft prosecution with the absurdity of contemporary misogyny. By the 1970s, the connection between witch-hunting and oppression was increasingly seen in feminist and Marxist terms, as activists such as Robin Morgan and Mary Daly began to reimagine witches as proto-feminists. A New York women's collective named their "guerrilla theatre" group "WITCH". New York academics Barbara Ehrenreich and Deirdre English wrote a pamphlet titled *Witches, Midwives and Nurses* (1973), as part of their anger at the contemporary American medical profession's view of female bodies. In California, Starhawk founded Witchcraft covens focused on feminism and eco-activism.[13] Meanwhile in Britain in 1970 to 1971, the historians Keith Thomas and Alan Macfarlane at Oxford University produced studies arguing that Tudor economic problems caused the Elizabethan upsurge of witchcraft prosecution to focus on indigent older women, and Macfarlane's *Witchcraft in Tudor and Stuart England* was Churchill's main source for *Vinegar Tom*'s historical details.[14] However, she incorporated these into a feminist framework influenced by Ehrenreich and English (whom she mentions, with Macfarlane, in her preface), producing a transatlantic fusion of political concerns embodied in a hybrid drama of witch-hunting.

Vinegar Tom was written for the agitprop group Monstrous Regiment and features women accused of witchcraft in mid-seventeenth-century England: some are healers, others are poor, all stand out in their community and suffer for it. The play's timing in the aftermath of the British Equal Pay Act (1970) and Sex Discrimination Act (1975) is not coincidental, and the Domestic Violence Act was passed in the year of its first performance.[15] It is thus a provocative mix, generically complex: "a play about witches with no witches in it", as Churchill called it.[16] Monstrous Regiment, meanwhile, described it as "a witch hunt with music". Texts and generic conventions are juxtaposed to create what Elaine Scarry calls "Brecht's alchemy of theatrical transformation, where anything can become a new thing".[17] And this method makes the play a more magical text than may initially appear: alongside scenes of seventeenth-century life are interludes sung in modern dress, where the authors of *Malleus Maleficarum* appear as a music hall act, played by crossdressing actresses. In the first production, Churchill recalls, they had also portrayed the recently hanged witches. The transformation of dead witches into live demonologists is a magical sleight that eerily dramatises the ways in which demonologies fed off trial accounts.

As well as transformative contradictions of genre and gender, there is also a deliberate confusion of tone. "Why is a greater number of witches found in the fragile feminine sex than in men?" asks Kramer, a line usually delivered as if setting up a "knock, knock" joke. "Why is a greater number of witches found in the fragile feminine sex than in men?" responds Sprenger, and Kramer answers with the punchline: "All wickedness is but little to the wickedness of a woman". The translation is that of Summers (see Chapter 3), whose florid prose adds to the distancing effect created. *Vinegar Tom* is thus a thoroughly Brechtian play, aiming to "isolate and manifest certain ideas and relationships that make ideology visible". Gillian Hanna of Monstrous Regiment recalls the need to create discomfort: "we didn't want to allow the audience to get off the hook by regarding it as a period piece, a piece of very interesting history". However, instead of inventing her historic basis, Churchill researched it exceptionally well and *Vinegar Tom*'s historically accurate scenes offer the audience the chance to rediscover Renaissance witchcraft in great detail. Using Macfarlane's academic study, Churchill dramatised moments from a number of witchcraft pamphlets very accurately, although like Bassett, Reeves and Conn she also made changes to history as required.[18]

For example, the first character whom we meet in *Vinegar Tom* is referred to as "Alice", but in scene two, we discover that her surname is "Noakes", thus she is an avatar of Alice Nokes, one of the subjects of the pamphlet *A Detection of Damnable Driftes*. It was in print in Barbara Rosen's 1969 edition *Witchcraft in England*, but Churchill told me she had no memory of Rosen's book and remembered using only Macfarlane's extracts from the pamphlets.[19] Indeed, the historical Alice Nokes is not fully named in the pamphlet: she is referred to only as "Mother" Nokes, so Churchill took her forename from Macfarlane, who gives this detail on pages 84 and 258. The real-life Alice Nokes was old enough to have a 28-year-old daughter, but it is to this younger figure that Churchill has transferred the name Alice in her play, whilst her mother is renamed Joan. So the historical Alice Nokes has re-emerged in *Vinegar Tom* younger, and more central to events than her original in 1579. Despite these changes, her story has analogies with that of the original Mother Nokes' daughter, told in *A Detection of Damnable Driftes*.

In the pamphlet, we read how a servant to Thomas Spycer snatched a pair of gloves from Mother Nokes' daughter, "which he protesteth to have done in jest". Mother Nokes was angry and bewitched him. Macfarlane retells this story, describing how "Mother Nokes' daughter had her gloves snatched away by a youth" and "the unfortunate young man was paralysed". This uneasy (playful? bullying? flirtatious?) relationship with Spycer's manservant seems echoed in the play in relationships between women and men. We first meet Alice with her lover, referred to as "Man". Man begins by teasing Alice about the sinful nature of their relationship. "Am I the devil?" he asks, ". . . didn't I lie on you so heavy I took your breath? Didn't the enormous size of me terrify you?" Alice teases back: "it seemed a fair size like other men's". But as the dialogue continues, the Man becomes angry. He calls Alice a "whore, damned strumpet" and "witch" and abandons her by the roadside. This scene suggests how what Macfarlane calls "rudeness, sexual jealousy, and quarrelling" led to accusation. Other examples he gives include *A True and Just Recorde*'s Richard Harrison who called the suspect Annis Heard a "vield strumpet": Heard too may have contributed to *Vinegar Tom*.

Further echoes of witchcraft pamphlets abound. The play's title comes from the familiar described in Hopkins' *Discovery*, mentioned by Macfarlane on page 139. Joan Noakes' cat also recalls the historical Mother Nokes who was said to have a "Feende" called Tom. Some of the conflicts between accusers and accused echo *A True and Just Recorde*, via Macfarlane. For example, Churchill's Margery Carter fears Noakes has stolen her bowl and bewitched her milk: "She still got my big bowl I give her some eggs in that time she was poorly . . . We'll get that bowl back off her . . . we'll heat a horseshoe red hot and put it in the milk to make the butter come". Here she echoes the 1582 pamphlet's Bennet Lane, who (as quoted by Macfarlane on page 108): "tooke a horse shoe and made it redde hot and put it into the milke" to combat witch-attack after a quarrel over a borrowed "dish".[20] There are also a witch-hunter and his searcher strongly reminiscent of Hopkins and his associates. Far more historically accurate than *Witchfinder General*'s characters, Churchill's Packer and Goody are earnest but misguided. The play refuses a sadistic stereotype, although it shows the evil done. Churchill thus rendered material from witchcraft pamphlets, as chosen by Macfarlane, directly into plot and dialogue to make a play with sharp topical relevance despite its historical specificity – an exemplary rediscovery. Although a pioneer, she is not alone: for example, Sarah Daniels' feminist *Byrthrite* (1986) also draws on witchcraft pamphlets, recalling Hopkins with its "Woman-Finder General".[21]

The witchcraft fictions of the 1960s and 1970s thus rediscovered some of the key themes and traits of the Romantic works that we examined in Chapters 3 and 4: an interest in the sublime experiences that prompted witchcraft accusation – especially war – a moral seriousness and/or radical political engagement. Like the witch-fictions of the "new spell", later twentieth-century texts used their chosen genres inventively, to introduce fantastical and surrealist elements. However, the tone of fictions written since the 1960s is not like that of earlier works. Witchcraft fictions post-1960 are grim rather than fey. Whilst they all recall *The Crucible* – and post-Miller witchcraft stories moved away from the novel towards the stage and film studio – all are also very unlike it. Writers such as Reeves, Conn and Churchill display a sharp self-awareness of the play of genres within their works, sometimes employing particular theoretical or generic models to distance aspects of witchcraft stories from their audiences. All three use music, in particular, in an unsettling way, and elements of humour, camp and self-reflexiveness break in. The relationship between immersion in the emotions of the story and reflection upon its meanings is thus problematised, and the response of viewers is less certain, and less directed, than in earlier works.

Writing back through witchcraft

Other aspects of the relationship between Renaissance and postmodern texts also changed during the twentieth century. As we saw, writers such as Benson and Matson had little knowledge of the real histories of witches: they repurposed the Renaissance witch-figure without its details. In the 1950s, historical novelists such as Lewis had to trawl record repositories and libraries painstakingly to acquire these details. But today, dramatists, novelists and film-makers can easily build knowledge of historical realities and the precursors of their own work, an ease that has grown since the advent of online book sales and Wikipedia. Post-modernism has also encouraged a focus on intertextuality, the notion that texts are in dialogue across history and that rewriting an earlier text is not only ethically praiseworthy as a political act but also marketable. One of the features of witchcraft fictions in the last few decades, therefore, is that they very often "write back" in some detail to a variety of earlier texts.

"Writing back" is a term coined by Salman Rushdie: it designates the ways that previously suppressed voices challenge canonical texts. Writing back can also challenge standard literary features such as linear narration and realism, exposing the sexism, racism, class and literary-critical snobbery that may underlie them. For example, Sycorax and Caliban have often been revisited in this context: Caliban symbolised the aspirations of colonised nations for Aimé Césaire, whilst versions of Sycorax have influenced such writers as Kamau Brathwaite and Marina Warner. In Warner's *Indigo*, Sycorax is transplanted to the Caribbean where she becomes an *obeah* woman. Some versions of Tituba, such as Maryse Condé's *I Tituba* (1986) also draw on Sycorax for their "magic of healing and revolution", as George Yancy puts it.[22] *Macbeth* has also been reimagined in ways influenced by "writing back" to imperial literatures and by magical realism. In 1986, Terry Eagleton provocatively stated that "the witches are the heroines" of *Macbeth* and Rebecca Reisert's *The Third Witch* (2001) makes this explicit. Her "third witch", Roah, is a child drawn into witchcraft by her adoptive guardians, Nettle and Mad Helga (Witches 1 and 2). Reisert uses these characters to write back to *Macbeth* and allow her subversive, young, female protagonist to wreak vengeance on the oppressive, older, male titular villain.[23]

Like the fictions of the 1960s and 1970s, writing back was influenced by the political climate of its heyday. The late 1980s and 1990s saw right-wing Conservative and Republican parties taking power for lengthy terms of office in Britain and America, prompting fictional responses demonstrating the power of magic to transcend social, gendered and generational barriers to empowerment. Despite Prime Minister Margaret Thatcher's femininity, she was seldom associated with feminism, and her government was characterised by leftists as militaristic, homophobic and responsible for both mass unemployment and retrogressive taxation. In America, President Ronald Reagan represented the liberal wing of a movement whose more extreme conservatives regarded women's liberation as disastrous for the American family and nation: figures such as Pat Robertson, who opined that feminism was "a socialist, anti-family political movement that encourages women to leave their husbands, kill their children, practice witchcraft, destroy capitalism and become lesbians".[24] In this climate of polarised rhetoric, writing back offered the possibility of unpicking conservative demonologies or gleefully drawing on their angry energies to produce a fittingly powerful response.

For Kate Pullinger, the Warboys witch of 1593, Agnes Samuel, offered these possibilities with regard to the Puritan patriarchy of her day, and its resonances of "mass hysteria . . . and blame, and misogyny, and fear of change, and class hatred". Animated by "a kind of feminist agenda at work", as in many of Pullinger's other novels, *Weird Sister* (note the *Macbeth*ian title) sees Agnes return to attack the descendants of her persecutors, the Throckmortons. And *Weird Sister* is a well-researched book. Pullinger's inspirations were very diverse, as she told me:

> the "sensation novels" from the 19th century, in particular the fabulous Mary Elizabeth Braddon and *Lady Audley's Secret* . . . witchcraft cases from

England in the 16th century . . . reading around fairytales, Marina Warner of course, and Jack Zipes. And of course Salem . . . [Husain's] *The Virago Book of Witches* . . . [Summers'] *The History of Witchcraft* . . . [Rosen's] *Witchcraft in England 1558–1618* . . . (which has the Warboys pamphlet in it, though I first found the pamphlet in the B[ritish] L[ibrary] on its own), *The Witch in History* [by] Diane Purkiss . . . *Lolly Willowes* most definitely, *The Crucible*, and the Alice Hoffman novels . . . John Updike [and] Stephen King . . .[25]

From this impressive list, Pullinger created her revenant Agnes, and wrote back to *The most strange and admirable discoverie of the three Witches of Warboys*. Yet for all the clarity of her revenge fantasy, Pullinger also wanted the "reader to not quite believe that [Agnes] is actually a witch, but then for it to become more and more apparent that she is". This ambiguity is often a feature of contemporary witchcraft novels.

For instance, early drafts of Janice Elliott's *The Sadness of Witches* (1987) survive, and show the author tweaking her depiction of the reality and historicity of her Cornish witch Martha Price's magic. Her dilemma is both how culpable but also how powerful to make Martha. Martha muses on the harms witches do – sinking ships, causing earthquakes and pandemics – but Elliott deleted a phrase linking this to Satan in the traditional way: "she alone in this place knew the mouths of hell and how close they all were to one". Later, when Martha bewitches her lover's wife Molly, Elliott considered how soon after the moment when Martha "had made up her mind" and "raised her arms" to place her description of Molly's sudden affliction. Originally, it was within a few lines, but in the final version, it was moved into the next section, breaking the clear connection between apparent magic and apparent result.[26] Whilst Martha really does seem to be a witch, there are also other explanations for the novel's events. Writing back to the notion of the woman as witch is thus sometimes a process of negotiation between empowerment and responsibility.

In *Weird Sister*, Agnes' apparent witchcraft raises issues about the endorsement of original accusations against her. In particular, Pullinger titles one chapter "Agnes is a witch and a whore", potentially rebutting the historical Agnes' assertion that she was neither of these. But Pullinger is quite clear about the historical Agnes' innocence. She told me that her thinking was that "if you were an innocent person executed for witchcraft that might, in fact, be enough to grant you wicked powers in the future". That many readers accept Agnes' right to choose to be a witch – in Purkiss' terms – and support her in her revenge makes the novel a more potent read than if she had been innocent in modernity as well as in 1593. The witch-hunters' descendants are rightly forced to admit their guilt and Agnes' right to bewitch them ("the Samuels were hanged, my family was responsible. It's enough to turn anyone toward evil" says Robert Throckmorton) and the novel ends with the suggestion that "she will return, won't she?" to keep exacting penance. But exactly how Agnes makes her return and revenge is not even discussed: how this "sister" is "weird" is wholly and satisfyingly unclear.[27] Thus fictions that write back to Renaissance witchcraft texts often leave open the nature and extent of their characters' magic, producing a delicate and suggestive magical realism that refuses to be tied down.

Magical realism is a vexed term, however. Broadly, the genre has flourished among Anglophone writers from the 1980s onward and is conventionally described as originating in South America in the 1930s. Chris Baldick defines it as:

> a kind of modern fiction in which fabulous and fantastical events are included in a narrative that otherwise maintains the "reliable" tone of objective realistic report, designating a tendency of the modern novel to reach beyond the confines of realism and draw upon the energies of fable, folk tale, and myth while maintaining a strong contemporary social relevance.

All these apply to Pullinger's, Elliott's and other similar novels where witchcraft appears to be present, but confirmation of that is strategically withheld. They also apply to Benson's *Living Alone* (1919), however, which is neither South American nor of the 1930s. But then again, the terms which have come to define postmodernism (listed by Theo D'Haen as "self-reflexiveness, metafiction, eclecticism, redundancy, multiplicity, discontinuity, intertextuality, parody, the dissolution of character and narrative instance, the erasure of boundaries, and the destabilization of the reader") also apply to *Living Alone*. Further, D'Haen points out that they also apply routinely to magical realist texts. It is also true that both these genres (if indeed they can be separated) attempt to put the previously marginal at the centre of fiction and oust the usually central from that position: what D'Haen calls "decentring privileged centres". In that sense, both are literatures of "becoming minoritarian" as discussed in my Introduction, with the witch as their ideal protagonist. Witchcraft novels thus often occupy the same territory as postmodern and magical realist texts, by nature of their elusive, subversive subject matter, and they are also minoritarian novels, almost by default.

This is particularly true of Jeanette Winterson's "Pendle" novel, *The Daylight Gate*, with its title not-coincidentally referring to a marginal state (twilight). *The Daylight Gate* is a good example of a contemporary witchcraft rediscovery that appears designed to be a minoritarian fiction, as much as it is also postmodern and magical realist.[28] It also continues the tradition of experimentation with the horror genre that was begun by *Witchfinder General*.

The Daylight Gate: from horror film to "horror" novel

Along with an increase in postmodern self-awareness among recent fictions, a mainstream and "highbrow" engagement with the horror genre has also flourished. Horror films are no longer regarded as pulp entertainments or straight-to-video nasties. Four decades after *Witchfinder General* and *Vinegar Tom*, similar liberal concerns and pamphlet sources prompted Jeanette Winterson to write her horror novel *The Daylight Gate*, published in 2012 for the 400th anniversary of the "Pendle" trial. As expected from the author of *Sexing the Cherry* and other

historical experiments, it is not a realist novel and, like Churchill's drama, fore-
grounds absurdity, anachronism and generic shifts. However, *The Daylight Gate* is
in some ways more like *Witchfinder General* than it is like *Vinegar Tom*, partly
because it was written by Winterson for the new owners of the Hammer horror
franchise. At first sight, then, *The Daylight Gate* is a branded text based on a
defined cultural toolkit. But instead of conforming, it challenges readers. For
example, the novel draws attention by its publication date and "Introduction"
to its commemorative basis, yet it contains unhistorical liberties, such as an
appearance by Shakespeare that Winterson admits is present because "it pleases
me".[29] It is beautifully presented in a black and silver jacket, illustrated with
silhouettes of black birds, resembling a gift book or children's title, yet it is ugly in
plot, adult in theme. *The Daylight Gate* is thus a text of inbetweenness, and it is
multiply intertextual too, based on diverse Renaissance sources that complicate
its genre further: comedy, tragedy, romance, demonology.

As a result of these provocative clashes, critics broadly agreed that it was "genre
fiction", but questioned which genre(s). Sinclair McKay's response was typical:
"because the novella is under the imprint of 'Hammer', the venerable horror
studio, initial expectations are all over the place: will this be finely-wrought
fiction or full-throated Grand Guignol? . . . it somehow manages to be both".
Danuta Kean agreed the novel was "a mash-up of historical fact and fiction that
expands the boundaries of horror", both "a literary thriller about bigotry" and "a
Hammer Horror creeper" with "love story and orgies". Sarah Hall also tried to
determine its genre, but for her it was closest to Potts' *Discoverie*, on which it was
based. Hall described Winterson's style as:

> like courtroom reportage, sworn witness testimony. The sentences are short,
> truthful – and dreadful. "Tom Peeper raped Sarah Device. He was quick.
> He was in practice". Absolutism is Winterson's forte, and it's the perfect
> mode to verify supernatural events when they occur. You're not asked to
> believe in magic. Magic exists.

Instead of, and as well as, horror, *The Daylight Gate*'s genre might therefore be
described as magical realism.

Readers can spot without difficulty magical influences: Potts, William Perkins'
Discourse of the Damned Art of Witches, *Daemonologie*, *Newes from Scotland*, *The
Tempest*, *Macbeth*, *Friar Bacon* and *Dr Faustus*, among others. The novel shuffles
motifs from these texts, cramming them together. The Pendle witches create a
speaking prophetic head, made from a grave-robbed skull and severed tongue,
which recalls Friar Bacon's brazen head. Like Bacon's machine, it utters a three-
part message: "Born in fire. Warmed by fire. By fire to depart". Its words are also a
prophecy for the protagonist – the witch Alice Nutter – like those of the apparitions created by *Macbeth*'s witches. Alice will die in fire, her advisor John Dee
tells her.[30] This introduction of Renaissance celebrities is a keynote of the book
too. Elizabeth Demdike, Alice Nutter, Dee and Edward Kelley become lovers.
Alice Nutter once saw Marlowe's *Doctor Faustus* in London, and later we see

Demdike as a female Faust, signing a devil-pact in her own blood. All these borrowings are accommodated in a short, densely allusive novella.

Most overtly intertextual is the moment when Potts confronts Shakespeare at a performance of *The Tempest*, using *Friar Bacon*'s author Robert Greene's words against him to call him "an upstart crow": "*Macbeth* – that was a ridiculous play", he concludes. Here, texts speak to each other through the mouths of Winterson's characters, as again when Shakespeare defends *The Tempest* against accusations of frivolity by referring to the events of *Newes from Scotland*: "I began this play ... with a shipwreck in sympathy with the King's own shipwreck by supernatural forces on his way back from Denmark to Berwick". The North Berwick witches recur repeatedly in conversation, Demdike has a familiar named Greymalkin like *Macbeth*'s First Witch, Nowell reads from Perkins, Potts cites *Daemonologie* and there are frequent direct quotations from Potts, both verbatim and altered. The longest is Demdike's instruction about "the speediest way to take a man's life away by witchcraft" from B3v. Winterson has added a line making it clear that "Picture of Clay" can equally well be "a Doll or Poppet" such as Elizabeth Device later uses against Nowell.[31] It is unusual for those rediscovering Renaissance witchcraft to display their sources so prominently: in the text, the quotations are often in italics too. Winterson wants us to notice her collage – just as Churchill wanted to alienate us from hers so that we confront the violence, misogyny and repressions inherent in hunting witches.[32]

Winterson wrote that she did not find this complex book easy to write. Interestingly, one of the things that bothered her most was the "horror" label. In interviews and blogposts she discussed *The Daylight Gate* as commissioned: "I don't know why I have agreed to write a Hammer Horror story when I am so easily scared to death" she said in 2010. In an August 2012 post, she explained: "*The Daylight Gate* was written as a kind of dare – can I write a Hammer Horror?" In her blog, Winterson also anticipated questions about the novel's relationship with the 1612 trial record: "It isn't history, although it is historically based. It is fiction; a story". In particular, there was a creative tension between historical re-creation and the novel's generic origin. So, as well as her knowledge of seventeenth-century texts, *The Daylight Gate* was influenced by Hammer-specific research: Winterson mentions *The Woman in Black* as well as *The Devil Rides Out* (both Hammer films). When she talked about the book, it was usually as "my Hammer Horror" – hers but theirs, in a genre marked by capital letters – and how this identity influenced choices about content.[33]

The Daylight Gate is thus shaped by the Hammer imprint, but more broadly, it is a novel written in a climate where postmodern magical realism has become common, thanks in part to Winterson's own previous fiction. As magical realism should, it attempts to recentre the marginal. Winterson, a committed socialist-feminist, has serious concerns with misogyny, sexual violence, sectarian hatred and poverty. Many of the women and girls in the novel are raped (the invented character Sarah, the historical Elizabeth Device), children are sexually abused (Jennet Device), the priest Christopher Southworth is tortured, raped and castrated.[34] The book is also shaped by Winterson's interest in astrology and dedicated to her friend Henri Llewelyn Davies.[35] Winterson calls Llewelyn Davies "her own witch and mine", aligning her with the women of 1612. *The Daylight Gate*'s witches are not just victims, after all: they really are witches. Alice is an alchemist, as well as an intelligent, sexy, wealthy woman, her magic real and metaphorical, and the Demdike family really do animate a prophetic head. In this way, despite other similarities, Winterson's novel is not like *The Crucible* or *Vinegar Tom*, because it does not explain magic away. Instead, it embraces it to create a witchcraft novel *with witches in it*. It thus incorporates elements of the other trend with which this chapter must deal: the post-*Witches of Eastwick* story of witches as empowered women.

The *Daylight Gate* is a heartfelt project. But it also draws attention to the commercial aspect of witchcraft fictions in the early twenty-first century, the fact that a witchcraft theme effectively sells cultural products across a number of clearly labelled, if not always clearly defined, genres. The long heritage of sublime feeling that surrounds witchcraft – the emotion that led the Romantics to it – does not preclude its packaging in ways that are equally interesting as their content. And noting this phenomenon in modernity prompts us also to notice it in history: at least one Renaissance witchcraft fiction has been described in similar, though less flattering, terms as "frankly exploitative", part of a "cultural moment" or "vogue" to which it responds with a "collage" of "bits of witch-lore". Diane Purkiss was writing angrily about *Macbeth*, but she might have been referring approvingly to *The Daylight Gate*.[36] In some ways, this book about rediscovering Renaissance witches ends where it started: in a moment where witchcraft has become important to some of the best writers of the age, who draw on diverse sources to create profoundly ambiguous and resonant texts, some of which are extremely popular.

With this popularity and marketability in mind, the final section of this chapter will look at the popular pleasures afforded by rediscoveries of witchcraft today.

Witchcraft for everyone

Contemporary writing about witchcraft challenges generic boundaries, as we have seen. And it also collapses boundaries between popular and highbrow fiction, in its own way another type of writing back. It is unfashionable to discuss the work of such writers as Churchill and Winterson alongside comic novels of witchcraft such as those by Terry Pratchett, but it is necessary in any serious work on witchcraft in contemporary culture. Pratchett sold over 70 million books in his lifetime, and cultural critics who dismiss his novels as "ordinary ... middlebrow ... trash" are now being challenged by more open-minded readers. Like Churchill, Pullinger, Conn and Winterson, Pratchett shares with the other writers discussed in this chapter, a desire for debate about the nature and meaning of magic in fiction and wider culture. To this end, like them, he meditates upon Renaissance witchcraft texts, most obviously in his 1988 *Wyrd Sisters* but also throughout his oeuvre. From the late 1980s until his death in 2015, he increasingly used his comic fiction to inform and educate, as well as entertain, readers through the medium of the fantastical novel.[37]

Pratchett's stories regularly set magical occurrences alongside the notion of magic-as-metaphor, using it to ask probing questions about the human mind, death, religiosity, social and political fictions in accessible, amusing ways. For example, Pratchett's witch, Granny Weatherwax, practises primarily the psychological manipulation she calls "headology":

> If you give someone a bottle of red jollop for their wind it may work, right, but if you want it to work for sure you let their mind *make* it work for them. Tell 'em it's moonbeams bottled in fairy wine or something.

Granny can also enter the minds of birds and animals, and fly, but her headology – auto-suggestion, treatment for psychosomatic disease – is her most potent weapon. Pratchett's witches are thus both magical and realist in a deliberate, earthy paradox, mocking – among other targets – literary-critical pretensions such as those towards an exclusive definition of the magical realist in fiction. Like Granny, Pratchett's novels are both magical (imaginative, moving, poetic, themed on witches and wizards, fae, grindylows and so on) and realist (sharply aware of human limitations, politically engaged, instructive, anchored in the mundane and intolerant of fancy and so on).[38]

A similar case can be made for J.K. Rowling's *Harry Potter* series as magical realist. For both Pratchett and Rowling, witches are ordinary human beings as well as possessing magical powers. Witches and wizards are regular schoolboys and schoolgirls, parents, teachers, journalists, professors, government ministers and so on. Unlike Muggles, they possess magical powers, but there the differences end. They are both good and bad, vulnerable and powerful, and their experience is often mundane. In this, they resemble the witches of *Vinegar Tom*, *The Crucible* and *Eastwick*, as well as all the other ordinary witches of recent American and British fiction and visual culture. The witches who are descended from the *Witches of Eastwick* film, and appear in *Charmed*, *Sabrina the Teenage Witch* and other relatively domesticated witch-fictions, are like Rowling's Harry, Hermione and Ron, and all of them offer audiences a popular magical realism.[39] It should be self-evident that magical realism can occur in fiction for children and popular fiction as well as in more exclusive works. The ordinariness of witches in such fictions as the *Harry Potter* books is magical realist, not in the purest literary-critical sense of the term, but in a way that is accessible to readers of all ages and levels of interest in literature, so much so that Rowling has sold around 500 million *Harry Potter* books.[40]

Looked at this way, the *Harry Potter* phenomenon is part of a much wider magical realist trend in contemporary fiction, particularly in the young adult market. That market interconnects across popular series and types of magical creature. For example, at Vue cinemas in 2012 to see one of the vampire-themed *Twilight* film series, visitors could pick up a postcard advertising a new witchcraft novel by Ruth Warburton. As she commented on her blog: "if you're watching *Breaking Dawn* next week then keep an eye out for *Witch in Winter* post-cards... they have a QR code on the back that takes you to an exclusive downloadable extract". As Warburton told me, "there does seem to be a strong interest in paranormal across the board – witches, fae, vampires", although she also pointed out that – as this book argues – "witches are an enduring fascination . . . a cornerstone of our imagination from Circe, through Morgan la Fay, through Shakespeare's weird sisters, Disney's glamorous enchantresses, the Witches of Eastwick". Drawing on the glamour and empowerment associated with these figures, Warburton's postcard and book cover show a beautiful girl against the backdrop of a storm ("in Thunder, Lightning, or in Raine").[41] Her trilogy follows a teenager, Anna Winterson, who, after finding a grimoire, realises that she can work spells, one of which causes her classmate Seth to fall in love with her. Anna and Seth's contemporary love story is the heart of the books – these magical realist novels are also magical romances in the broad and narrow senses of the word – but they also have Renaissance roots.

The greatest threat to witches such as Anna comes from the Malleus Maleficorum (sic), a society of witch-hunters. Anna awakes in *A Witch in Love* to find a "person bending over my bed, pinning my arms to my sides". He smells of "sweat, tobacco, beer", is dressed in black and wears a hood with eye-slits. Warburton's witch-hammering haters are "ordinary men. Workers, fishermen, dads, uncles". As their name suggests, they draw inspiration from the *Malleus Maleficarum*. One man quotes it, with variations: "like the book says: *If she be a witch she will not be able to weep: although she will assume a tearful aspect and smear her cheeks and eyes with spittle to make it appear that she is weeping*" and "*All wickedness is but little to the wickedness of a woman*, as the book says".[42] Readers are encouraged to identify with Anna as a silenced, abused young woman, but also with her accuser, Caroline, a school rival. Although she has brought Anna to court, Caroline refuses to testify, stammering "I didn't mean . . . I didn't want . . . I was angry . . . I thought they'd just scare you, I'm so . . .". Later the two girls achieve reconciliation, driving home the simple but effectively made point that women only empower their common misogynistic enemies by being mean girls. It is one familiar from American fictions such as *The Witches of Eastwick* and its filmic successors.[43]

Witchcraft novels also appear regularly among self-published fiction, which is largely ignored in academia but is thriving. For example, in 2012, Dulcinea Norton-Smith, a teaching assistant from Lancashire, published in Kindle format a novel named *Blood and Clay*. Her protagonist is Alizon Device, here known as Lizzie, and the novel follows her attempts to escape her family tradition of witchcraft.[44] Norton-Smith told me that:

> what interested me about Alizon's story was that she was little more than a child at the time of her trial . . . and that she came from a family of witches . . . When we look at families in the twenty-first century we can often see the influence of past generations. Coming from several generations of witches and living in a village where her name was "bad" from birth, what hope did Alizon Device have in a seventeenth-century world of being different from her mother and grandmother?[45]

Norton-Smith's Alizon is a victim, brought up by people regarded as "a scrounging evil family" by neighbours and whom Norton-Smith speculates may be based on originals with "a mental health issue".

In her desperate plight, Lizzie resembles the abused children whose stories created a publishing phenomenon in the 1990s, and her tragic innocence also recalls Harrison Ainsworth's Alizon in *The Lancashire Witches*. She is the antithesis of the Alizon of Neill's *Mist over Pendle*. Both these books inspired Norton-Smith, and it is easy to see with which one her sympathies lay. Her Alizon also follows the tradition of the campaigning works discussed in this chapter in using a story of witchcraft to make a social statement about an issue important to the author: here, child welfare.[46] Other examples of witch-fiction based on early modern sources and self-published electronically include Cecilia Gausden's *We Three* (the story of Jennet Timble, one of the witches accused by Edward Fairfax, 2012) and Sarah L. King's *The Gisburn Witch* and *A Woman Named Sellers* (the story of Jennet Preston, 2015 and 2016). In this way, stories by new and amateur writers are constantly emerging, often dramatising the authors' social, religious or political interests and writing back both to Renaissance texts and to the notion that magical realism is an elitist or easily delimited genre.

Within academia, witchcraft studies is flourishing, with a number of new journals (*Magic, Ritual and Witchcraft, Preternature, Supernatural Studies, Revenant*) devoted wholly or in part to the topic. Perhaps not surprisingly, therefore, some of the successful popular rediscoveries of Renaissance witchcraft are by writers working within or close to academic settings. Kate Pullinger is Professor of Creative Writing at Bath Spa University.[47] The author of the bestselling witchcraft fiction the *All Souls Trilogy* is Deborah Harkness, Professor of History at the University of Southern California. Harkness' fictional work is a romantic fantasy with a witch protagonist, Diana Bishop, who, among other adventures, travels in time to 1590, is attacked by the witch-hunting Christopher Marlowe, collaborates with the alchemist Mary Sidney and marries a vampire geneticist. Diana is descended from the Salem victim Bridget Bishop, with a nod to the magical romance genre's American past, but draws on both her magical heritage and her knowledge as a scholar of alchemical texts to recover a lost Book of Life containing both magical and evolutionary secrets. Not coincidentally, Harkness is also the author of two scholarly monographs on the interface between mysticism and natural philosophy in Elizabethan England – in which ideas of nature as a book, and about human ability to access supernatural knowledges and powers, are explored.

Harkness' foray into popular fiction draws on her scholarly intelligence and creativity in a variety of ways. For example, one reading of her story of Diana and her fusion of witchcraft and science, fiction and academic fact might be alchemical. Her novels link their real and fictional female scholars together in a work of transformative re-enchantment of scholarship, reversing (as do so many texts discussed in this book) the notion of the "decline of magic" as conceptualised by previous historians in Harkness' field. As if writing back to Keith Thomas, Diana asks "how humans came up with a view of the world that had so little magic in it... how they convinced themselves that magic wasn't important". In fact, she decides, "they failed... the magic never really went away. It waited, quietly, for people to return to it when they found the science wanting". Anticipating this insight, Diana's creator ended her first scholarly book, *John Dee's Conversations with Angels*, with a discussion of Thomas' ideas in *Religion and the Decline of Magic*, explaining how, in her own work, it was possible to trace a "comprehensible" relationship between ideas now regarded as delusionally magical and ones regarded as scientific. Identifying that relationship meant that magical ideas could be rehabilitated in academic study, work that she continued in her second book, *The Jewel House*. Thus, the renewed interest in magic fictionalised in Diana's discovery of her witchcraft parallels that of the scholarly world. In modernity, Harkness pointed out to me, "there is no evidence that we've outgrown magic. Instead, the opposite is true".[48] Her *All Souls* series, its forthcoming TV adaptation and the All Souls Con fan convention in 2017 testify to that.

Notes

1 Hunt, 82–4.
2 *Curse of the Crimson Altar* is known in the US as *The Crimson Cult*; it also exists in several versions.
3 *Straw Dogs* shares *Witchfinder General*'s cinematographer, John Coquillon, while *Peeping Tom* was cited by an anonymous reviewer as a context in the *Monthly Film Bulletin*; see also Cooper, 29, 31, 74.
4 Bassett, 22, 28, 36, 38, 39, 49–54, 98, 100, 106–20, 122–4, 173–8, 172, 183, 188, 221, 246–50, 253, 254; Halligan, 107.
5 Although others, like Russell Taylor, accepted that it contained elements of documentary truth: see also Halligan 121, 197–9 and Murray, *Michael Reeves* 262, 263 for reactions. On the politics of "seventeenth century" "folk horror" as a genre see Harmes, although the films are not as directly comparable as is suggested. *Cry of the Banshee* is an outlier in that it is set in Henrician times, its costumes and religious politics suggest, not the seventeenth century, and it may be set in Ireland, not England, as witness character names such as Oona, Sean, Maureen and so on, and the culturally specific references to the *sidhe*.
6 Reeves, quoted in Halligan 155, 157, 197; Trevor-Roper (especially May issue, 7, and June issue, 23); Halligan, 162; Cooper, 9, quoting Kim Newman; Gaskill, "Witchcraft and Evidence" 33. See also Sharpe, "Cinematic".
7 "Love Theme from *Witchfinder General*" by Roberto Mann and his Orchestra, Deram, 19 July 1968 (www.45cat.com/record/dm200).
8 "Windmill girls" worked at the Windmill Theatre.
9 Albert Steptoe, in *Steptoe and Son*.
10 Cooper, 75.
11 Reeves, quoted in Halligan, 156; aspects were reworked in *Cry of the Banshee*, set in the mid-sixteenth century; Price quoted in Cooper, 37. Witches, however, remained a staple of the horror and exploitation genres, as in Hammer's Wheatley films (see Chapter 5), or Romero's *Season of the Witch*.
12 Conn, 8, 11, 48–55; personal communications 12–15 December 2016, 1–3 April 2017. Conn's sources included the National Library of Scotland's copy of Pitcairn, his own copy of Harrison's edition of *Daemonologie*, Davidson's *Rowan Tree*, a Scottish

"witchcraft miscellany" including material from *Newes* (e.g. 65, 66), Tytler (the witches are discussed in volume 9, 57–62 of the 1843 edition, with the edition Conn consulted dating from 1864), and McElwee.

13 See "W.I.T.C.H"; Morgan continues to publish fiction about witches; Starhawk is the coven name of the activist Miriam Simos.

14 Purkiss, *Witch* 68.

15 For the British context see the British Library oral history of activism, online history of *Shrew* magazine and Monstrous Regiment online archive.

16 Churchill, 130.

17 Monstrous Regiment online archive; Scarry, 16.

18 Reinelt, 154; Hanna quoted in Reinelt, 161; Churchill, 130.

19 Churchill, 138, 139; Churchill, personal communications 18 and 19 August 2016.

20 Macfarlane, 84, 107, 108, 139; *True and Just Recorde* F3, E8v; Churchill, 129, 130, 141.

21 Daniels, 373.

22 Rushdie's term was popularised among literary critics by Ashcroft, Griffiths and Tiffin, eds, Zabus, 149, 150; Yancy, especially chapter three and 85; Jalalzai. Both Zabus and Alden T. and Virginia Mason Vaughan have explored the many afterlives of *The Tempest*; Sycorax also appears as a medieval Yorkshire witch in Aspinall. Other witches, such as Mary Webster of Hadley, have avatars in contemporary literature too: Webster is the heroine of Margaret Atwood's poem "Half-Hanged Mary", and the dedicatee of her feminist dystopia *The Handmaid's Tale*.

23 Eagleton, 2; Reisert, 15, 16, 149, 150.

24 For example, Gelb, 59; Smith, "Centering"; Blundell, *passim*; Anonymous, "Robertson Letter".

25 Pullinger, personal communication, 26 April 2014; Warner and Zipes have both written on folk tales, whilst King is best-known for his horror fiction; Hoffman's best-known magical novel is *Practical Magic*.

26 Elliott, 63–5, 68, 163–5; Janice Elliott Papers, Exeter University Library, EUL MS279/3/1 76, 196, quoted by kind permission of Exeter University Library and Sheil Land.

27 Pullinger, personal communication, and *Weird* 225, 307, 308.

28 Baldick, 146; D'Haen, 192, 193, 201.

29 Winterson, *Daylight* vii, viii; interview with Appleyard. Quotations by kind permission of Jeanette Winterson.

30 Winterson, *Daylight* 48, 17, 110 and see below.

31 Winterson, *Daylight* 46, 48, 50, 59, 62, 96, 81, 149 (Potts appears to read from *Daemonologie* but is, in fact, quoting his own work, which draws on *Daemonologie* 1.2 and 2.3 for its categories of witch) 102, 106, 112–14, 122, 127, 134, 188, viii.

32 See also Potts and Nowell as witch-hunters, the latter unexpectedly attractively, like Neill's Nowell: Winterson, *Daylight* 19, 45, 46, 64, 134, 135; Winterson also reread the "crazy old" *The Devil Rides Out* as part of her research (Winterson, blogpost "January 2011").

33 Winterson, blogposts "November 2012", "August 2012", "January 2011", "September 2011", "November 2010"; see also www.jeanettewinterson.com/ *passim* and interview with Appleyard.

34 Winterson, *Daylight* 11, 26, 49, 74, 180, etc.

35 Llewelyn Davies; Winterson, blogpost "Astrology (Vogue)" (undated); anonymous obituary "Henrietta Llewelyn Davies".

36 For example, Purkiss, *Witch* 207; Kinney, chapter 1 and *passim*; Rickard, 231.

37 As reported by ITV: www.itv.com/news/2015-03-12/terry-pratchett-sold-more-than-70-million-books/; Jones, "Get Real" (who admitted he had not read Pratchett's

work); in response see Cottrell Boyce, who likens Pratchett to Swift, and Jones' partial recantation "I've Read Pratchett Now".

38 Pratchett, *Wyrd*; *Equal* 45, 64; Butler, James and Mendlesohn, eds.
39 Rowling, *Philosopher's Stone* and sequels; see also Gibson, *Witchcraft Myths* chapter five.
40 According to: https://en.wikipedia.org/wiki/List_of_best-selling_fiction_authors.
41 Warburton, blogposts "A Witch on Tour" and "A Witch in Winter in cinemas next week! (sort of)". Postcard: Boomerang/bookswithbite/Hodder Children's Books. Warburton, personal communication, 3 February 2014.
42 Warburton, *Winter*; *Love* 325, 337, 339; *Alone*.
43 *Love* 325–7, 352–4. In Warburton's follow-up series, *Witchfinder* and its sequels, understanding is also extended to *Malleus* members.
44 www.knowonder.com/dulcinea-norton-smith/; Norton Smith, *Blood*.
45 Norton-Smith, personal communication, 11 February 2014.
46 For more of Norton-Smith's other blogging and self-publishing work see: https://typeaparent.com/author/dulcinea and www.knowonder.com/tag/adventurous/.
47 www.katepullinger.com/; https://en.wikipedia.org/wiki/Kate_Pullinger.
48 Harkness, *John Dee's* 225, and *Jewel*; *Discovery* 11, 87 and sequels; http://deborahharkness.com/; http://deborahharkness.com/discovery-of-witches-tv-news-notes/.

Conclusion

In contemporary culture, witches are being rediscovered in multiple ways, re-creating Renaissance originals in new forms. Where once there were news pamphlets, now there are videos, webpages, blogs and other electronic ephemera to represent them. Witchcraft plays continue into films and television, whilst the popularisation of the novel as a middlebrow form in the twentieth century did most to rediscover the witch in modernity, during and after the First World War. It too continues in print and online.

Many contemporary rediscoveries draw on the first, Romantic, rediscovery of witches in the late eighteenth and early nineteenth centuries. As this book has shown in detail for the first time, this was a politicised rediscovery *and* a poetic one, because it emphasised the intersection of witchcraft with sublimity in the form of terror, passion and, ultimately, revolutionary thinking about law, society and authority. The second rediscovery, after 1917, focused on these notions once again, as I have shown, driven in particular by the trauma of the War. It added specific concerns with gender and age, and began a conversation about witchcraft and the philosophies of science and technology that continues today. Witchcraft's association with gender in twentieth- and twenty-first-century fiction has been well documented, but its wider associations have often been overlooked. And it is easy to assume that witches would always have come to represent empowered women. In fact, the book shows that this was not predetermined. It depended for its development beyond flippancy upon war and dislocation, and relied upon creative writers such as Stella Benson, Norman Matson, Sylvia Townsend Warner and Una Silberrad to make the link imaginatively meaningful. Recall Oliver Madox Hueffer's 1908 suggestion that: "there could be no more appropriate or deserving figure to be chosen as Patroness of the great fight for [women's] freedom than the much-libelled, much-martyrised, long-enduring, eternally misunderstood Witch". How fresh and unexpected that sounds once one strips away the sense of inevitability from its outcome.

The book has thus documented a series of literary and political choices over a century of writing in Britain and America. This focus on the cultural history of the witch, documenting specific episodes and trends, shows that there have been peaks and troughs of investment in the witch-figure. I have shown that witchcraft recurs in modern fiction most frequently during periods where radical and conservative forces are in negotiation, the radical in the ascendant. Here, witchcraft embodies a type of Romanticism that is enchanted by the past and is associated with mysticism or pagan exploration, but is rebellious against the constraints of conservative societies. However, witchcraft is also of interest to conservative mythmakers, who have built around the figure of the witch new demonologies, focused on gender, race, political ideologies and identities in opposition to the mainstream or the author's views. Even in periods between the Romantic rediscoveries, the writing of witchcraft fictions thus never altogether ceases – and there are significant overlaps between such periods, where the witch-figure embodies the debate. Across the whole period, the diversity, as well as the proliferation, of witchcraft fictions is striking: it demonstrates the resilience and inventive potential of witchcraft, which is both real and unreal, teasing the mind with the possibilities of story and unable to be closed down.

In generic terms, the central contribution of magic to fiction in the twentieth and twenty-first centuries has also been examined here, with the intention of broadening our understanding of the notion of magical realism to encompass the significant and lucrative contribution of witchcraft fictions to Britain's culture, economy and global influence. As I suggested in the Introduction, witchcraft fictions such as the *Harry Potter* books project a magical "soft power" that far outweighs Britain's "harder" political or military influence on the world stage today. Examining the self-conscious generic blending of postmodern literatures has also led me to suggest that we live in a newly Romantic phase of witchcraft fictions, and one that is democratised and multiplicitous in ways that the original Romantics might well have found pleasing. Recent cultural productions such as the television series' *Outlander* (2014–present) and *American Horror Story: Coven* (2013), Radiohead's "Burn the Witch" song and video (2016), Ben Wheatley's film *A Field in England* (2013) and Anna Biller's film *The Love Witch* (2016) all suggest that witchcraft is capable of endless, and often ideologically pointed, rediscovery.

It remains to be seen how the liberal and empowered figure of the witch – usually female, usually subversive – will withstand the pressures of contemporary reactionary politics and social conservatism. In defending minoritarian and inclusive identities, we may find the witch and the sublime passions that animate witchcraft stories a useful site of resistance.

Select bibliography

Primary sources

A Detection of Damnable Driftes (London, 1579).
A Most Wicked Work of a Wretched Witch (London, 1592).
A True and Impartial Relation of the Informations against Three Witches (London, 1682).
A True and Just Recorde (London, 1582).
A True Relation of the Araignment of Eighteene Witches (London, 1645).
A Tryal of Witches (London, 1682).
Calef, Robert, *More Wonders of the Invisible World* (London, 1700).
Davenport, John, *The Witches of Huntingdon* (London, 1646).
F.H., *A True and Exact Relation of the Severall Informations, Examinations, and Confessions of the Late Witches* (London, 1645).
Fairfax, Edward, *Daemonologia* (Manuscript 1621; Harrogate, 1882).
Galis, Richard, *A Brief Treatise* (London, 1579).
Gardiner, Ralph, *England's Grievance Discovered in Relation to the Coal-Trade* (London, 1655).
Gaule, John, *Select Cases of Conscience Touching Witches and Witchcraft* (London, 1646).
Gifford, George, *A Dialogue concerning Witches and Witchcraftes* (London, 1593).
Glanvill, Joseph, *Saducismus Triumphatus* (London, 1681).
Goodcole, Henry, *The Wonderfull Discovery of Elizabeth Sawyer* (London, 1621).
Grant, Francis, *A True Narrative of the Sufferings and Relief of a Young Girle* (Edinburgh, 1698).
Greene, Robert, *Friar Bacon and Friar Bungay* (London, 1594).
Hale, John, *A Modest Inquiry into the Nature of Witchcraft* (Boston, 1702).
Heywood, Thomas and Richard Brome, *The Late Lancashire Witches* (London, 1634).
Holinshed, Raphael, *Chronicles* (London, 1577, 1587).
Hopkins, Matthew, *The Discovery of Witches* (London, 1647).
Hutchinson, Francis, *An Historical Essay concerning Witchcraft* (London, 1718).
James VI and I, *Daemonologie* (Edinburgh, 1597).
Jonson, Ben, *The Masque of Queenes* (1609) Royal MS 18 A XLV.
Lyly, John, *Mother Bombie* (London, 1594).
Marlowe, Christopher, *The Tragicall History of Doctor Faustus* (London, 1604).
Marston, John, *Sophonisba* (London, 1606).
Mather, Cotton, *Memorable Providences* (Boston, 1689).
Mather, Cotton, *Wonders of the Invisible World* (Boston and London, 1692).
Mather, Increase, *Cases of Conscience* (Boston, 1693).

Middleton, Thomas, *The Witch* (London, 1778).

Newes from Scotland (London, 1591).

Peele, George, *The Old Wives Tale* (London, 1595).

Potts, Thomas, *The Wonderfull Discoverie* (London, 1612).

Rowley, William, Thomas Dekker, John Ford *et al.*, *The Witch of Edmonton* (1621; London, 1658).

Scot, Reginald, *The Discoverie of Witchcraft* (London, 1584).

Shakespeare, William, *The First Part of Henry the Sixt*, from *Mr. William Shakespeare's Comedies, Histories & Tragedies* (London, 1623).

Shakespeare, William, *The Second Part of Henry the Sixt*, from *Mr. William Shakespeare's Comedies, Histories & Tragedies* (London, 1623).

Shakespeare, William, *The Tragedie of Macbeth*, from *Mr. William Shakespeare's Comedies, Histories & Tragedies* (London, 1623).

Shakespeare, William, *The Tempest*, from *Mr. William Shakespeare's Comedies, Histories & Tragedies* (London, 1623).

Spenser, Edmund, *The Faerie Queene* (London, 1596).

Stearne, John, *A Confirmation and Discovery of Witch-Craft* (London, 1648).

The Full Trials, Examination and Confession of Four Notorious Witches (London, 1690).

The Lawes against Witches and Conjuration . . . Also The Confession of Mother Lakeland (London, 1645).

The Most Strange and Admirable Discoverie of the Three Witches of Warboys (London, 1593).

The Most Wonderfull and True Storie of a Certaine Witch Named Alse Gooderidge (London, 1597).

The Wonderfull Discoverie of the Witchcrafts of Margaret and Phillip Flower (London, 1619).

Wyntoun, Andrew of, *De Orygynale Cronykil of Scotland*, David Macpherson, ed. (London, 1795).

Archival materials cited

Cambridge University Library, Stella Benson Diaries, MJ MF 11391.

Dennis Wheatley Museum, www.denniswheatley.info/museum/, texts and artefacts.

Dorset County Museum, Sylvia Townsend Warner Archive, MSS and library.

Edinburgh University Library, John Buchan Papers, Gen. 1728/B/14/111-31.

Exeter University Library Special Collections, Janice Elliott Papers, EUL MS 279, 280.

Lancashire Archives, Robert Neill Archive DDX 177/ACC7655 Boxes 1–9.

National Archives, Kew, PRO ASSI 35/21/4, PRO ASSI 35/24/1.

National Archive of Scotland, NAS JC2/2, JC2/3, JC26/2, NAS GD16/41/117.

Nottingham University Library Manuscripts and Special Collections, Hilda Lewis Papers, GB 159 Lw H3.

University of Leeds Special Collections, Dennis Wheatley Archive, MS 1942 Boxes 1–22.

Rediscoveries

A Field in England, dir. Ben Wheatley, Rook Films (2013).

A Puritan Courtship, n.d., Pathé Frères (1911).

A Study in Terror, dir. James Hill, Compton-Tekli (1965).

Ackland, Valentine, "The Village Witch", *West Country Magazine* 4:3 (1949) 190–2.

Adam, Isabel, *Witch Hunt: The Great Scottish Witchcraft Trials of 1697* (London: Macmillan, 1978).

Addison Roberts, Jeanne, "The Crone in English Renaissance Drama", *Medieval and Renaissance Drama in England* 15 (2003) 116–37.

Adelman, Janet, "Born of Woman: Fantasies of Maternal Power in *Macbeth*", Garber, Marjorie, ed., *Cannibals, Witches and Divorce* (Baltimore: Johns Hopkins University Press, 1985) 90–121.

Adelman, Janet, *Suffocating Mothers* (London: Routledge, 1992).

Adger Law, Robert, "The Composition of *Macbeth* with Reference to Holinshed", *University of Texas Studies in English* 31 (1952) 35–41.

Adorno, Theodor, *Prisms*, trans. Samuel and Shierry Weber (Cambridge, MA: MIT, 1981).

Ahmed, Rollo, *I Rise* (London: John Long, 1937).

Ahmed, Rollo, *The Black Art* (1934; London: Senate, 1994).

Ainsworth, W. Harrison, *The Lancashire Witches* (London, 1849).

Almond, Philip, *England's First Demonologist* (London: I.B. Tauris, 2014).

Almond, Philip, "The Lancashire Witches" (8 August 2012), https://theibtaurisblog. com/2012/08/08/infanticide-cannibalism-and-an-english-sabbath-the-story-of-the-samlesbury-witches/

Almond, Philip, *The Lancashire Witches* (London: I.B. Tauris, 2016).

Almond, Philip, *The Witches of Warboys* (London: I.B. Tauris, 2008).

American Horror Story: Coven, Prod. Ryan Murphy and Brad Falchuk, 20th Century Fox/FX (2013).

Andrews, Martin J., *The Life and Work of Robert Gibbings* (Bicester: Primrose Hill, 2003).

Anonymous, *A Collection of Rare and Curious Tracts on Witchcraft* (Edinburgh, 1820).

Anonymous, "A Mirror for Witches", *Spectator* (28 September 1928) 25.

Anonymous, "Battle of the Aisne", *The Times* (18 April 1917) 5.

Anonymous, "First Meatless Day in Hotels", *The Times* (18 April 1917) 8.

Anonymous, "George William Outram Addleshaw" *Project Canterbury Bibliographic Directory*, http://anglicanhistory.org/england/gwoaddleshaw/

Anonymous, "Helen Ann Mins Robbins", www.library.rochester.edu/robbins/helenann

Anonymous, "Henrietta Llewelyn Davies", *Telegraph* (10 May 2011), www.telegraph.co. uk/news/obituaries/8505523/Henrietta-Llewelyn-Davies.html

Anonymous, *History of the Witches of Renfrewshire* (Paisley, 1809).

Anonymous, Interview with Robert Neill, *Burnley Express and News* (1 August 1951) n.p.

Anonymous, "Obituary: Christopher Fry", *The Economist* 376: 8435 (2005) 83.

Anonymous, "Review of Arnot, *Collection*", *English Review* (October 1785) 286–91.

Anonymous, "Review of Arnot, *Collection*", *Monthly Review* 77 (September 1787) 213–16.

Anonymous, "Review of Arnot, *Collection*", *Edinburgh Magazine* (September 1785) 155–58.

Anonymous, "Review of Kirkpatrick Sharpe, *Memorialls*", *Edinburgh Monthly Review* 1:6 (June 1819) 681–707.

Anonymous, "Review of *Mist over Pendle*", *Bristol Evening World* (22 June 1951) n.p.

Anonymous, "Review of *Mist over Pendle*", *Burton Daily News* (25 July 1951) n.p.

Anonymous, "Review of *Mist over Pendle*", *Newcastle Journal* (22 May 1951) n.p.

Anonymous, "Review of *Mist over Pendle*", *Preston Guardian* (19 May 1951) n.p.

Anonymous, "Review of *Mist over Pendle*", *Saturday Review* (no date, 1952) n.p.

Anonymous, "Review of *Mist over Pendle*", *TLS* (8 June 1951) n.p.

Anonymous, "Robertson Letter Attacks Feminists", *New York Times* (26 August 1992), www.nytimes.com/1992/08/26/us/robertson-letter-attacks-feminists.html

Anonymous, "Rossell Hope Robbins", www.library.rochester.edu/robbins/rossell

Anonymous, "Some Books to Read", *Michigan Alumnus* 36 (1929).

Anonymous, "Superstition in Essex", *The Times* (3 September 1915) 5.

Anonymous, "Superstition in London", *The Times* (26 January 1914) 5.

Anonymous, "The Belief in Charms", *The Times* (5 March 1917) 5.

Anonymous, "The Trial of Joan of Arc", *The Times* (20 November 1911) 3.

Anonymous, "Threatening Letters and Witchcraft", *The Times* (21 February 1912) 9.

Anonymous, "Witchfinder General", *Monthly Film Bulletin* 25:414 (July 1968) 100.

ApIvor, Denis, and Andrée Howard, *A Mirror for Witches*, Sadler's Wells Ballet (1952).

Ardolino, Frank, "Greene's Use of the History of Oxford in *The Honourable History of Friar Bacon and Friar Bungay*", *ANQ* 18:2 (2005) 20–5.

Ardolino, Frank, "The Protestant Context of George Peele's 'Pleasant Conceited' *Old Wives Tale*", *Medieval and Renaissance Drama in England* 18 (2005) 146–65.

Arnold, Matthew, "On the Study of Celtic Literature" (1867), R.H. Super, ed., *Lectures and Essays in Criticism* 11 vols. (Ann Arbor: University of Michigan Press, 1960–77) vol. 3 (1962) 291–386.

Arnot, Hugo, *A Collection and Abridgement of Celebrated Criminal Trials* (Edinburgh, 1785).

Arnot, Hugo, *The History of Edinburgh* (1779; 2nd ed. Edinburgh, 1816).

Ashcroft, Bill, Gareth Griffiths, and Helen Tiffin, eds, *The Empire Writes Back* 2nd ed. (1989; London: Routledge, 2002).

Atwood, Margaret, "Half-Hanged Mary", *Morning in the Burned House* (Toronto: McClelland and Stewart, 1995) 58–69.

Atwood, Margaret, *The Handmaid's Tale* (Toronto: McClelland and Stewart, 1985).

Atwood, Margaret, "Wondering What It's Like to be a Woman", *New York Times* (13 May 1984) Section 7: 1.

Baillie, Joanna, *Witchcraft in Dramatic and Poetical Works* 2nd ed. (London, 1853) 613–43.

Baker, Carlos, and David Lee Clark, "Literary Sources of Shelley's *The Witch of Atlas*", *PMLA* 56:2 (1941) 472–94.

Baker, Phil, *The Devil is a Gentleman* (Sawtry: Dedalus, 2009).

Baldick, Chris, *The Oxford Dictionary of Literary Terms* 3rd ed. (Oxford: Oxford University Press, 2008).

Barber, C.L., *Shakespeare's Festive Comedy*, with a "Foreword" by Stephen Greenblatt (1959; Princeton: Princeton University Press, 2012).

Bardsley, Alyson, "Belief and Beyond: The Law, the Nation, and the Drama in Joanna Baillie's *Witchcraft*" *Yale Journal of Law and the Humanities* 14:2 (2002) 231–69.

Barker, Shirley, *Peace, My Daughters* (New York: Crown, 1949).

Barr, Amelia, *The Black Shilling* (New York: Dodd, Mead, 1903).

Barrie, James Matthew, *Peter Pan* (1911; London: HarperCollins, 2015).

Barry, Jonathan, Marianne Hester and Gareth Roberts, eds, *Witchcraft in Early Modern Europe* (Cambridge: Cambridge University Press, 1996).

Bassett, Ronald, *Witchfinder General* (1966; London: Pan, 1968).

Bates, Jack, *Esther Forbes* (Lanham, MD, and London: Scarecrow, 1998).

Baum, Lyman Frank, *The Wonderful Wizard of Oz* (Chicago: George M. Hill, 1900).

Baym, Nina, "Review of *The Witches of Eastwick*", *Iowa Review* 14:3 (1984) 165–70.

Beatty, Charles, *Gate of Dreams* (London: Geoffrey Chapman, 1972).

Begley, Adam, *Updike* (New York: HarperCollins, 2014).

Bell, Book and Candle, dir. Richard Quine, Columbia (1958).

Bellany, Alastair, *The Politics of Court Scandal in Early Modern England* (Cambridge: Cambridge University Press, 2002).

Belton, Ellen R., "When No Man was His Own: Magic and Self-Discovery in *The Tempest*", *University of Toronto Quarterly* 55:2 (1985/6) 127–40.

Bemrose, John, "Drama that Delivers", *Maclean's* 111:23 (1998) 51.

Benecke, Ingrid, "The Shorter Stage Version of Shakespeare's *Macbeth* as Seen through Simon Forman's Eyes", *Notes and Queries* 61:2 (2014) 246–53.

Bennett, Alan, "Views", *Listener* (23 May 1968) 657–8.

Benson, Stella, *Living Alone* (1919; London: Macmillan, 1920).

Bewitched, dir. William Asher, ABC (1964–72).

Blundell, John, ed., *Remembering Margaret Thatcher* (New York: Algora, 2013).

Bonnett, Alastair, "The Dilemmas of Radical Nostalgia in British Psychogeography", *Theory, Culture and Society* 26:1 (2009) 47–72.

Borman, Tracy, *Witches* (London: Vintage, 2014).

Bostridge, Ian, *Witchcraft and its Transformations c.1650–c.1750* (Oxford: Clarendon, 1997).

Bostridge, Ian, "Witchcraft Repealed", Jonathan Barry, Marianne Hester and Gareth Roberts, eds, *Witchcraft in Early Modern Europe* (Cambridge: Cambridge University Press, 1996) 309–34.

Bourke, Angela, *The Burning of Bridget Cleary* (London: Penguin, 2001).

Bourke, Joanna, *Dismembering the Male: Men's Bodies, Britain and the Great War* (London: Reaktion, 1996).

Bourne, Lois, *Conversations with a Witch* (Kindle, 2014).

Bowers, Maggie Ann, *Magic(al) Realism* (London and New York: Routledge, 2004).

Braddon, Mary Elizabeth, *Lady Audley's Secret* (London, 1862).

Breslaw, Elaine G., *Tituba, Reluctant Witch of Salem* (New York: New York University Press, 1996).

Briggs, Katherine M., *Pale Hecate's Team* (New York: Humanities Press, 1962).

Brion, Marcel, *Dürer* (New York: Garland, 2000).

British Library Learning, "Sisterhood", www.bl.uk/learning/histcitizen/sisterhood/browsesubcategories.html#id=143441

Brochard, Thomas, "Scottish Witchcraft in a Regional and Northern European Context", *Magic, Ritual and Witchcraft* 10:1 (2015) 41–74.

Brodie Innes, John William, *For the Soul of a Witch* (London: Rebman, 1910).

Brodie Innes, John William, *Scottish Witchcraft Trials* (London, 1891).

Brodie Innes, John William, *The Devil's Mistress* (London: William Rider, 1915).

Bromham, A.A., "The Date of *The Witch* and the Essex Divorce Case", *Notes and Queries* 225 (1980) 149–52.

Brontë, Charlotte, *Jane Eyre* (London, 1847).

Buchan, John, *Witch Wood* (1927; London: Hodder & Stoughton, 1941).

Buell, Lawrence, *New England Literary Culture* (Cambridge: Cambridge University Press, 1986).

Burke, Edmund, *A Philosophical Inquiry into the Origin of Our Ideas of the Sublime and Beautiful*, Adam Phillips, ed. (1757; Oxford: Oxford University Press, 1990).

Burr, George Lincoln, *Narratives of the Witchcraft Cases* (New York: Scribner's Sons, 1914).

Busia, Abena P.A. "Silencing Sycorax: On African Colonial Discourse and the Unvoiced Female", *Cultural Critique* 14 (1989) 81–104.

Butler, Andrew, M., Edward James, and Farah Mendlesohn, eds, *Terry Pratchett* (n.p.: Science Fiction Foundation, 2008).

Butler, Catherine, "Modern Children's Fantasy", James and Mendlesohn, eds, 224–35.

Buyandelger, Manduhai, *Tragic Spirits* (Chicago: University of Chicago Press, 2013).

Byville, Eric, "How to Do Witchcraft Tragedy with Speech Acts", *Comparative Drama* 45:2 (2011) 1–33.

Cabell, Craig, *Dennis Wheatley and the Occult* (Kindle, rev. ed. 2014).

Cabell, Craig, *Witchfinder General* (Stroud: History Press, 2006).

Caine, Hall, *The Supernatural in Shakespeare* (London, 1880).

Calhoun, Howell V., "James I and the Witch Scenes in *Macbeth*", *Shakespeare Association Bulletin* 17:4 (1942) 184–9.

Callaghan, Dymphna, "Wicked Women in *Macbeth*", Mario Di Cesare, ed., *Reconsidering the Renaissance* (Binghampton, NY: Medieval and Renaissance Texts and Studies, 1992) 355–69.

Campbell, Jeff, *Updike's Novels* (Wichita Falls, TX: Midwestern State University Press, 1987).

Carpenter, Edward, *Civilisation, Its Cause and Cure* (London, 1889).

Carter, Harold, "From Slums to Slums in Three Generations: Housing Policy and the Political Economy of the Welfare State 1945-2005", Discussion Papers in Economic and Social History 98 (University of Oxford, 2005), www.nuffield.ox.ac.uk/economics/History/Paper98/carter98.pdf

Cassirer, Manfred, *Medium on Trial* (Stansted: PN Publishing, 1996).

Castleton, D.R., *Salem* (New York, 1874).

Cat People, dir. Jacques Tourneur, RKO (1942).

Chaemsaithong, Krisda, "Analysis of Interactive Speaking Roles in a Paratextual Genre: The Case of Witchcraft Pamphlets' Prefaces (1566–1621)", *Language and Literature* 25:4 (2016) 343–62.

Chaemsaithong, Krisda, "Discursive Control and Persuasion in Early Modern News Discourse: The Case of English Witchcraft Pamphlets and their Prefaces (1579–1621)", *English Text Construction* 4:2 (2011) 228–56.

Chaemsaithong, Krisda, "Interaction in Early Modern News Discourse: The Case of English Witchcraft Pamphlets and their Prefaces (1566–1621)", *Text and Talk* 33:2 (2013) 167–88.

Chakrabarty, Dipesh, *Provincializing Europe* 2nd ed. (2000; Princeton and Oxford: Princeton University Press, 2007).

Chamberlain, Stephanie, "Fantasising Infanticide: Lady Macbeth and the Murdering Mother in Early Modern England", *College Literature* 32:3 (2005) 72–91.

Charmed, Prod. Constance M. Burge, Spelling (1998–2006).

Chase Coale, Samuel, *In Hawthorne's Shadow* (Lexington: University Press of Kentucky, 1985).

Cheney, Patrick, "And Doubted Her to Deeme an Earthly Wight: Male Neoplatonic 'Magic' and the Problem of Female Identity in Spenser's Allegory of the Two Florimells", *Studies in Philology* 86:3 (1989) 310–40.

Child, Lydia Maria, *The Rebels* (Boston, 1825).

Churchill, Caryl, *Plays: One* (New York: Routledge, 1985).

Clark, Sandra and Pamela Mason, eds, *Macbeth*, by William Shakespeare (London: Bloomsbury/Arden, 2015).

Clark, Stuart, "Inversion, Misrule and the Meaning of Witchcraft", *Past and Present* 87:1 (1980) 98–127.

Clark, Stuart, *Thinking with Demons* (Oxford: Clarendon, 1997).

Coffin, Charlotte, "Theatre and/as Witchcraft: A Reading of *The Late Lancashire Witches* (1634)", *Early Theatre* 16:2 (2013) 91–119.

Cohen, Debra Rae, *Remapping the Home Front: Locating Citizenship in British Women's Great War Fiction* (Chicago: Northeastern University Press, 2002).

Cohn, Norman, *Europe's Inner Demons* (Brighton and London: University of Sussex Press/Heinemann, 1975).

Coleridge, Samuel Taylor, *Christabel* (London, 1816).

Collins, Mabel, *The Blossom and the Fruit* (London, 1889).

Comensoli, Viviana, "Witchcraft and Domestic Tragedy in *The Witch of Edmonton*", Jean R. Brink, Allison P. Coudert and Maryanne C. Horowitz, eds, *The Politics of Gender in Early Modern Europe* (Kirksville, MO: Sixteenth Century Journal, 1989) 43–60.

Condé, Maryse, *I, Tituba* (New York: Ballantine, 1994).

Cooper, Ian, *Witchfinder General* (2011; New York: Columbia University Press, 2017).

Cope, Jackson Irving, "Peele's *Old Wives Tale:* Folk Stuff into Ritual Form", *ELH* 49:2 (1982) 326–38.

Corbin, Peter and Douglas Sedge, eds, *Three Jacobean Witchcraft Plays* (Manchester: Manchester University Press, 1986).

Cordey, Anna, "Reputation and Witch-Hunting in Seventeenth-Century Dalkeith", Goodare, ed., *Scottish Witches* 103–20.

Corfield, Cosmo, "Why Does Prospero Abjure his Rough Magic?", *Shakespeare Quarterly* 36:1 (1985) 31–48.

Cottrell Boyce, Frank, "Terry Pratchett was a True Great, the Equal of Swift", *Guardian* (15 March 2015), www.theguardian.com/commentisfree/2015/mar/15/terry-pratchett-death-literature

Craig, Hardin, "Magic in *The Tempest*", *Philological Quarterly* 47 (1968) 8–15.

Crossley, James ed., *Potts' Discovery of Witches* (Chetham Society, 1845).

Crowley, Aleister, *Moonchild* (1929; San Francisco: Red Wheel/Weiser, 1970).

Cry of the Banshee, dir. Gordon Hessler, AIP (1970).

Curry, W.C., *Shakespeare's Philosophical Patterns* (Baton Rouge: Louisiana State University Press, 1936).

Curse of the Crimson Altar, dir. Vernon Sewell, Tigon (1968).

Curtis, Peter (Norah Lofts) *The Devil's Own* (1960; retitled *The Witches*, London: Pan, 1966).

D'Haen, Theo, "Magical Realism and Postmodernism: Decentering Privileged Centres", Lois Parkinson Zamora and Wendy B. Faris, eds, *Magical Realism* (Durham, NC, and London: Duke University Press, 1995) 191–208.

Dahlquist, Mark, "Love and Technological Iconoclasm in Robert Greene's *Friar Bacon and Friar Bungay*", *ELH* 78:1 (2011) 51–77.

Daly, Mary, *Gyn/Ecology* (Boston: Beacon, 1978).

Daly, Mary, *Pure Lust* (Boston: Beacon, 1984).

Dalyell, John Graham, *The Darker Superstitions of Scotland* (Edinburgh, 1834).

Dana, Marvin, *The Puritan Witch* (New York and London: Smart Set, 1903).

Daniels, Sarah, *Plays: One* (London: Bloomsbury, 2013).

Das, Santanu, *Touch and Intimacy in First World War Literature* (Cambridge: Cambridge University Press, 2005).

Davidson, Jane P. "Review", *Sixteenth Century Journal* 27:3 (1996) 898–9.

Davidson, Thomas, *Rowan Tree and Red Thread* (Edinburgh and London: Oliver & Boyd, 1949).

Davies, Owen, *America Bewitched* (Oxford: Oxford University Press, 2013).

Davies, Owen, *Witchcraft, Magic and Culture 1736–1951* (Manchester: Manchester University Press, 1999).

Davis, Elizabeth R., "English Imperial Selfhood and Semiperipheral Witchcraft in *The Faerie Queene, Daemonologie,* and *The Tempest*", MA thesis, Wake Forest University (Proquest, 2016).

Dawson, Anthony B., "Witchcraft/Bigamy: Cultural Conflict in *The Witch of Edmonton*", *Renaissance Drama* 20 (1989) 77–98.

de Bellis, Jack, *The John Updike Encyclopaedia* (Westport, CT: Greenwood, 2000).

De Forest, John William, *Witching Times* (New York, 1856–7).

De Lisser, Herbert George, *The White Witch of Rosehall* (London: Ernest Benn, 1929).

Deacon, Richard, *Matthew Hopkins* (London: Frederick Muller, 1976).

Dean, Paul, "*Friar Bacon and Friar Bungay* and *John of Bordeaux:* A Dramatic Diptych", *English Language Notes* 18:4 (1981) 262–6.

Dodd, Catherine Isabella, *Three Silences* (London: Jarrolds, 1927).

Dolan, Frances, *Dangerous Familiars* (Ithaca: Cornell University Press, 1994).

Doran, Madeleine, "The *Macbeth* Music", *Shakespeare Studies* 16 (1983) 153–73.

Eagleton, Terry, *William Shakespeare* (Oxford and New York: Basil Blackwell, 1986).

Eastwick, Prod. Maggie Friedman, Marc David Alpert *et al.*, Warner Bros (2009).

Egan, Robert, "This Rough Magic: Perspectives of Art and Morality in *The Tempest*", *Shakespeare Quarterly* 23:2 (1972) 171–82.

Egerton, George (Mary Dunne), *Keynotes* (London: Elkin Mathews, John Lane, 1894).

Ehrenreich, Barbara and Deirdre English, *Witches, Midwives and Nurses* (New York: Feminist Press, 1973) and 2nd ed. (2010).

Elkins, Caroline, *Britain's Gulag* (London: Pimlico, 2005).

Elliott, Janice, *The Sadness of Witches* (1987; London: Sceptre, 1988).

Elmer, Peter, *The Later English Trial Pamphlets* vol. 5 of James Sharpe and Richard Golden, eds, *English Witchcraft 1560–1736*, 6 vols (London: Pickering & Chatto, 2003).

Elmer, Peter, *Witchcraft, Witch-Hunting and Politics in Early Modern England* (Oxford: Oxford University Press, 2016).

Empson, Patience, *The Wood Engravings of Robert Gibbings* (London: J.M. Dent, 1959).

Engelbrecht, Helmuth Carol and Frank Cleary Hanighen, *Merchants of Death* (New York: Dodd, Mead, 1934).

Ettin, Andrew V. "Magic into Art: The Magician's Renunciation of Magic in English Renaissance Drama", *Texas Studies in Literature and Language* 19:3 (1977) 268–93.

Ewing, Murray, "*Witch Wood* by John Buchan" (2010), www.murrayewing.co.uk/mewsings/2010/08/15/witch-wood-by-john-buchan/

Fabian, Robert, *Fabian of the Yard* (London: Naldrett, 1950).

Fabian, Robert, *London after Dark* (London: Naldrett, 1954).

Favret-Saada, Jeanne, *Deadly Words* trans. Catherine Cullen (1977; Cambridge: Cambridge University Press, 1980).

Fishlin, Daniel, "Counterfeiting God: James VI (I) and the Politics of *Daemonologie* (1597)", *Journal of Narrative Technique* 26:1 (1996) 1–29.

Fishman, Nina, "Tanner, Frederick John Shirley", *Dictionary of Labour Biography* 13 vols. Keith Gildart, David Howell, and Neville Kirk, eds (Basingstoke: Palgrave Macmillan, 2003) vol. 11 274–83.

Floyd, Carlisle, *Bilby's Doll*, Houston Grand Opera (1974).

Forbes, Esther, *A Mirror for Witchcraft* (Boston: Houghton Mifflin, 1928) and 2nd ed. (Bath: Cedric Chivers, 1973).

Forster, Edward Morgan, *Aspects of the Novel* (1927; London: Penguin, 2000).

Fortey, Neil and Stanley Blackmore, "Bottesford Rectory: As It Was" (2011), www. bottesfordhistory.org.uk/content/places/buildings-and-houses/bottesford-rectory-as-it-was

Fortune, Dion, *The Demon Lover* (1927; San Francisco: Red Wheel/Weiser, 2010).

Foster Madison, Lucy, *A Maid of Salem Towne* (Philadelphia, PA, 1906).

Foucault, Michel, "Of Other Spaces, Heterotopias" (1967) trans. Jay Miskowiec, *Architecture, Mouvement, Continuité* 5 (1984) 46–9.

Frazer, James George, *The Golden Bough*, Robert Fraser, ed. (Oxford: Oxford University Press, 1994).

Fry, Christopher, *The Lady's Not for Burning* 2nd ed. (1949; New York and London: Oxford University Press, 1950).

Gabaldon, Diana, *Outlander,* originally published as *Cross Stitch* (1991; London: Arrow, 1994).

Galbraith, John Kenneth, *The Affluent Society* (Boston: Houghton Mifflin, 1958).

Gardner, Gerald, *The Meaning of Witchcraft* (1959; York Beach, ME, and Boston: Red Wheel/Weiser, 2004).

Garrett, Julia M., "Dramatising Deviance: Sociological Theory and *The Witch of Edmonton*", *Criticism* 49:3 (2007) 327–75.

Garrett, Julia M., "Witchcraft and Sexual Knowledge in Early Modern England", *Journal for Early Modern Cultural Studies* 13:1 (2013) 32–72.

Garrity, Jane, *Step-Daughters of England* (Manchester: Manchester University Press, 2003).

Garth, John, *Tolkien and the Great War* (London: HarperCollins, 2003).

Gaskell, Elizabeth, *Lois the Witch and Other Tales* (London, 1861).

Gaskill, Malcolm, *Hellish Nell* (London: Fourth Estate, 2001).

Gaskill, Malcolm, ed., *The Matthew Hopkins Trials* vol. 3 of James Sharpe and Richard Golden, eds, *English Witchcraft 1560–1736*, 6 vols. (London: Pickering & Chatto, 2003).

Gaskill, Malcolm, "Witchcraft and Evidence in Early Modern England", *Past and Present* 198:1 (2008) 33–70.

Gaskill, Malcolm, "Witchcraft and Power in Early Modern England: The Case of Margaret Moore", Jenny Kermode and Garthine Walker, eds, *Women, Crime and the Courts in Early Modern England* (London: Routledge, 1994) 131–52.

Gaskill, Malcolm, *Witchfinders* (London: John Murray, 2005).

Gaspey, Thomas, *The Witch-Finder* (London, 1824).

Gausden, Cecelia, *We Three* (Kindle, 2012).

Gazeley, Ian, *Poverty in Britain 1900–65* (Basingstoke: Palgrave Macmillan, 2003).

Geis, Gilbert, and Ivan Bunn, *A Trial of Witches* (London and New York: Routledge, 1997).

Gelb, Joyce, *Feminism and Politics* (Berkeley: University of California Press, 1989).

Gent, Frank, *The Trial of the Bideford Witches* (1982; rev. ed. Crediton: Gent, 2001), http://gent.org.uk/bidefordwitches/tbw.pdf

George, David, "The Problem of Middleton's *The Witch* and its Sources", *Notes and Queries* 212 (1967) 209–11.

Gerard, Louise, *The Witch Child* (London: Mills & Boon, 1928).

Geschiere, Peter, *Witchcraft, Intimacy and Trust* (Chicago: University of Chicago Press, 2013).

Geschiere, Peter, "Witchcraft, Shamanism and Nostalgia", *Comparative Studies in Society and History* 58:1 (2016) 242–65.

Gibson, Marion, ed., *Early English Trial Pamphlets* vol. 2 of James Sharpe and Richard Golden, eds, *English Witchcraft 1560–1736*, 6 vols (London: Pickering & Chatto, 2003).

Gibson, Marion, ed., *Early Modern Witches* (London: Routledge, 2000).

Gibson, Marion, "Greene's *Friar Bacon and Friar Bungay* and *A Most Wicked Work of a Wretched Witch:* A Link" *Notes and Queries* 44:1 (1997) 36–7.

Gibson, Marion, *Imagining the Pagan Past* (London and New York: Routledge, 2013).

Gibson, Marion, "Kissing the Medium: The Spiritualist-Witch as Countercultural Heroine in *The Thirty-Nine Steps* (1959)" in Benjamin Poore, ed., *Neo-Victorian Villains* (Amsterdam: Rodopi, forthcoming).

Gibson, Marion, *Possession, Puritanism and Print* (London: Pickering & Chatto, 2006).

Gibson, Marion, *Reading Witchcraft* (London: Routledge, 1999).

Gibson, Marion, *Witchcraft Myths in American Culture* (New York and London: Routledge, 2007).

Gibson, Marion and Jo Ann Esra, *Shakespeare's Demonology* (London: Bloomsbury, 2015).

Gilbert, Sandra and Susan Gubar, *The Madwoman in the Attic* (New Haven: Yale University Press, 1979).

Gilman, Charlotte Perkins, *Herland* (1915; New York: Dover, 2000).

Gilman, Charlotte Perkins, *The Forerunner* 1 (1909–10), https://catalog.hathitrust.org/Record/000544186

Gilman, Charlotte Perkins, "When I was a Witch", Ann J. Lane, ed., *The Charlotte Perkins Gilman Reader* (London: Women's Press, 1981) 21–31.

Giorno, Gabriella T., "The Reflected Tempest and Prospero's 'Calling Word'", *Hungarian Journal of English and American Studies* 11:1 (2005) 203–10.

Go, Kenji, "Montaigne's 'Cannibals' and *The Tempest* Revisited", *Studies in Philology* 109:4 (2012) 455–73.

Goodare, Julian, "Bibliography of Scottish Witchcraft" in Goodare, ed., *Scottish Witches* 234–45.

Goodare, Julian, "Introduction" to Goodare, ed., *Scottish Witch-Hunt* 11–15.

Goodare, Julian, ed., *Scottish Witches and Witch-Hunters* (Basingstoke: Palgrave Macmillan, 2013).

Goodare, Julian, ed., *The Scottish Witch-Hunt in Context* (Manchester: Manchester University Press, 2002).

Goodrick-Clarke, Nicholas, *Black Sun* (New York: New York University Press, 2002).

Goodrick-Clarke, Nicholas, *The Occult Roots of Nazism* (Wellingborough: Aquarian Press, 1985).

Goudge, Elizabeth, *The White Witch* (London: Hodder & Stoughton, 1958).

Gould, Philip, *Covenant and Republic* (Cambridge: Cambridge University Press, 1996).

Grant, Joan, *Life as Carola* (London: Methuen, 1939).

Grant, Joan, *Winged Pharoah* (London: Arthur Barker, 1937).

Grant, Joy, *Stella Benson: A Biography* (London and Basingstoke: Macmillan, 1987).

Greenblatt, Stephen, "Shakespeare Bewitched", Jeffrey N. Cox and Larry J. Reynolds, eds, *New Historical Literary Study* (Princeton: Princeton University Press, 1993) 108–35.

Greenblatt, Stephen, "Toil and Trouble", *New Republic* 211:20 (1994) 32.

Greig, J. C. G., "Introduction", John Buchan, *Witch Wood* (Oxford: Oxford University Press, 1993) iv–xvii.

Grinstead, Durward, *Elva* (New York: Covici Friede, 1929).

Gross, Kenneth, *Spenserian Poetics* (Ithaca and London: Cornell University Press, 1985).

Guenther, Genevieve, *Magical Imaginations* (Toronto: University of Toronto Press, 2012) 89–94.

Haining, Peter, *The Anatomy of Witchcraft* (London: Souvenir, 1972).

Hall, Sarah, "*The Daylight Gate* by Jeanette Winterson: Review", *Guardian* (16 August 2012), www.theguardian.com/books/2012/aug/16/daylight-gate-jeanette-winterson-review

Halliday, William Reginald, "Review", *Folklore* 33:2 (1922) 224–30.

Halligan, Benjamin, *Michael Reeves* (Manchester: Manchester University Press, 2003).

Hämmerle, Christa, Oswald Überegger and Birgitta Bader Zaar, eds, *Gender and the First World War* (Basingstoke: Palgrave Macmillan, 2014).

Hansen, Chadwick, "The Metamorphosis of Tituba, or Why American Intellectuals Can't Tell an Indian Witch from a Negro", *New England Quarterly* 47:1 (1974) 3–12.

Handley, Janet, "Scripting the Witch: Voice, Gender and Power in *The Witch of Edmonton* (Rowley, Dekker and Ford, 1621) and *Witchcraft* (Baillie, 1836)", MA thesis, UIT Arctic University of Norway (2016).

Hapgood, Lynne, *Margins of Desire: The Suburbs in Fiction and Culture 1880–1925* (Manchester and New York: Manchester University Press, 2005).

Hardy, Thomas, "The Withered Arm", *Wessex Tales* (1888; Ware: Wordsworth, 1995) 43–68.

Harker, James, "'Laura was Not Thinking': Cognitive Minimalism in Sylvia Townsend Warner's *Lolly Willowes*", *Studies in the Novel* 46:1 (2014) 44–62.

Harkness, Deborah, *A Discovery of Witches* (New York: Viking Penguin, 2011).

Harkness, Deborah, *John Dee's Conversations with Angels* (Cambridge: Cambridge University Press, 1999).

Harkness, Deborah, *Shadow of Night* (New York: Viking Penguin, 2012).

Harkness, Deborah, *The Book of Life* (New York: Viking Penguin, 2014).

Harkness, Deborah, *The Jewel House* (New Haven: Yale University Press, 2007).

Harkness, Deborah, webpages at http://deborahharkness.com/

Harman, Claire, *Sylvia Townsend Warner* (London: Penguin, 1989).

Harmes, Marcus, "The Seventeenth Century on Film: Patriarchy, Magistracy and Witchcraft in British Horror Films 1968–1971" *Canadian Journal of Film Studies* 22:2 (2013) 64–80.

Harris, Anthony, *Night's Black Agents* (Manchester: Manchester University Press, 1980).

Harrison, G.B., ed., *Daemonologie and Newes from Scotland* (London and New York: Bodley Head, Dutton, 1924).

Harvie, Christopher, "Introduction", John Buchan, *Witch Wood* (Edinburgh: Canongate, 2001) i–xii.

Hattaway, Michael, "Women and Witchcraft: The Case of *The Witch of Edmonton*", *Trivium* 20 (1985) 49–68.

Hatton, Timothy J. and Roy Bailey, "Seebohm Rowntree and the Postwar Poverty Puzzle", *Economic History Review* 53:3 (2000) 517–43.

Hawthorne, Nathaniel, *The House of the Seven Gables* (1851; London: Everyman, 1954).

Hawthorne, Nathaniel, *The Scarlet Letter* ed. Leland S. Person (1850; New York: W.W. Norton, 2004).

Hawthorne, Nathaniel, "Young Goodman Brown" (1835), Charles L. Crow, ed., *American Gothic* 2nd ed. (Oxford: Wiley Blackwell, 2012) 80–8.

Hazlitt, William Carew, *Fairy Tales, Legends and Romances Illustrating Shakespeare* (London, 1875).

Heale, M.J., *McCarthy's Americans* (Atlanta: University of Georgia Press, 1998).

Henderson, Lizanne, *Witchcraft and Folk Belief in the Age of Enlightenment* (Basingstoke: Palgrave Macmillan, 2016).

Herbert, Henry William, *The Fair Puritan* (Philadelphia, 1844–1845).

Herrington, H.W., "Witchcraft and Magic in the Elizabethan Drama", *Journal of American Folklore* 32:126 (October–December 1919) 447–85.

Hieatt, Charles, "A New Source for *Friar Bacon and Friar Bungay*", *Review of English Studies* 32:126 (1981) 180–7.

Higonnet, Margaret, Jane Jenson, Sonya Michel and Margaret C. Weitz, eds, *Behind the Lines* (New Haven: Yale University Press, 1987).

Hill, Susan, *The Woman in Black* (London: Hamish Hamilton, 1983).

Hoffman, Alice, *Practical Magic* (New York: G.P. Putnam, 1995).

Holland, Josiah Gilbert, *The Bay Path* (New York, 1857).

Hope, Jonathan and Michael Witmore, "The Language of *Macbeth*", Ann Thompson, ed., *Macbeth: The State of Play* (London: Arden Bloomsbury, 2014) 183–208.

Hope Robbins, Rossell, *Encyclopaedia of Witchcraft and Demonology* (New York: Crown and London: Spring Books, 1959).

Hopkins, Lisa, "Reading Between the Sheets: Letters in Shakespearean Tragedy", *Critical Survey* 14:3 (2002) 5–13.

Hopkins, Lisa and Helen Ostovich, eds, *Magical Transformations on the Early Modern English Stage* (Farnham and Burlington, VT: Ashgate, 2014).

Horner, Avril and Sue Zlosnik, "Releasing Spirit from Matter", *Gothic Studies* 2:1 (2000) 136–47.

House of Lords Journal vol. 24 1732–7 (London: HMSO, 1767–1830), *British History Online*, www.british-history.ac.uk/lords-jrnl/vol24/

Hoyer, Linda Grace, *Enchantment* (London: André Deutsch, 1971).

Hughes, Charles James Pennethorne, *Witchcraft* (1952; London: Penguin, 1965).

Hughes, Paula, "Witch-Hunting in Scotland 1649–1650" in Goodare, ed., *Scottish Witches* 85–102.

Hunt, Leon, "Necromancy in the UK: Witchcraft and the Occult in British Horror", Steve Chibnall and Julian Petley, eds, *British Horror Cinema* (London and New York: Routledge, 2002) 82–98.

Husain, Shahrukh, ed., *The Virago Book of Witches* (London: Virago, 1993).

Hutchison, I.G.C., "Scottish Issues in British Politics, 1900–1939", Chris Wrigley, ed., *A Companion to Early Twentieth Century Britain* (Oxford: Blackwell, 2003) 72–86.

Hutton, Ronald, *The Triumph of the Moon* (Oxford: Oxford University Press, 1999).

I Married a Witch, dir. René Clair, Paramount (1942).

Jackson, Louise, "Witches, Wives and Mothers: Witchcraft Persecution and Women's Confessions in Seventeenth-Century England", *Women's History Review* 4:1 (1995) 63–84.

Jackson, Louise A. and Angela Bartie, *Policing Youth* (Manchester: Manchester University Press, 2014).

Jackson, Rosemary, *Fantasy* (1981; London: Routledge, 2003).

Jacobs, Mary, "Sylvia Townsend Warner and the Politics of the English Pastoral 1925–34", Gill Davies, David Malcolm and John Simons, ed., *Critical Essays on Sylvia Townsend Warner* (Lampeter: Edwin Mellen, 2006) 61–82.

Jalalzai, Zubeda, "Historical Fiction and Maryse Condé's *I Tituba: Black Witch of Salem*", *African American Review* 43:2–3 (2009) 413–25.

James, Edward, and Farah Mendlesohn, eds, *The Cambridge Companion to Fantasy Literature* (Cambridge: Cambridge University Press, 2012).

Jarcke, Karl Ernst, "Ein Hexenprozess", *Annalen der Deutschen und Ausländischen Criminal-Rechts-Pflege* 1(1828) 450.

Jenkins, Clive, "B.O.A.C.: The Anatomy of a Strike", *Universities and Left Review* 6 (1959) 30–34.

Jenkins, Richard, 'Disenchantment, Enchantment and Re-Enchantment', *Max Weber Studies* 1 (2000) 11–32.

Johnson, Diane, "Warlock", *New York Review* (14 June 1984), www.nybooks.com/articles/1984/06/14/warlock/

Johnson, Greg, "Weird Sisters" *Southwest Review* 69:3 (1984) 342–4.

Johnston, Mary, *The Witch* (Boston: Houghton Mifflin, 1914).

Jones, Jonathan, "Get Real: Terry Pratchett is Not a Literary Genius", *Guardian* (31 August 2015), www.theguardian.com/artanddesign/jonathanjonesblog/2015/aug/31/terry-pratchett-is-not-a-literary-genius

Jones, Jonathan, "I've Read Pratchett Now: It's More Entertainment than Art", *Guardian* (11 September 2015), www.theguardian.com/artanddesign/jonathanjones-blog/2015/sep/11/jonathan-jones-ive-read-terry-pratchett-now-its-more-enter-tainment-than-art

Josiffe, Christopher, "British Voodoo: The Black Art of Rollo Ahmed", *Fortean Times* 316 (2014) 28–35.

Joyce, James, *Ulysses* ed., J. Johnson (1922; Oxford: Oxford University Press, 1998).

Juhasz, Tamas, "Witch is Which, or the Selfsame Words in *Macbeth*", *Hungarian Journal of English and American Studies* 3:2 (1997) 59–69.

Kean, Danuta, *"The Daylight Gate* by Jeanette Winterson" *Independent* (12 August 2012), www.independent.co.uk/arts-entertainment/books/reviews/the-daylight-gate-by-jeanette-winterson-8034588.html

Kermode, Frank, ed., *The Tempest* (London: Methuen, 1954).

King, Sarah L., *A Woman Named Sellers* (Kindle, 2016).

King, Sarah L., *The Gisburn Witch* (Kindle, 2015).

Kinney, Arthur, *Lies like Truth* (Detroit: Wayne State University Press, 2001).

Kirkpatrick Sharpe, Charles, ed., *Robert Law's Memorialls* (Edinburgh, 1818).

Kittredge, George Lyman, *Witchcraft in Old and New England* (Cambridge, MA: Harvard University Press, 1929).

Knight, Damon, *In Search of Wonder* 2nd ed. (London: Hachette, 2013).

Knights, Lionel Charles, *Explorations* (Manchester: Manchester University Press, 1946).

Knoll, Bruce, "'An Existence Doled Out': Passive Resistance as a Dead End in Sylvia Townsend Warner's *Lolly Willowes*", *Twentieth-Century Literature* 39:3 (1993) 344–63.

Knox, E. V., *This Other Eden* (London: Methuen, 1929).

Knox, Robert, *The Races of Men* (London, 1850).

Kocher, Paul, "The Witchcraft Basis in Marlowe's *Faustus*", *Modern Philology* 38:1 (1940) 9–36.

Kranz, David L., "The Sounds of Supernatural Soliciting in *Macbeth*", *Studies in Philology* 100:3 (2003) 346–83.

Krueger, Christine, *Reading for the Law* (Charlottesville: University of Virginia Press, 2010).

L'Estrange Ewen, C. *Witch-Hunting and Witch-Trials* (New York: Dial Press, 1929).

L'Estrange Ewen, C, *Some Witchcraft Criticisms* (London: Printed for the Author, 1938).

Laary, Dasmani, "Ghana Shuts Down Witches' Camp", *Africa Report* (19 December 2014), www.theafricareport.com/Society-and-Culture/ghana-shuts-down-witches-camp.html

Laing, David ed., *The Bannatyne Club* (Edinburgh, 1867).

Lamb, Charles, "On a Passage in *The Tempest*", Thomas Noon Talfourd, ed., *Works* 5 vols. (1884) vol. 5 70–4.

Lamb, Mary Ellen, "Old Wives Tales, George Peele and Narrative Abjection", *Critical Survey* 14:1 (2002) 28–43.

Lancashire, Anne, *"The Witch:* Stage Flop or Political Mistake?", Kenneth Friedenreich, ed., *Accompanying the Players* (New York: AMS, 1983) 161–81.

Landy, Joshua and Michael Saler, eds, *The Re-Enchantment of the World* (Stanford: Stanford University Press, 2009).

Laoutaris, Chris, *Shakespearean Maternities* (Edinburgh: Edinburgh University Press, 2008).

Larner, Christina, *Enemies of God* (Oxford: Blackwell, 1981).

Larner, Christina, *Witchcraft and Religion* (Oxford: Blackwell, 1984).

Laski, Marghanita, "New Novels", *Observer* (20 May 1951) 7.

Le Hardy, Esther, *Agabus* (London, 1851).

Leeney, Cathy, *Irish Women Playwrights 1900–39* (New York: Peter Lang, 2010).

LeGrandeur, Kevin, "Brasenose College's Brass Head and Greene's *Friar Bacon and Friar Bungay*", *Notes and Queries* 47:1 (2000) 48–50.

Leimberg, Inge, "Shakespeare De-Witched", *Connotations* 11:1 (2001–2), 60–77, www.connotations.de/pdf/articles/leimberg01101.pdf

Lellock, Jasmine, "Boiled Brains, 'Inward Pinches' and Alchemical Tempering in *The Tempest*", Hopkins and Ostovich, eds, 123–38.

Levack, Brian, *Witch-Hunting in Scotland* (London: Routledge, 2007).

Levine, Nina S., "The Case of Eleanor Cobham: Authorizing History in *2 Henry VI*", *Shakespeare Studies* 22 (1994) 104–21.

Lewis, Hilda, *The Witch and the Priest* (1956; London: Sphere, 1975).

Lieberman, Robbie and Clarence Lang, eds, *Anticommunism and the African American Freedom Movement* (New York: Palgrave Macmillan, 2009).

Lindley, David, *The Trials of Frances Howard* (London: Routledge, 1993).

Llewelyn Davies, Henri, "Horoscopes: Jeanette Winterson's Website" (18 March 2009), www.henrillewelyndavies.blogspot.co.uk/

Loudermilk, Kim, *Fictional Feminism* (London: Routledge, 2009).

Louis, Margot, *Persephone Rises 1860–1927* (Aldershot: Ashgate, 2009).

Lovecraft, Howard Phillips, *The Necronomicon*, ed. Stephen Jones (London: Gollancz, 2008).

Lovett, Edward, *Magic in Modern London* (London: Folklore Society, 1925).

Lowe Thompson, R., *A History of the Devil* (London: Kegan Paul Trench Trubner, 1929).

Lucy, Margaret, *Shakespeare and the Supernatural* (Liverpool: Shakespeare Press, 1906).

Lurie, Alison, "Widcraft", *New York Review* (15 January 2009), www.nybooks.com/articles/2009/01/15/widcraft/#fn-1

Lynn Linton, Eliza, *Witch Stories* (London, 1861).

Mac Cárthaigh, Críostóir, "The Ship-Sinking Witch: A Maritime Folk Legend from North-West Europe", *Béaloideas* 60/61 (1992/3) 267–86.

Macardle, Dorothy, *Dark Enchantment* (1953; London: Bantam, 1966).

Macardle, Dorothy, ed., *Defence of Poesy* (London: Macmillan, 1927).

Macardle, Dorothy, *Shakespeare: Man and Boy* (London: Faber, 1961).

Macardle, Dorothy, *Uneasy Freehold* (London: Peter Davies, 1941).

Macardle, Dorothy, *Witch's Brew* (London: Year Book Press, 1931).

Macbeth, dir. Roman Polanski, Columbia (1971).

Macdonald, James Ross, "Calvinist Theology and 'Country Divinity' in Marlowe's *Doctor Faustus*", *Studies in Philology* 111:4 (2014) 821–44.

Macdonald, Kate, "Edwardian Transitions in the Fiction of Una L. Silberrad (1872–1955)", *English Literature in Transition* 54:1 (2011) 212–33.

Macdonald, Kate, "Witchcraft and Non-Conformity in Sylvia Townsend Warner's *Lolly Willowes* (1926) and John Buchan's *Witch Wood* (1927)", *Journal of the Fantastic in the Arts* 23:3 (2012) 215–38, www.thefreelibrary.com/Witchcraft+and+non-conformity+in+Sylvia+Townsend+Warner%27s+Lolly...-a0318999973

Macfarlane, Alan, *Witchcraft in Tudor and Stuart England* (1970; Prospect Heights, IL: Waveland, 1991).

MacGregor Mathers, Samuel Liddell, *The Key of Solomon* (1889; Mineola, NY: Dover, 2009).

Mackay, Charles, *Extraordinary Popular Delusions and the Madness of Crowds* (London, 1841).

Mackay, Sinclair, "*The Daylight Gate* by Jeanette Winterson: Review", *Telegraph* (23 August 2012), www.telegraph.co.uk/culture/books/bookreviews/9494923/The-Daylight-Gate-by-Jeanette-Winterson-review.html

Mackie, Pauline, *Ye Lyttle Salem Maide* (Boston, 1898).

Maclaurin, Colin, *Arguments and Decisions in Remarkable Cases* (Edinburgh, 1774).

Madox Ford, Ford, *The Half Moon* (New York: Doubleday, 1909).

Madox Ford, Ford, *The Young Lovell* (London: Chatto & Windus, 1913).

Madox Hueffer, Oliver, *The Book of Witches* (London: Nash, 1908).

Madsen, Deborah L., "Witch-Hunting: American Exceptionalism and Global Terrorism", Sylvia Söderlind and James Taylor Carson, *American Exceptionalisms* (Albany: SUNY Press, 2011) 15–29.

Maguire, Laurie E., *Shakespearean Suspect Texts* (Cambridge: Cambridge University Press, 1996).

Maid of Salem, dir. Frank Lloyd, Paramount (1937).

Mallon, Thomas, "The Devil's Own", *New York Times* (4 October 2013), www.nytimes.com/2013/10/06/books/review/jeanette-wintersons-daylight-gate.html?pagewanted=2&_r=1

Mallowan, Max, "Murray, Margaret Alice (1863–1963)", rev. R. S. Simpson, *Oxford Dictionary of National Biography*, Oxford University Press, 2004, 0-www.oxforddnb.com.lib.exeter.ac.uk/view/article/35169

Mantel, Hilary, "Unhappy Medium", *LRB* (3 May 2001), www.theguardian.com/books/2001/may/03/londonreviewofbooks

Mappen, Marc, *Witches and Historians* 2nd ed. (Malabar, FL: Krieger, 1996).

Marcus, Leah, *Puzzling Shakespeare* (Berkeley: University of California Press, 1988).

Marcus, Leah, *Unediting the Renaissance* (New York: Routledge, 1996).

Martin, Lauren, "The Witch, the Household and the Community: Isobel Young in East Barns 1580–1629", Goodare, ed., *Scottish Witches* 67–84.

Marvell, Holt, *The Passionate Clowns* (London: Duckworth, 1927).

Maschwitz, Eric, *No Chip on My Shoulder* (London: Herbert Jenkins, 1957).

Maslin, Janet, "Film: *The Witches of Eastwick*", *New York Times* (12 June 1987), www.nytimes.com/movie/review?res=9B0DE4DD143CF931A25755C0A961948260

Match, Richard, "Review of *Mist over Pendle*", *New York Times* (23 March 1952) n.p.

Matson, Norman, *Flecker's Magic* (New York: Boni & Liveright, 1926).

Maugham, W. Somerset, *The Magician* (London: Heinemann, 1908).

Maxwell Stuart, P.G., *An Abundance of Witches* (Stroud: Tempus, 2005).

Maxwell Stuart, P.G., *The British Witch* (Stroud: Amberley, 2014).

Maxwell Stuart, P.G., *Witch Hunters* (Stroud: Tempus, 2003).

McCormick, Donald, *Murder by Witchcraft* (London: Long, 1968).

McElwee, William, *The Wisest Fool in Christendom* (New York: Harcourt Brace, 1958).

McInnes, Paul, "*The Witches of Eastwick*: Striking a Blow for Womankind. Or Not", *Guardian* (14 October 2009), www.theguardian.com/film/2009/oct/14/witches-of-eastwick-digested-watch

Michelet, Jules, *La Sorcière* (1862; trans. A.R. Allinson as *Satanism and Witchcraft*, London: Tandem, 1965).

Millar, Charlotte Rose, *The Devil is in the Pamphlets* (London: Routledge, forthcoming).

Miller, Arthur, *Plays: One* (London: Bloomsbury Methuen, 2010).

Mitchell, John and John Dickie, *The Philosophy of Witchcraft* (Paisley, Glasgow, Edinburgh, Montrose, 1839).

Mitchell, Laurence J., "In Another Country: Sylvia Townsend Warner at Large", Rosemary Colt and Janice Rossen, eds, *Writers of the Old School* (Basingstoke: Macmillan, 1992) 120–37.

Moir, George, *Magic and Witchcraft* (London, 1852).

Mone, Franz Josef, "Über das Hexenwesen", *Anzeiger für Kunde der Teutschen Vorzeit* 5 (1839) 271–5, 444–5.

Monstrous Regiment at www.unfinishedhistories.com/history/companies/monstrous-regiment/

Moore, Caroline, "The Widows of Eastwick", *Telegraph* (29 October 2008), www.telegraph.co.uk/culture/books/fictionreviews/3562653/The-Widows-of-Eastwick-by-John-Updike-review.html

Morgan, Robin, *The Burning Time* (New York and London: Melville House, 2006).

Moseley, Rachel, "Glamorous Witchcraft: Gender and Magic in Teen Film and Television", *Screen* 43:4 (2002) 403–22.

Mowat, Barbara, "Prospero's Book", *Shakespeare Quarterly* 52:1 (2001) 1–33.

Murray, John B., *The Remarkable Michael Reeves* (London: Cinematics, 2002).

Murray, Margaret Alice, *My First Hundred Years* (London: Kimber, 1963).

Murray, Margaret Alice, "The 'Devil' of North Berwick", *Scottish Historical Review* 15:60 (July 1918) 310–21.

Murray, Margaret Alice, *The Witch-Cult in Western Europe* (Oxford: Clarendon, 1921).

Mushat Frye, Roland, "Launching the Tragedy of *Macbeth*: Temptation, Deliberation and Consent in Act I", *Huntington Library Quarterly* 50:3 (1987) 249–61.

My Bare Lady, dir. Arthur Knight, Union (1962).

Mzeil, Ahmad H., "The Ambivalence of the Colonial Project in *The Tempest*", *Journal of Advanced Social Research* 3:3 (2013), 113–21, www.sign-ific-ance.co.uk/index.php/JASR/article/viewFile/196/198

Naked as Nature Intended, dir. George Harrison Marks, Markten Compass (1961).

Nancy, Jean-Luc, *The Ground of the Image* trans. Jeff Fort (New York: Fordham University Press, 2005).

Neal, John, *Rachel Dyer* (Portland, 1829).

Neele, Henry, "Shakespeare's Supernatural Characters", *Lectures on English Poetry* (London, 1839) 221–9.

Neill, Robert, *Mist over Pendle* (London: Hutchinson, 1951).

Neill, Robert, *The Devil's Door* (London: Hutchinson, 1979).

Neill, Robert, *Witch Bane* (1967; London: Arrow, 1980).

Neill, Robert, *Witchfire at Lammas* (1977; London: Arrow, 1988).

Newman, Judie, *John Updike* (Basingstoke: Macmillan, 1988).

Newsinger, John, "Fantasy and Revolution: An Interview with China Miéville", *International Socialism Journal* 88 (2000): http://pubs.socialistreviewindex.org.uk/isj88/newsinger.htm

Night of the Demon, dir. Jacques Tourneur, Columbia (1957).

Night of the Eagle, dir. Sidney Hayers, Independent Artists (1962).

Nilan, Mary M., "*The Tempest* at the Turn of the Century: Cross Currents in Production", Patrick Murphy, ed., *The Tempest: Critical Essays* (London: Routledge, 2010) 341–56.

Normand, "Modernising Scottish Witchcraft Texts", *EnterText* 3:1 (2003) 227–37.

Normand, Lawrence and Gareth Roberts, eds, *Witchcraft in Early Modern Scotland* Exeter: University of Exeter Press, 2000).

Norton Smith, Dulcinea, *Blood and Clay* (Kindle, 2012).

Norton Smith, Dulcinea, webpages at www.knowonder.com/dulcinea-norton-smith/

Nosworthy, J.M., "Macbeth, Doctor Faustus and the Juggling Fiends", J.C. Gray, ed., *The Mirror up to Shakespeare* (Toronto: University of Toronto Press, 1984) 208–22.

Notestein, Wallace, *A History of Witchcraft in England* (Washington: American Historical Association, 1911).

Nussbaum, Emily, "Updike and the Women", *New York* (19 October 2008) 1–3, http://nymag.com/arts/books/profiles/51366/

Nutt, Alfred, *The Fairy Mythology of Shakespeare* (London, 1900).

O'Brien, Sheilagh Ilona, "The Discovery of Witches: Matthew Hopkins' Defense of his Witch-Hunting Methods", *Preternature* 5:1 (2016) 29–58.

O'Mahoney, Katherine, "The Witch Figure: The Witch of Edmonton", *The Seventeenth Century* 24:2 (2009) 238–59.

Oates, Caroline, and Juliette Wood, *A Coven of Scholars* (London: Folklore Society, 1998).

Outlander, prod. Ronald D. Moore, Sony Pictures (2014–present).

Owen, Alex, *The Darkened Room* (London: Virago, 1989).

Owen, Alex, *The Place of Enchantment* (Chicago: University of Chicago Press, 2004).

Peeping Tom, dir. Michael Powell, Anglo-Amalgamated (1960).

Peterson, Henry, *Dulcibel* (Philadelphia: John C. Winston 1907).

Pettitt, Tom, "Categorical Transgression in Marlovian Death and Damnation", *Orbis Litterarum* 65:4 (2010) 292–317 (300–3).

Pettitt, Tom, "The Folk-Play in Marlowe's *Doctor Faustus*", *Folklore* 91:1 (1980) 72–7.
Pettitt, Claire, "Time Lag and Elizabeth Gaskell's Transatlantic Imagination", *Victorian Studies* 54:4 (2012) 599–623.
Pitcairn, Robert, ed. *Ancient Criminal Trials in Scotland*, 10 vols. (Edinburgh, 1829–33).
Plath, James, "Giving the Devil His Due: Leeching and Edification in *The Scarlet Letter* and *The Witches of Eastwick*", James Yerkes, ed., *John Updike and Religion* (Grand Rapids: Eerdmans, 1999) 208–27.
Poe, Edgar Allen, "The Conqueror Worm", *Graham's Lady's and Gentleman's Magazine* 25 (January 1843).
Pollitt, Katha, "Bitches and Witches", *The Nation* (23 June 1984) 773.
Pomfret, Richard, "Poison had the Last Word", *Evening Chronicle* (16 May 1951) n.p.
Poole, Robert, ed., *The Lancashire Witches* (Manchester: Manchester University Press, 2003).
Poole, William Frederick, "Cotton Mather and Salem Witchcraft", *North American Review* 108:223 (1869) 337–97.
Poulos Nesbitt, Jennifer, "Footsteps of Red Ink: Body and Landscape in *Lolly Willowes*", *Twentieth-Century Literature* 49:4 (2003) 449–71.
Powers, Alan, *Eric Ravilious* (London: Imperial War Museum/Philip Wilson, 2003).
Pratchett, Terry, *Equal Rites* (1987; London: Gollancz, 2014).
Pratchett, Terry, *Wyrd Sisters* (London: Gollancz, 1988).
Psycho, dir. Alfred Hitchcock, Paramount (1960).
Pudney, Eric, "Scepticism and Belief in English Witchcraft Drama 1538–1681", PhD thesis, Lund University (2016).
Pullinger, Kate, *Weird Sister* (London: Phoenix House, 1999).
Pullinger, Kate, texts at www.katepullinger.com/.
Punt, Steve, "Who Put Bella in the Wych Elm", *Punt PI* 7:4 (2014), www.bbc.co.uk/programmes/b04c9dfn
Purkiss, Diane, "Desire and its Deformities: Fantasies of Witchcraft in the English Civil War", *Journal of Medieval and Early Modern Studies* 27:1 (1997) 103–32.
Purkiss, Diane, *The Witch in History* (London and New York: Routledge, 1996).
Quiller Couch, Arthur, "The Workmanship of *Macbeth*", 3 parts, *North American Review* 200:707–9 (October–December 1914) 576–91, 758–70, 923–30.
Quinault, Roland, "Britain 1950", *History Today* 51:4 (2001), www.historytoday.com/roland-quinault/britain-1950
Ra'ad, Basem L., "Updike's New Versions of Myth in America", *Modern Fiction Studies* 37:1 (1991) 25–33.
Radiohead, *Burn the Witch*, dir. Chris Hopewell, YouTube (2016).
Raine, Allen, *A Welsh Witch* (1902; Dinas Powys: Honno, 2013).
Raine, Craig, "Sisters with the Devil in Them", *TLS* (28 September 1984) 1084.
Raymond, John, "Review of *Mist over Pendle*", *New Statesman* (9 June 1951) n.p.
Redman, Ben Ray, "Christopher Fry: Poet-Dramatist", *English Journal* 42:1 (1953) 1–7.
Rees, Celia, *Sorceress* (London: Bloomsbury, 2002).
Rees, Celia, *Witch Child* (London: Bloomsbury, 2000).
Reeves, Michael, "Alan Bennett's Views", *The Listener* (30 May 1968) 704.
Reid, Desmond, *Witch Hunt!* (London: Fleetway, 1960).
Reid, Robert L., "Sacerdotal Vestiges in *The Tempest*", *Comparative Drama* 41:4 (2007–8) 493–513.

Reinelt, Janelle, "Beyond Brecht: Britain's New Feminist Drama", *Theatre Journal* 38:2 (1986) 154–63.

Reisert, Rebecca, *The Third Witch* (London: Hodder & Stoughton, 2001).

Rembold, Elfie, "Home Rule All Round: Experiments in Regionalizing Great Britain 1886–1914", Peter Catterall, Wolfram Kaiser and Ulrike Walton-Jordan, eds, *Reforming the Constitution* (2000; London: Routledge, 2014) 201–24.

Renwick, Roger DeV., "The Mummers' Play and *The Old Wives Tale*", *Journal of American Folklore* 94:374 (1981) 433–55.

Richards, Jeffrey, "The 'Lancashire Novelist' and the Lancashire Witches", Poole, ed., 166–87.

Richardson, Anthony, *The Barbury Witch* (London: Constable, 1927).

Richardson, Anthony, *Word of the Earth* (London: Heinemann, 1923).

Richardson, Shelby, "Witches and Actors in Early Modern Theatre", PhD thesis, Tulane University (ProQuest, 2012).

Rickard, Jane, *Writing the Monarch in Jacobean England* (Cambridge: Cambridge University Press, 2015).

Roberts, Gareth, "A Re-Examination of the Magical Material in Middleton's *The Witch*", *Notes and Queries* 221 (1976) 216–19.

Roberts, Gareth, "The Descendants of Circe: Witches and Renaissance Fiction", Barry, Hester and Roberts, eds, 183–206.

Roche, Thomas P., ed., *The Faerie Queene* by Edmund Spenser (London: Penguin, 2003).

Rosemary's Baby, dir. Roman Polanski, Paramount (1968).

Rosen, Barbara, *Witchcraft in England 1558–1618* (1969; Amherst: University of Massachusetts Press, 1991).

Rosenthal, Bernard, *Salem Story* (Cambridge and New York: Cambridge University Press, 1993).

Rothenberg, Molly Anne, Dennis Foster and Slavoj Žižek, eds, *Perversion and the Social Relation* (Durham, NC, and London: Duke University Press, 2003).

Rowling, J.K., *Harry Potter and the Philosopher's Stone* (London: Bloomsbury, 1997).

Rubin, Merle, "The Witches of Eastwick", *Christian Science Monitor* (18 July 1984), www.csmonitor.com/Books/Book-Reviews/2008/1026/the-witches-of-eastwick

Russell Taylor, John, "Horror and Something More", *The Times* (11 May 1968) 39.

Sabrina the Teenage Witch, "The Crucible", Season 1, Episode 23, dir. Gary Halvorson (1997).

Salem: An Eastern Tale (New York, 1820).

Scarry, Elaine, *Resisting Representation* (Oxford and New York: Oxford University Press, 1994).

Schafer, Elizabeth, ed., *The Witch* (London: A & C Black, 1994).

Schelling, Felix, "Some Features of the Supernatural as Represented in Plays of the Reigns of Elizabeth and James", *Modern Philology*, 1:1 (1903) 31–47.

Schiff, James A., "Updike's Scarlet Letter Trilogy: Recasting an American Myth", *Studies in American Fiction* 20:1 (1992) 17–31.

Scott, Walter, *Letters on Demonology and Witchcraft* (London, 1830).

Scott, Walter, *Novels and Tales by the Author of Waverley* (Edinburgh, 1823).

Scragg, Leah, ed. *Mother Bombie* by John Lyly (Manchester: Manchester University Press, 2010).

Scragg, Leah, "Re-editing Lyly for the Modern Reader, or the Case of Mother Bombie's Stool", *Review of English Studies* 63: 258 (2012) 20–33.

Season of the Witch, dir. George A. Romero, Latent Image (1973).

Secrets of a Windmill Girl, dir. Arnold Miller, Searchlight (1966).

Seebohm Rowntree, Benjamin and G.R. Lavers, *Poverty and the Welfare State* (London: Longman, Green, 1951).

Seltzer, Daniel, ed., *Friar Bacon and Friar Bungay* by Robert Greene (London: Edward Arnold, 1964).

Senn, Werner, "Robert Greene's Handling of Source Material in *Friar Bacon and Friar Bungay*", *English Studies* 54:6 (1973) 544–53.

Sermin Meskill, Lynn, "Exorcising the Gorgon of Terror: Jonson's *Masque of Queenes*", *ELH* 72:1 (2005) 181–207.

Sharpe, James, "The Cinematic Treatment of Early Modern Witchcraft Trials", Mark Thornton-Burnett and Adrian Streete, ed., *Filming and Performing Renaissance History* (Basingstoke: Palgrave Macmillan, 2011) 83–98.

Sharpe, James, "The Devil in East Anglia: The Matthew Hopkins Trials Reconsidered", Barry, Hester and Roberts, eds, 237–56.

Sharpe, James, "Witch-Hunting and Witch Historiography: Some Anglo-Scottish Comparisons", Goodare, ed., *Scottish Witch-Hunt*, 182–97.

Sharpe, James, *Instruments of Darkness* (London: Hamish Hamilton, 1996).

Shelley, Percy, "The Witch of Atlas", *Posthumous Poems* ed. Mary Shelley (London, 1824).

Shrew magazine, webpages, www.bl.uk/learning/histcitizen/21cc/counterculture/liberation/shrew/shrew.html

Siegel, James, *Naming the Witch* (Stanford: Stanford University Press, 2006).

Silberrad, Una Lucy, *Keren of Lowbole* (London: Constable, 1913).

Silberrad, Una Lucy, *The Book of Sanchia Stapleton* (London: Hutchinson, 1927).

Simkin, John, "Eric Maschwitz", http://spartacus-educational.com/SPYmaschwitz.htm

Simpson, Jacqueline, "Margaret Murray: Who Believed Her and Why?", *Folklore* 105: 1–2 (1994) 89–96.

Sisson, C.J., "The Magic of Prospero", *Shakespeare Survey* 11 (1958) 70–7.

Smith, Anna Marie, "The Centering of Right-Wing Extremism through the Construction of an 'Inclusionary' Homophobia and Racism" in Shane Phelan. Ed., *Playing with Fire* (New York and London: Routledge, 1997) 113–38.

Smith, Nadia Clare, *Dorothy Macardle* (Dublin: Woodfield, 2007).

Snow, C.P., "Atmospherics", *The Times* (20 May 1951) 3.

Somerset, Anne, *Unnatural Murder* (London: Weidenfeld & Nicolson, 1997).

Spalding, T.A., *Elizabethan Demonology* (London, 1880).

Starhawk, *The Spiral Dance* (New York: Harper & Row, 1979).

Starkey, Marion, *The Devil in Massachusetts* (New York: Doubleday, 1947).

Stebner, Beth, "Americans Baffled by 'Left-Wing Tribute' to Free Healthcare", *Daily Mail* (28 July 2012), www.dailymail.co.uk/news/article-2180227/London-2012-Olympics-Some-Americans-left-baffled-tribute-NHS-Mary-Poppins-Opening-Ceremony.html

Stephens, Walter, "Skepticism, Empiricism and Proof in Gianfrancesco Pico della Mirandola's *Strix*", *Magic, Ritual and Witchcraft* 11:1 (2016) 6–29.

Stephens, Walter, *Demon Lovers* (Chicago and London: University of Chicago Press, 2002).

Steptoe and Son, created by Ray Galton and Alan Simpson, BBC (1962–74).

Stevens, Andrea, "A Triple Spell", *New York Times* (13 May 1984) section 7, 1.

Stevenson, Ruth, "The Comic Core of Both A- and B-Editions of *Doctor Faustus*", *SEL* 53:2 (2013) 401–19.

Straw Dogs, dir. Sam Peckinpah, ABC (1971).

Streete, Adrian, "Consummatum Est: Calvinist Exegesis, Mimesis and *Doctor Faustus*", *Literature and Theology* 15:2 (2001) 140–58.

Stymeist, David, "'Must I be . . . Made a Common Sink?' Witchcraft and the Theatre in *The Witch of Edmonton*", *Renaissance and Reformation* 25:2 (2001) 33–53.

Sugar, Gabrielle, "Falling to a Divelish Exercise: The Copernican Universe in Christopher Marlowe's *Doctor Faustus*", *Early Theatre* 12:1 (2009) 141–9.

Suhr, Carla, "Portrayal of Attitude in Early Modern English Witchcraft Pamphlets" *Studia Neophilologica* 84:Sup1 (2012) 130–42.

Summers, Montague, *Antinous* ed. Timothy D'Arch Smith (1907; London: Cecil Woolf, 1995).

Summers, Montague, *The Galanty Show*, ed. Brocard Sewell (London: Cecil Woolf, 1980).

Summers, Montague, *The Geography of Witchcraft* (London: Kegan Paul, 1927).

Summers, Montague, *The History of Witchcraft* (1925; London: Senate, 1994).

Swinburne, Algernon, *Poems and Ballads* (London, 1866).

Swinburne, Algernon, *Songs before Sunrise* (London, 1871).

Tate, Trudi, *Modernism, History and the First World War* (Manchester: Manchester University Press, 1998).

Tate, Trudi, *Women, Men and the Great War* (Manchester: Manchester University Press, 1995).

Tate, Trudi and Suzanne Raitt, eds, *Women's Fiction and the Great War* (Oxford: Oxford University Press, 1997).

Tayler, Christopher, "Every Witch Way", *Guardian* (25 October 2008), www.theguardian.com/books/2008/oct/25/updike

Tennyson, Alfred, *Idylls of the King* ed. J.M. Gray (1859–85; London: Penguin, 1983).

The Curse, dir. Edward V. Spencer, Mutual Film (1913).

The Devil Rides Out, dir. Terence Fisher, Hammer (1968).

The Judgment, dir. Edward V. Spencer, Mutual Film (1913).

The Love Witch, dir. Anna Biller, Oscilloscope Laboratories (2016).

The Salem Belle: A Tale of Love and Witchcraft (Boston, 1842).

The Simpsons, "Rednecks and Broomsticks", dir. Bob Anderson and Rob Oliver, Fox (2009).

The Simpsons, "Treehouse of Horror VIII: Easy-Bake Coven", dir. Mark Kirkland, Fox (1997).

The Tempest, dir. Percy Stow, Clarendon (1908).

The Witch of Salem, dir. Raymond B. West, Mutual Film (1913).

The Witches, dir. Cyril Frankel, Hammer (1966).

The Witches of Eastwick, dir. George Miller, Warner Bros. (1987).

The Wizard of Oz, dir. Victor Fleming *et al.*, Metro-Goldwyn-Mayer (1939).

The Woman in Black, dir. James Watkins, Hammer (2012).

Thiselton Dyer, Thomas Firminger, *The Folk-Lore of Shakespeare* (London, 1883).

Thomas, Keith, *Religion and the Decline of Magic* (London: Peregrine, 1971).

Thorne Smith, James, *Topper* (London: Robert Holden, 1926).

Thorne Smith, James and Norman Matson, *The Passionate Witch* (London: Tandem, 1942).

Thurber, James, "The Secret Life of Walter Mitty", *My World and Welcome to It* (New York: Harcourt Brace, 1942) 72–81.

Tiedemann, Rolf, ed., *Can One Live after Auschwitz?* (1997; Stanford: Stanford University Press, 2003).

Timbers, Frances, "Witches' Sect or Prayer Meeting? Matthew Hopkins Revisited", *Women's History Review* 17:1 (2008) 21–37.

Times Digital Archive, http://gale.cengage.co.uk/times-digital-archive/times-digital-archive-17852006.aspx

Tolman, Albert, "Notes on *Macbeth*", *PMLA* 11:2 (1896) 200–19.

Took, Barry, "(Albert) Eric Maschwitz (1901–1969)", *Oxford Dictionary of National Biography* (Oxford: Oxford University Press, 2004), 0-www.oxforddnb.com.lib.exeter.ac.uk/view/article/38408

Towne, Frank, "'White Magic' in *Friar Bacon and Friar Bungay*", *Modern Language Notes* 67:1 (1952) 9–13

Townsend Warner, Sylvia, *King Duffus and Other Poems* (Wells: Clare, 1968).

Townsend Warner, Sylvia, *Lolly Willowes* (1926; London: Virago, 2012).

Townsend Warner, Sylvia, "Modern Witches" (*Eve* 18 August 1926), republished in *The Sylvia Townsend Warner Society Newsletter Number Ten* (2005) 12–14.

Toye, Richard, *Lloyd-George and Churchill* (London: Pan, 2008).

Traister, Barbara, "Magic and the Decline of Demons: A View from the Stage", Hopkins and Ostovich, eds, 19–30.

Trevor-Roper, Hugh Redwald, "Witches and Witchcraft", *Encounter* (May and June 1967) 3–25, 13–34, www.unz.org/Pub/Encounter-1967may-00003 and www.unz.org/Pub/Encounter-1967jun-00013

Tricomi, Albert H., "Joan la Pucelle and the Inverted Saints' Play in *1 Henry VI*", *Renaissance and Reformation* 25:2 (2001) 5–31.

Tylee, Edward, *The Witch Ladder* (London: Duckworth, 1911).

Tynan, Kenneth, "Christopher Fry", *Telegraph* (4 July 2005) n.p.

Tytler, Patrick Fraser, *History of Scotland* 9 vols. (1828; Edinburgh, 1843).

Updike, John, "A 'Special Message' for the Franklin Library's First Edition Society printing of *The Witches of Eastwick*", *Odd Jobs* (1991; London: Penguin, 1992) 853–6.

Updike, John, "Dürer and Christ", *New York Review of Books* (2 November 2000), www.nybooks.com/articles/2000/11/02/durer-and-christ/

Updike, John, "Lolly and Jake Opt Out", *Hugging the Shore* (New York: Random House, 1983) 284–5.

Updike, John, *Rabbit, Run* (1960; New York: Knopf, 1970).

Updike, John, "The Mastery of Miss Warner", *Picked-Up Pieces* (Greenwich, CT: Fawcett Crest, 1975) 229–34.

Updike, John, *The Widows of Eastwick* (New York: Knopf, 2008).

Updike, John, *The Witches of Eastwick* (New York: Knopf, 1984).

Upham, Charles Wentworth, *Salem Witchcraft and Cotton Mather: A Reply* (Morrisania, NY, 1869).

Upham, Charles Wentworth, *Salem Witchcraft* (1867; Mineola, NY: Dover, 2000).

Vaizey, Ed and Department for Culture, Media and Sport, "Creative Industries Worth Almost £10 Million an Hour to Economy", *Gov.uk* (26 January 2016), www.gov.uk/government/news/creative-industries-worth-almost-10-million-an-hour-to-economy

Vale, Allison, "Is this the Bella in the Wych Elm?", *Independent* (22 March 2013), www.independent.co.uk/news/uk/home-news/is-this-the-bella-in-the-wych-elm-unravelling-the-mystery-of-the-skull-found-in-a-tree-trunk-8546497.html

Valiunas, Algis, "The 'Magic' of Gabriel García Márquez", *Commentary* 117:4 (2004) 51–5.

Veldman, Meredith, *Fantasy, the Bomb and the Greening of Britain* (Cambridge: Cambridge University Press, 1994).

Verduin, Kathleen, "Sex, Nature and Dualism in *The Witches of Eastwick*", *Modern Language Quarterly* 46:3 (1985) 293–315.

Walker, Hugh, ed, *The Merry Devil of Edmonton* (London: Aldine House, 1897).

Walker, Michael D., blogposts at www.thornesmith.net

Wallraven, Miriam, *Women Writers and the Occult in Literature and Culture* (London and New York: Routledge, 2015).

Walsh, Brian, "Deep Prescience: Succession and the Politics of Prophecy in *Friar Bacon and Friar Bungay*", *Medieval and Renaissance Drama in England* 23 (2010) 63–85.

Walsham, Alexandra, *The Catholic Reformation in Protestant Britain* (2014; London and New York: Routledge, 2016).

Walton Williams, George, "Time for Such a Word: Verbal Echoing in *Macbeth*", *Shakespeare Survey* 47 (1991) 153–9.

Warburton, Ruth, *A Witch Alone* (London: Hodder, 2013).

Warburton, Ruth, *A Witch in Love* (London: Hodder, 2012).

Warburton, Ruth, *A Witch in Winter* (London: Hodder, 2012).

Warburton, Ruth, blogposts at www.ruthwarburton.com/blog/page/

Warburton, Ruth, *Witchfinder* (London: Hodder, 2014).

Warner, Marina, *Indigo* (1992; London: Vintage, 1993).

Wasser, Michael, "Scotland's First Witch-Hunt: The Eastern Witch-Hunt of 1568–9", Goodare, ed., *Scottish Witches* 17–33.

Waters, Sarah, "'The Most Famous Fairy in History': Antinous and Homosexual Fantasy", *Journal of the History of Sexuality* 6:2 (1995) 194–230.

Waugh, Robert H., "Dr. Margaret Murray and H.P. Lovecraft: The Witch-Cult in New England", *Lovecraft Studies* 31 (1994) 2–10.

Weber, Max, *From Max Weber*, trans. H.H. Gerth and C. Wright Mills, (New York: Oxford University Press, 1946).

Webster, David, ed. (?), *A Collection of Rare and Curious Tracts on Witchcraft* (Edinburgh, 1820).

Weigand, Kate, *Red Feminism* (Baltimore: Johns Hopkins University Press, 2002).

Weisman, Richard, *Witchcraft, Magic and Religion in Seventeenth-Century Massachusetts* (Amherst: University of Massachusetts Press, 1984).

West, Robert H., "Ceremonial Magic in *The Tempest*", Alwin Thaler and Norman Sanders, eds, *Shakespearean Essays* (Knoxville: University of Tennessee Press, 1964) 63–78.

Wheatley, Dennis, *Gateway to Hell* in *The Devil Rides Out/Gateway to Hell* (London: BCA, 2005).

Wheatley, Dennis, *Gunmen, Gallants and Ghosts* (London: Arrow, 1975).

Wheatley, Dennis, *Strange Conflict* (1941; London: Mandarin, 1991).

Wheatley, Dennis, *The Devil and All His Works* (1971; London: Arrow, 1973).

Wheatley, Dennis, *The Devil Rides Out* (1934; London: Orbit, 1980).

Wheatley, Dennis, *The Haunting of Toby Jugg* (1948; London: Wordsworth, 2007).

Wheatley, Dennis, *The Irish Witch* (1973; London: Arrow, 1975).

Wheatley, Dennis, ed., *Satanism and Witches* (London: Sphere, 1974).

Wheatley, Dennis, *The Satanist* (1960; London: Arrow, 1974).

Wheatley, Henry, "The Folklore of Shakespeare", *Folklore* 27:4 (December 1916) 378–407.

Whitaker, Kati, "Ghana Witch Camps: Widows' Lives in Exile", *BBC News* (1 September 2012), www.bbc.co.uk/news/magazine-19437130

Whitworth, Charles, ed., *The Old Wives Tale* by George Peele, republished as *The Old Wife's Tale* (London: New Mermaids, 2014).

Wickwar, J.W., *Witchcraft and the Black Art* (republished as *Handbook of the Black Arts* (1925; London: Senate, 1996).

Wilby, Emma, *Cunning Folk and Familiar Spirits* (Brighton: Sussex Academic Press, 2005).

Wilby, Emma, *The Visions of Isobel Gowdie* (Brighton: Sussex Academic Press, 2010).

"W.I.T.C.H", www.jofreeman.com/photos/witch.html

Williams, William Carlos, *Many Loves and Other Plays* (New York: New Directions, 1982).

Willis, Deborah, *Malevolent Nurture* (Ithaca and London: Cornell University Press, 1995).

Willis, Deborah, "The Witch-Family in Elizabethan and Jacobean Print Culture", *Journal for Early Modern Cultural Studies* 13:1 (2013) 4–31.

Wills, Garry, *Witches and Jesuits* (New York: Oxford University Press, 1995).

Winick, Mimi, "Modernist Feminist Witchcraft: Margaret Murray's Fantastic Scholarship and Sylvia Townsend Warner's Realist Fantasy", *Modernism/Modernity* 22:3 (2015) 565–92.

Winterson, Jeanette, blogposts at www.jeanettewinterson.com/archive/ and www.jeanettewinterson.com/pages/

Winterson, Jeanette, interview with Brian Appleyard, *Sunday Times* (5 August 2012) at http://bryanappleyard.com/wintersons-world/

Winterson, Jeanette, *Sexing the Cherry* (1989; London: Vintage, 1990).

Winterson, Jeanette, *The Daylight Gate* (London: Hammer, 2012).

Witchcraft, dir. Don Sharp, Twentieth Century Fox (1964).

Witchfinder General, dir. Michael Reeves, Tigon (1968).

Wolcott, James, "Caretaker/Pallbearer", *London Review of Books* 31:1 (2009) 9–10.

Woolf, Virginia, *A Room of One's Own* (New York: Harcourt Brace, 1929).

Wordsworth, William, *The Complete Poetical Works* ed. Henry Reed (Philadelphia, 1849).

Wordsworth, William, *The Pedlar, Tintern Abbey, The Two-Part Prelude* ed. Jonathan Wordsworth (Cambridge: Cambridge University Press, 1985).

Wordsworth, William, and Samuel Taylor Coleridge, *Lyrical Ballads* ed. Fiona Stafford (Oxford: Oxford World's Classics, 2013).

Wright, Thomas, *Narratives of Sorcery and Magic* (London, 1851).

Wright, Thomas, *The Worship of the Generative Powers* (London, 1865).

Wynne, Deborah, "Hysteria Repeating Itself: Elizabeth Gaskell's 'Lois the Witch'", *Women's Writing* 12:1 (2006) 85–97.

Yancy, George, *Look, a White!* (Philadelphia: Temple University Press, 2012).

Yeoman, Louise, "Hunting the Rich Witch", Goodare, ed., *Scottish Witch-Hunt* 106–21.

Yeoman, Louise, "North Berwick Witches (*act.* 590–1592)", *Oxford Dictionary of National Biography* (Oxford: Oxford University Press, 2004), 0-www.oxforddnb.com.lib.exeter.ac.uk/view/article/69951

Zabus, Chantal, *Tempests after Shakespeare* (New York and Basingstoke: Palgrave, 2002).

Index